The Future of
CHRISTIANITY

The Future of CHRISTIANITY

Can It Survive?

Arthur J. Bellinzoni

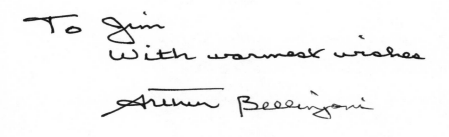

To Jim
With warmest wishes

Arthur Bellinzoni

Prometheus Books

59 John Glenn Drive
Amherst, New York 14228-2197

Published 2006 by Prometheus Books

Inquiries should be addressed to
Prometheus Books
59 John Glenn Drive
Amherst, New York 14228–2197
VOICE: 716–691–0133, ext. 207
FAX: 716–564–2711
WWW.PROMETHEUSBOOKS.COM

10 09 08 07 06   5 4 3 2 1

Library of Congress Cataloging-in-Publication Data

Bellinzoni, Arthur J.
    The future of Christianity : can it survive? / by Arthur J. Bellinzoni.
        p. cm.
    Includes bibliographical references and index.
    ISBN 1–59102–406–4 (hardcover : alk. paper)
    1. Christianity—Forecasting. 2. Church history—21st century. 3. Twenty-first century—Forecasts. I. Title.

BR121.3.B45 2006
230.01'12—dc22
                                                                            2006003369

Printed in the United States of America on acid-free paper

CONTENTS

PART 4: MYTH

PREFACE

To some extent, this book is an autobiography, although not as one ordinarily understands that literary genre. It is autobiographical because it reflects in significant measure my own personal religious journey, and, I suspect, the religious journeys of many people, young and old, Catholics and Protestants, Jews and Muslims.

A friend reminded me that this type of autobiographical reflection is not altogether unusual in a tradition that notably includes Augustine's *Confessions* and James Joyce's *Portrait of an Artist as a Young Man*. Although I am almost embarrassed to mention my modest contribution in the same breath as these literary masterpieces, what is similar is the way in which a person's life becomes a spiritual journey and a mirror of the people, the society, and the culture.

I was born to parents of a mixed marriage, a Scottish American Presbyterian mother and an Italian American Roman Catholic father, at a time when such marriages were still relatively rare and generally disapproved. Neither of my parents was a particularly observant Christian, although my father regularly attended midnight mass on Christmas Eve. Nevertheless, they agreed to be married in St. Patrick's Church in the Fort Hamilton neighborhood of Brooklyn. The marriage took place in the church's rectory, because it was then "unlawful," according to some man-made religious canon, for them to be married in the church itself. At the time of the marriage, my Protestant mother had to sign an agreement to raise me in the Catholic Church. And so she did.

Almost three years after my parents' marriage, I was born in the Methodist Hospital in the Park Slope neighborhood of Brooklyn, and subsequently baptized, received my first communion, and was later confirmed in the Holy Name of Jesus Roman Catholic Church in the same neighborhood. Although educated in a public elementary school, PS 154, I was dutifully shipped off to religious instructions every Wednesday afternoon from 2:00 to 3:00 PM to be instructed and indoctrinated in the Catholic faith by the sisters and brothers, who taught me for an hour a week over a period of eight years. I took it all very seriously and attended mass every Sunday. I went to confession and received communion almost every week and observed all of the holy days of obligation. I was a very good Catholic boy all those years.

I remember being troubled during the course of my childhood religious education when one of the nuns broke the news that my dear mother would probably go to hell when she died because she was not Catholic. That disturbed me deeply, but I never told my mother. I didn't want her to know the bad news, so I kept it to myself. Instead, I prayed for her conversion, as I was told to do by the very strict, intimidating, and unapproachable nuns. I was convinced that this mixed marriage was really a terrible mistake, unacceptable in God's eyes. But I knew that I loved both of my parents, who were extremely good to me and to everyone else for that matter. I also knew that my father's failure to go to church every Sunday would likely cost him his immortal soul as well. I faced the unhappy prospect of being alone in heaven without my parents. Somehow heaven without my parents seemed to this impressionable only child a fate worse than hell.

My parents continued my secular education at Poly Prep, a private country day school in Brooklyn, where I had a rigorous and sound secondary education. If I had developed the skills of reading, writing, and arithmetic in elementary school, at Poly I was exposed at a relatively young age to the rigor of the liberal arts. I was taught how to think, how to reason, how to evaluate evidence and make sound decisions. I excelled at Poly and graduated first in my class. I was exceptionally well prepared when I entered Princeton University in the fall of 1953 as a premed student, on my way to being a medical doctor—for reasons that were never really clear to me.

I did very well in my studies during my first two years at Princeton as a premed student. Along the way, I had to satisfy certain liberal arts requirements, as everyone does in such programs. More specifically, I had to take a course in history, philosophy, or religion. I chose to take a religion course and enrolled in Professor Paul Ramsay's Basic Christian Ethics. For the first time ever, I was expected to ask questions about issues that had been firmly implanted in my brain by the good sisters and brothers at Holy Name Church years earlier. It was a disquieting semester. I was even beginning to question the concept of God as a cosmic Santa Claus, although I didn't really understand the issue that clearly at the time.

Perhaps another course or two in religion would help me to answer some of the questions raised in this first religion course. So I enrolled in Professor George Thomas' Major Problems of Religious Thought. A major mistake! Many more questions than answers! Perhaps I should learn a bit more about the Bible, so I enrolled in An Introduction to the Old Testament with Professor R. B. Y. Scott, and subsequently in An Introduction to the New Testament with Professor William David Davies. These men were all giants in their respective fields. I was getting an extraordinary education, but my childhood faith was slowly but surely slipping away.

At the end of my sophomore year, I decided to major in religion, even as I continued my premed studies as an upperclassman, still set on medical school and a career as a doctor. Along the way, I went to see Princeton's Roman Catholic chaplain,

Hugh Horton, an Oxford DPhil, to talk to him about my growing crisis of faith. Father Horton's advice was simple: I shouldn't be majoring in religion at a place like Princeton, and I certainly shouldn't be reading many of the required books in the courses in which I was enrolled. They were on some index of forbidden books. What were the options? To fail my courses, or to continue to slip further from my faith! Neither seemed particularly acceptable to this ingenuous Princeton undergraduate. I thought back to the day that I first learned that my mother was going to hell for all eternity. The choices seemed unacceptable. I was certainly not prepared to pass over required reading and, therefore, fail courses in my major field, but neither was I interested in going to hell. Maybe, I thought, I should just become a generic Protestant and start going to the Princeton Chapel on Sunday mornings rather than to Father Horton's Newman Society mass. In those days, Princeton required us all to go to chapel, or church, or synagogue, or somewhere else of our choice, whatever our personal religious belief. I don't think there were any exceptions to this rule, even for agnostics or atheists, if there were any at Princeton in those days.

I excelled at Princeton and graduated magna cum laude in religion (with great praise in religion). I had studied both Latin and French for four years at Poly Prep and had begun to study Hebrew and Greek at Princeton to enable me to read the Bible in the original languages, something I deemed important at the time. I'm not even sure that I knew before my days at Princeton that the Bible wasn't written originally in English.

Come senior year, it was time for this premed religion major to apply to medical school. Even as I was filling out applications, I was beginning to wonder whether it might be better for me to go to graduate school to study more about religion, if for no other reason than to try to save my immortal soul. By now, I was a member of the Church of Total Confusion, not knowing what to believe, no longer sure at what church, if any, I should worship each Sunday. In many ways, I was already in hell, because I took it all extremely seriously.

It was not until late spring of my senior year that I decided to accept the invitation of Harvard University to enroll in their PhD program in the history and philosophy of religion rather than in their MD program. And so in the fall of 1957, I trudged off to Cambridge, Massachusetts, the first student Harvard had ever accepted into their PhD program in religion directly out of an undergraduate institution. My peers in the doctoral program were almost all about twenty years my senior, a situation which I found very intimidating.

At Harvard I opted to concentrate in the area of New Testament studies, although I was expected to pass general examinations in world religions and philosophy of religion before narrowing my focus in the third year of the program. I studied with a plethora of Harvard's best professors. Arthur Darby Nock, G. Ernest Wright, Krister Stendahl, and Helmut Koester constituted the committee before which I defended my doctoral dissertation on *The Sayings of Jesus in the Writings of Justin Martyr*.

My personal and religious journey had, of course, really just begun. I sometimes wonder how that journey might have progressed had I grown up after, rather than before, the Second Vatican Ecumenical Council of 1962–1965. By the time of the opening of the council and the subsequent adoption of some of its liberating reforms, I was already beginning my professional career. In the fall of 1962, I went to Wells College, a small women's college in Aurora, New York, to join the religion department as an instructor. At Wells I taught over a period of thirty-eight years a rich array of courses covering virtually the whole field of religious studies: Old and New Testaments, church history, philosophy of religion, theology, world religions, and for almost twenty years a course in the contemporary Middle East in historical and religious perspective. Although I published several books as a New Testament specialist, I remained throughout my career a generalist, covering some subjects much better than others.

Throughout my Wells years, I was also an evolving soul, a growing spirit, involved in my personal quest for religious truth, wherever I could find it. This book reflects my intellectual and spiritual journey over many decades. Once I retired from Wells College in June 2000, I was determined to write something like this book, although its scope and form were not yet clear to me.

As I began to collect my thoughts for this book in 2001, I was invited to deliver a lecture at the Rothko Chapel in Houston, Texas. The Rothko Chapel, dedicated in 1971 as an intimate interfaith sanctuary, is available to people of every belief and of no belief. The chapel welcomes people from all parts of the world and is a place that is alive with religious ceremonies of all faiths. It is a space where the experience and understanding of all traditions are encouraged and made available, and it has become a rallying place for people concerned with peace, freedom, human rights, and social justice. I had been invited by respected friend and board chair Frances Tarlton "Sissy" Farenthold to join the board of directors of the Rothko Chapel, and this seemed like the perfect setting for me to begin to hone my thoughts on a few subjects. The fourfold outline of this book emerged in the process of preparing for the Rothko lecture.

I returned from Venice late on September 9, 2001, and was scheduled to fly to Houston on September 12 to deliver on the thirteenth what was essentially an early, much briefer version of the introduction to this volume. Of course no one flew on September 12, 2001, and I didn't lecture at the Rothko Chapel on the thirteenth. I finally delivered my lecture in November of 2001 with the title "A Christianity for the New Millennium." My lecture was well received, and work on this volume began in earnest.

After a fifty-year career in religious studies, focused primarily in New Testament studies, I have concluded that Christianity is in need of serious self-reflection regarding its future. The issue is particularly critical, because I am convinced that Christianity cannot, will not, and should not survive if it refuses to embrace new truths and to address earnestly and honestly the question of its relevance in the third millennium. The changes that I propose in this volume are not subtle; they are fundamental and dramatic and go to the heart of Christian orthodoxy.

Another decisive force in my deciding to write this book has been my personal involvement with People For the American Way. In 1980, television and movie producer Norman Lear began searching for an appropriate response to a new and disturbing political movement in America. The Religious Right, in the form of Jerry Falwell, Pat Robertson, and others, was determined to impose a radical and extremist religious and political agenda, one that acknowledged only its leaders' narrow religious beliefs, on the whole of America, seeking thereby to diminish Americans' fundamental freedoms. The Religious Right called those who dared to dissent from their narrow orthodoxy "atheistic," "immoral," "anti-Christian," and "antifamily." Lear invited me to join the board of directors of People For the American Way in 1998, and I have been honored to serve this premier visionary organization in its dedication to the separation of church and state and the advancement of human equality in America—civil rights, women's rights, and gay and lesbian rights. I have learned a great deal from Norman and my distinguished colleagues on the staff and board of this extraordinary organization.

Although I am ultimately responsible for everything that I have gathered into this book, this final version is much better because of the generous suggestions and criticisms of two good friends and colleagues: Marvin A. Breslow, professor of history emeritus at the University of Maryland and my roommate of four years at the Harvard University Graduate School of Arts and Sciences; and David M. Reis, formerly visiting assistant professor of religion at Wells College and currently assistant professor of religion at the College of Santa Fe. Both of these men labored tirelessly and unselfishly over every word of every chapter and made invaluable contributions to this volume. Wells College alumna and friend Phyllis Wender, a literary agent in New York specializing in trade books, read the manuscript and encouraged me to find a publisher whose interests matched the theme of this book. I shared the manuscript with R. Joseph Hoffmann, Robert D. and Henrietta T. Campbell '12 Professor of Religion at Wells College. It was he who recommended my manuscript to Prometheus Books for publication.

This volume is dedicated to Dimitrios Dimopoulos, who provided tireless and unselfish moral support as well as generous technical expertise on the computer during this book's three-year period of gestation.

Arthur J. Bellinzoni
Aurora, New York
March 13, 2006

INTRODUCTION

It would be presumptuous for anyone to try to envision what Christianity might look like at the end of its third millennium in the year 3000. Frankly, I am not even sure that Christianity will survive for another thousand years. Neither am I convinced that Christianity deserves to survive, even to the end of this twenty-first century, at least in its present form. I do not have a crystal ball for gazing into the future; no one does. However, if Christianity does, in fact, manage to endure for another millennium, I assure you that by the year 3000 it will either be an insignificant religious sect or substantially different from the religion that you and I were taught in Sunday school.

There is no turning back the clock to recover a past that Christianity should have abandoned and discarded during the twentieth century; and there is no standing still, frozen in an untenable and indefensible present. There is no way for Christians to continue to evade and escape the insights and truths of the past two centuries that contradict much of what many believers still consider to be the essence of Christianity. It is time to move on. My confidence in the preeminence of human reason as the primary criterion of most truth is the basis for most of what appears on the pages of this book and for this forthright call to renovate Christianity substantially for the challenges of this new millennium.

Unfortunately, the quest for temporal power dominates much of the history of Christianity. In fact, the quest for power continues to play a leading role in most current disagreements and differences, both among the world's religions and even among Christian denominations. I have titled the opening chapter of this book "Religious Authority and Reason: Conflicting Modes for Attaining Truth." As the title suggests, I have cast the subject of that lead chapter principally as a political issue, not primarily as a philosophical or intellectual question. The matter of religious authority and reason involves much more than the traditional conflict between faith and reason, which is already the subject of multiple tomes.

The quest for temporal power has some bearing, either directly or indirectly, on many of the issues raised in this volume. That is what makes change so difficult, even in the third millennium. I urge Christians, and any others reading this book, to prepare for the intellectual and political challenges of the future, not by entrenching yourselves more deeply in past traditions and in untenable religious fundamentalisms, but rather by opening yourselves to the future and to new truths, wherever you find them, and however disconcerting and disturbing they may be.

Although my focus in this volume is on Christianity, because that is the religious tradition out of which I come and which I know best, this book can be understood as speaking, as well, to Judaism and Islam, sister religions of Christianity. Many of the same issues are equally applicable to them.[1]

*   *   *   *   *

Christianity had its origins in Roman Palestine as an insignificant sect within first-century Judaism. The nascent movement spread quickly into the Greco-Roman world, where it became a very different religion, a religion largely, but not entirely, divorced from its Jewish roots.

To understand Christianity's origins and growth, one must be aware of the historical, cultural, and religious contexts in which Jesus lived and into which the new religion was born and later spread, the one Jewish, the other Greco-Roman or Hellenistic; and one must also be aware of the historical, cultural, and religious contexts of subsequent generations in the church's two-thousand-year history.

The best scholarly research into the life and ministry of Jesus suggests that he was probably an apocalyptic prophet who preached the imminent end of history as we know it and the arrival of a new age, the Kingdom of God or the period of God's rule. Jesus apparently believed that this new order would be ushered in by a supernatural angelic figure, whom he and others of his generation called the Son of Man.

Following Jesus' death, his earliest followers apparently believed that when that angelic supernatural Son of Man arrived, presumably within their lifetimes, he would be none other than Jesus himself, whom, they claimed, God had raised from the dead and elevated to his right hand to a position of honor and authority. In his

---

1. When I first delivered the substance of these remarks in a lecture in November 2001 at the Rothko Chapel in Houston, Texas, I spoke to a rather large and diverse audience, which received my comments warmly, and even enthusiastically. In the audience was an ambassador from a predominantly Muslim country (whose anonymity I will preserve), who spoke to me afterward and volunteered that he agreed with the substance of what I had said and believed that it applied as well, and perhaps even more so, to Islam. Ironically, I was originally scheduled to fly to Houston on September 12, 2001, to deliver these remarks on September 13. Of course, no one flew anywhere on September 12, and I did not deliver the lecture on the thirteenth, but I was deeply moved by the ambassador's remarks and by the irony that my comments unintentionally spoke volumes to the tragic events of September 11: unenlightened religion anywhere is a danger to humankind everywhere.

earliest letter, probably written in 50–51 CE[2] from Corinth to the nascent Christian community in Thessalonica, Paul made it clear that he expected Jesus to return very soon, probably during his lifetime.[3]

It is widely understood that the first generation of Christians, and certainly Paul, effectively changed the religion *of* Jesus into a religion *about* Jesus. Contrary to the radical ethical teachings of the historical Jesus, early Christian communities believed that if an individual simply believed that Jesus had been raised from the dead and that he was Lord and Messiah, he or she could share in Jesus' resurrection and would after death be united with him and the Father in glory. Even today, that belief survives in some form in most mainstream Christian communities. Although individual denominations differ on the timetable for the second coming, most Christians continue to expect the future return of Jesus in glory to judge the living and the dead, and to terminate the present world order. Many Christians, especially in the United States, expect Jesus' second coming to occur very soon.

In the first three or four centuries, Christians struggled to find the appropriate language required to explain the relationship between Jesus the Messiah and God the Father, and the relationship of the two of them to the Holy Spirit or the spirit of God, who, they believed, continued to live with the church and inspire its members with supernatural power.

In the year 325 CE, about three hundred years after Jesus' death, 318 fathers of the church, bishops who were considered to be faithful witnesses to the Christian tradition, assembled at Nicaea in modern Turkey. That first ecumenical council was summoned by the Roman emperor Constantine to settle the dispute among contending parties about the person of Christ and his relationship to the Father.

The emperor himself presided over the council even though he had not yet been baptized. Under his guidance—some would say under his direction—the assembled bishops adopted language that, they maintained, expressed the correct or orthodox definition of the relationship of the Father, the Son, and the Holy Spirit in a formula still recited today in most Christian churches as the Nicene Creed. This creed expresses the authoritative understanding of the Trinity, most specifically that the Son is of the *same substance* as the Father (whatever that might mean). The Council of Nicaea was not only an important theological event; it was also a major political

---

2. Following current practice, I use throughout this volume the more neutral and inclusive abbreviations CE (of the Common Era) and BCE (Before the Common Era) rather than the specifically Christian terms AD (*Anno Domini*, in the year of the Lord) and BC (Before Christ).

3. See, for example, 1 Thessalonians 4:15 ("For this we declare to you by the word of the Lord, that *we who are alive, who are left until the second coming the Lord*, will by no means precede those who have died" [italics mine]). This verse indicates that Paul expected to live until the time of Jesus' second coming. So, too, 1 Corinthians 15:51–52, written about three or four years later in about 54 CE ("Listen, I will tell you a mystery! *We will not all die*, but we will all be changed, in a moment, in the twinkling of an eye, at the last trumpet. For the trumpet will sound, and the dead will be raised imperishable, and we will be changed" [italics mine]) reiterates Paul's belief that many of his generation would not die before Jesus' second coming.

event. It effectively united the church for the benefit of the empire, a move that led to the centralization of the Roman Empire in Constantinople.

The fourth ecumenical council was convened in 451 CE in Chalcedon, also in modern Turkey. The five hundred to six hundred bishops present adopted a statement of faith called the Chalcedonian Definition, which affirmed the existence in Christ of Two Natures, which are united "unconfusedly, unchangeably, indivisibly, and inseparably" (whatever that might mean). That formula maintains that Jesus Christ is in other words *wholly* human and *wholly* divine.

Subscribing to these two confessions, the Nicene Creed of 325 and the Chalcedonian Definition of 451, has become throughout most of the history of Christianity the principal test of orthodoxy—a word that means "correct teaching," as opposed to heresy, which means "choice" and which implies a "schism" or a "division" or a "faction" that knowingly and consciously deviates from the "correct teaching" of the universal church. Accepting the correct teaching of the universal or catholic church has been the principal measure of determining whether one is, indeed, a Christian or not, orthodox or heretical.

Christianity has generally required, first and foremost, personal subscription to the correct definitions of the Godhead, on the one hand, and of the dual nature of Jesus Christ, on the other hand. Christianity is, consequently, unique among the religions of the world in being first and foremost a belief system, that is, a subscription to correct or orthodox theology (teaching about the nature of God) and correct or orthodox Christology (teaching about the dual nature of Jesus Christ).

In the West, the period of the Middle Ages from 476 to the end of the fifteenth century is the age that approached most nearly the achievement of Christendom as a cultural unity. This period was characterized by the consolidation of ecclesiastical authority in the bishops of the west and, in particular, in the bishop of Rome as the first among the church's bishops. During this period there was, effectively, no separation between church and state, as we in the West have come to understand that principle in recent centuries.

Much of that unity in the West changed with the advent of the Reformation. Beginning in the fourteenth century with the attacks of the English reformer John Wycliffe and his followers, the Lollards, and their Czech associates Jan Hus and the Hussites, an involved series of changes began with assaults on the hierarchical and legalistic structure of the church as a whole, and on the papacy specifically.

From the beginning, the strongest criticism fell upon the papacy, since that institution was, more than any single thing, most responsible for that structure of the church. Consequently, when Martin Luther in the sixteenth century protested against the corruption of Rome and the serious abuses that attended the sale of indulgences, he was breaking no new ground but was, rather, advancing the earlier criticism of his fourteenth-century forbears.

John Calvin and Ulrich Zwingli in Switzerland challenged the authority of the bishops and, in particular, the authority of the pope, and identified authority as being vested instead in the Bible, the sixty-six books of the Old and New Testaments. The reformers saw themselves not as innovators, but as men who were returning to the state of primitive excellence that characterized the earliest church. In due course, Luther's study of Augustine led him to question the emphasis of late medieval theology upon "good works," and his historical studies, based on those of the fifteenth-century Italian humanist Lorenzo Valla, raised serious doubts regarding the validity of the claim of papal supremacy. The reformers believed that they were returning to the theology of Paul when they claimed that salvation came through faith rather than through works of the law, a position they associated with Roman Catholicism.

In affording this brief and imperfect sketch of a few critical periods in the history of the church, I am trying to call attention to the fact that the church and, in particular, the focus of the church's teaching and authority have changed or shifted significantly over the past twenty centuries. Christianity has not been static over its two-thousand-year history. It has rather been dynamic and has shown enormous adaptability in meeting the needs and the challenges of each new age. In each age there has been a strong political dimension both to the church and to its faith.

Looking to the future and trying to imagine what Christianity might be like by the end of its third millennium, a thousand years from now, I assume the following:

(1) The impact of the Enlightenment, which appeared in an especially unambiguous form in eighteenth-century Europe, will continue to have an even greater influence on Christianity in the future than it has had until now. Set within the increasing tendency to rationalism, the Enlightenment combined opposition to all supernatural religion and belief in the all-sufficiency of human reason with an ardent desire to promote the happiness of humankind in this life. One of the Enlightenment's chief ideals was religious toleration, although subsequent history makes that difficult to believe. Most representatives of the Enlightenment preserved the belief in God as the Creator who set the universe in motion, but they basically rejected the personal God of Western religion. They also believed that human freedom was consistent with reason, but they rejected Christian dogma and were hostile to both Catholicism and Protestant orthodoxy, which they regarded as powers of spiritual darkness that deprive humanity of the use of its rational faculties.

Their fundamental belief in the goodness of human nature produced an easy optimism and absolute faith in the progress and perfectibility of human society once the principles of enlightened reason were widely recognized. The spirit of the Enlightenment penetrated deeply into German Protestantism, where it disintegrated faith in the Bible and encouraged the development of biblical criticism, on the one hand, and fostered a reaction in emotional "Pietism," on the other hand. Both of these tendencies survive today.

I submit that increased acceptance of the principles of the Enlightenment in future centuries will mean that the fastest-growing denominations of this generation lack the rational foundation that will be needed to survive into Christianity's fourth millennium. To be quite blunt, pietistic tendencies like evangelical Christianity and twentieth-century American biblical fundamentalist denominations and sects have no long-term future. They are anomalies, even in this age. Like the Amish and the

Hasidic Jews, these reactionary movements have survived and flourished beyond their time. In spite of cycles of reformist fundamentalism, including the eighteenth-century Great Awakening and nineteenth-century movements near my home in upstate New York, history is against these movements. I cannot imagine fundamentalism of any kind surviving for very long into Christianity's third millennium, and certainly not into its fourth millennium.

(2) We live in a world of diversity in which people everywhere will continue to have increasing contact with people who are different from them—racially, culturally, and religiously. Christians (and others) will continue to assimilate ideas from secular movements and other religious movements, even as Christianity has done throughout its two-thousand-year history. Further assimilation will mean even more and more significant change in Christianity over the next millennium.

(3) Christianity *must* evolve in a way that will meet the needs and challenges of future generations. Otherwise, Christianity will diminish and possibly even disappear because of its irrelevance, as has been the case with countless religions that flourished in the past but that are now known largely from archaeological remains or textbooks. Much of what survives of these ancient religions is found in museums and art galleries, curiosities from humankind's ancient past. Much of mainstream Christianity is already irrelevant in these first years of its third millennium, but old things die hard. Establishment religions tend, by their very nature, to be conservative.

What kinds of things must change in Christianity? What kinds of accommodations will Christianity have to make in order to survive? I will indicate two rather recent developments to illustrate Christianity's success or failure at adaptation to new circumstances: (1) the ordination of women, and (2) the acceptance of gay men and lesbian women into the church and even more recently into the clergy. In both of these instances, the church or some denominations at least have responded positively to cultural changes that have challenged the social and religious status quo. To be sure, many denominations still refuse to ordain women, and even more continue to treat homosexuality as a sin and refuse to ordain gay men and lesbian women. It is my conviction that only those movements or denominations that adapt to changing times will survive. Those that do not adapt in a reasonable period of time will lose members and become insignificant sects, well outside the mainstream—like the Shakers, the Amish, and Hasidic Jews.

One question I have is whether the church will lead or just follow during times of significant social change. It is essential that the church understand when change is required and what kind of change is appropriate. By their very nature, religions tend to resist change, but from time to time prophetic figures in virtually every religious tradition challenge the status quo and introduce revolutionary ideas that bring necessary change, often quickly and quite dramatically.

Let's look together at issues that are far more challenging to the future of Christianity than the status of women or gays and lesbians in the church. In my opinion, those issues are no-brainers. It's time to get over it and catch up with the future. There are, however, four matters that come to mind that lie at the heart of Christianity and that need to be revisited and addressed over the next decades or centuries, and certainly before Christianity enters its fourth millennium. If not, I predict, Christianity will simply not make it through this, its third, millennium.

1. THE QUESTION OF GOD

Are Christians prepared to understand that God is not an anthropomorphic being, that God may not be a *He*, or even a *She* for that matter? (So much of feminist theology, in my opinion, substitutes bad theology with even worse theology.) Are we prepared to desist from creating God in *our* image? Do we understand that the concept of a personal God is too limiting? Too archaic?

I like to believe that Moses got it right almost 3,300 years ago when he told his followers not to make any images of their god. I think the problem is that not only carved images, but also conceptual images, are idolatrous. Unlike Judaism and Islam, Christianity has generally ignored Moses' commandment against making images of God. The history of Christian art and Christian theology is replete with representations of God, both *physical* representations and, maybe even more important, *conceptual* representations that taint the way in which we understand that word "God."

I submit to you that Moses was correct: our God is frankly too small. We must learn how to deconstruct God, or, more accurately, to deconstruct the outdated Christian concept of God.

2. THE QUESTION OF THE BIBLE

What about our understanding of the Bible, the canon of sacred scriptures? What does it mean to call this collection of sixty-six (or more) books "authoritative," especially when professional biblical scholarship makes it increasingly more clear that these books are human creations that reflect the teachings and the values of the time and place in which each was written?

We are surrounded by biblical fundamentalists, especially in America's South and in the form of TV evangelists—what I call "The Electronic Church." Fundamentalism is a movement in various Protestant denominations, which developed after World War I, especially in the United States. It rigidly upholds what it believes to be traditional orthodox Christian doctrines, and especially the doctrine of the literal inerrancy of the Bible. Biblical fundamentalism attracted widespread public attention in 1925, when William Jennings Bryan, the American Democratic leader, assisted in the prosecution of J. T. Scopes, a Tennessee schoolteacher, who was convicted of violating Tennessee state law by teaching biological evolution.

In a wider sense the term is applied to all profession of strict adherence to religious orthodoxy, especially in the matter of biblical interpretation. Recent evidence of the strength of the movement is manifest in the 1999 decision of the Kansas

Board of Education to delete the teaching of biological evolution and the big bang theory of the origin of the universe from the state's science curriculum. After considerable lobbying by liberal groups, that decision was overturned. But religious fundamentalism is still strong, especially in the South in the United States.

In future generations will Christians be increasingly open to understanding what the Bible is and what it is not? We know that Genesis is *not* a science manual in spite of those who persist in dismissing biological evolution and the big bang theory because they appear to contradict the account of creation in Genesis 1–2. It is interesting to speculate about how Christians will understand their scriptures a thousand years from now. I promise you that it will be quite different from the way in which most Christians currently understand the Bible. I trust that biblical fundamentalism will most assuredly be dead, a curiosity of twentieth-century reaction against the thrust of science and the Enlightenment.

Rather, Christians can and must understand more clearly how to distinguish in the Bible that which is truly *timeless* from that which was simply *timely*. The exercise is difficult, and sometimes painful, but it is essential to the future of Christianity. We must understand more clearly what the Bible is and what it is not.

3. THE QUESTION OF JESUS

And what about Jesus? Who was he anyway? What kind of man was he? Are we prepared to reexamine the question of Jesus' divinity and deal with him exclusively in his humanity? Will Christians be able to understand that phrases like "Son of God" may have symbolic meaning beyond trying to establish the genealogical or biological relationship of Jesus to God? I hope so, or I fear that Christianity will face extinction by virtue of irrelevance. Do we really need to believe that God or the Holy Spirit provided the sperm (or its spiritual equivalent) for Mary's impregnation?

We saw earlier that the Christian doctrine of the Trinity was carved out of fourth-century theological and Christological disputes within the Church that borrowed and adopted philosophical language then current in the Greco-Roman intellectual world. The form of the Nicene Creed was as much the result of a political decision on the part of Emperor Constantine as it was the victory of the followers of Bishop Athanasius over the followers of Arius. The Council of Nicaea has been characterized as an ecclesiastical dispute over a single iota, the Greek letter *i*. Are the Father and the Son of the same substance (*homoousia* in Greek) or are they of similar substance (*homoiousia* in Greek)? Interestingly, the "same substance" theologians prevailed at the council, with considerable help or encouragement from the emperor. Ironically, much of contemporary Christian theology is more of the "similar substance" variety. Ultimately, Arianism may prevail over what has been orthodoxy for almost seventeen centuries. In any case, we must begin to understand more clearly the role of a de-divinized Jesus, a Jesus who was, in life, fully human, but whom the church increasingly divinized.

4. THE QUESTION OF MYTH

What about Christianity's mythical view of the world and its mythical understanding of salvation and redemption? About sixty years ago German New Testament scholar and theologian Rudolf Bultmann recognized that the cosmology of the New Testament is essentially mythical in character. The world of the Bible is viewed as a three-storied structure, with the earth in the center, heaven above, and the underworld beneath. Heaven is the abode of God and the angels; the underworld is hell, the abode of Satan, the devil, and the place of torment and punishment for human evil-doers.

Even the earth is not simply the scene of everyday natural events. It is the scene of the supernatural activity of God and his angels on the one hand, and of Satan and his demons on the other. The New Testament presupposes this mythical view of the world in its preaching:

> In the fullness of time God sent forth his Son, a pre-existent divine Being, who appears on earth as a man. He dies the death of a sinner on the cross and makes atonement for the sins of [humankind]. His resurrection marks the beginning of the cosmic catastrophe. Death, the consequence of Adam's sin is abolished, and the demonic forces are deprived of their power. The risen Christ is exalted to the right hand of God in heaven and made "Lord" and "King." He will come again on the clouds of heaven to complete the work of redemption, and the resurrection and judgment of everyone will follow. Sin, suffering, and death will then be finally abolished. All this is to happen very soon; indeed, St. Paul thinks he himself will live to see it. All those who belong to Christ's Church and are joined to the Lord by Baptism and the Eucharist are certain of resurrection to salvation, etc., etc., etc.[4]

This all sounds very familiar, doesn't it? It is at the heart of the church's creeds; it is what is regularly preached in Christian churches every Sunday and daily on TV. Bultmann claims that this preached message is couched in mythological language whose origin can easily be traced to the mythology of first-century Jewish and Hellenistic thought. Bultmann, a Lutheran minister, maintained that Christianity's preaching is incredible and unbelievable for modern men and women, because the ancient mythical view of the world that it assumes is pure and simply obsolete.

It was Bultmann's view that there is, in fact, nothing specifically Christian in this mythical view of the world as such. It is nothing more or less than the cosmology of a prescientific age that was assumed and embraced by our religious forbears. Bultmann pointed out that the real purpose of myth is not to present an objective picture of the world as it is, but to express an understanding of *our* place in the world. Are we prepared to set aside or reinterpret ancient mythologies, or are we

---

4. Quoted from Rudolf Bultmann, "New Testament and Mythology: The Mythical Element of the New Testament and the Problem of Its Re-interpretation," *Kerygma and Myth*, ed. Hans Werner Bartsch, trans. Reginald H. Fuller (London: S.P.C.K., 1953–62), p. 2. Bultmann provides in fourteen footnotes dozens of passages in the New Testament to support this summary of what he calls the church's kerygma, or apostolic preaching.

bound to embrace, as Christians, a worldview that we know to be untrue? Should we continue to put our religion in one pocket and our science in another and continue to lead our personal lives as intellectual schizophrenics? I trust not!

These four issues are the focus of the four sections of this volume: the deconstruction of the Christian concept of God, the meaning and role of the Bible in Christianity, the role of Jesus in Christianity, and the role of myth in the past, the present, and the future. In my opinion, addressing these four questions fully, openly, and honestly is essential to the future of Christianity. Accordingly, our understanding of these issues will necessarily serve as the foundation of a Christianity for the new millennium.

Part 1
GOD

Chapter 1

RELIGIOUS AUTHORITY AND REASON

Conflicting Modes for Attaining Truth

*I*t was originally my intention to open this volume by rehearsing still one more time the familiar but now tedious discussion of the perceived conflict between faith and reason. In fact, I had already written this chapter with focus on that theme when I realized that I wanted to recast the issue in a somewhat different form. Far too often, it is the quest for power that resides near the center of most religions; hence, I decided to recast my discussion by acknowledging just that, but specifically in the case of Christianity.

It is beyond the scope of this chapter to trace the two-thousand-year history of the Christian church, or even the history of Christian theology. Suffice it to state at the outset that, beginning with the earliest community of believers, the church moved in a direction that diverged significantly from the teachings of the historical Jesus and that it has continued along that misdirected detour for the past two thousand years.[5]

Following Jesus' death in about 30 CE, it was not at all clear that a community of his followers would or should survive intact. Furthermore, even after the assembly of Jesus' disciples (the church) began to gather and to take shape, it was unclear where within that community authority should be vested. Contrary to popular belief, Jesus most assuredly never intended to establish a church or a new religion, hence, the dilemma. During his lifetime, Jesus made no unambiguous or unmistakable provision for what should happen after his death. The passage in Matthew 16:17–19 appears to contradict my claim:

> 17And Jesus answered him [Peter], "Blessed are you Simon son of Jonah! For flesh and blood has not revealed this to you, but my Father in heaven. 18And I tell you, you are Peter [Greek *petros*], and on this rock [Greek *petra*] I will build my church, and the gates of Hades will not prevail against it. 19I will give you the keys of the

---

5. The case for this claim will be made in the two chapters in part 3, "Jesus."

kingdom of heaven, and whatever you bind on earth will be bound in heaven, and
whatever you loose on earth will be loosed in heaven."

The Roman Catholic Church has historically pointed to this passage as the basis for
its claim that Jesus established the church with Peter as its first head (or pope), to
whom he then assigned the authority to bind and to loose.[6] Roman Catholics and
Protestants have argued for centuries over the meaning of this passage, specifically
whether Peter (the Roman Catholic view) or Peter's confession of faith that Jesus is
the Messiah (the Protestant view) is the "rock" on which the church is built. The disagreement is largely irrelevant, because few reputable New Testament scholars
believe that these so-called words of institution actually come from the historical
Jesus. Inasmuch as most scholars agree that Jesus never intended to establish a new
religion, it is particularly imperative, therefore, to look at one fascinating feature of
the history of the Christian church: the struggle on the part of the church to acquire
and maintain temporal authority, or power.

In this chapter, I intend to look at the question of authority within the church by
focusing on three issues:

1. The church's investment of authority in its ecclesiastical hierarchy and the
   resulting development of Christian orthodoxy. The emergence in the West of
   the Roman Catholic Church and the concentration of authority in the bishop
   of Rome, the pope, is an important component of this picture.
2. The Protestant Reformation's challenge to the authority of the Roman Catholic
   Church and the pope and the ensuing Protestant shift of authority from the
   pope to the Bible, those books that the church has historically considered
   inspired writings and identified as its canon of sacred scriptures. Luther's claim
   of *sola scriptura* (only the scriptures) is critical in this regard.
3. The emergence of an entirely different authority in the wake of the Enlightenment's establishment of the primacy of human reason. The emergence of
   modern science and philosophy, working in tandem, challenged both the
   Roman Catholic claim to the authority vested in the pope, and the Protestant
   claim of the authority vested in the Bible.

Another way of looking at this chapter might be to refer to it as "The Construction
and Deconstruction of the Claim to Authority in the Christian Church." The issue
involves not only the struggle between faith and reason as conflicting models for
attaining truth. It involves, as well, and maybe even more, the human quest for
power and the claim to authority, even when that claim involves using or abusing
religion as a means to power. The claim to authority and the acquisition of power

---

6. The play on words between the name "Peter" (Greek *petros*) and the word "rock" (Greek
petra) is important in this passage. In fact, in the (original) Aramaic they are actually the same
word *kepha*, hence in the New Testament the Greek name "Peter" is sometimes rendered by the
Aramaic original "Cephas" (see, for example, 1 Corinthians 15:5 and Galatians 1:18; 2:9, 11, 14).

have been all too rampant in the history of Christianity—Roman Catholic, Protestant, and Eastern Orthodox alike—and have led not only to the corruption of individuals but to the corruption and distortion of Christianity as well.

THE ORIGINS AND DEVELOPMENT OF RELIGIOUS AUTHORITY AND CHRISTIAN ORTHODOXY

From its modest beginnings just weeks after Jesus' death, the Christian community began the process of changing the religion *of* Jesus into a religion *about* Jesus. From the earliest stage in the life of the church, Jesus ceased being the great prophet and celebrated teacher that he was in life and was instead transformed by his disciples and their successors into the subject matter and focus of a new religion. The transforming events were Jesus' death by crucifixion and the church's subsequent claim that Jesus had been raised from the dead and elevated to a position of honor and authority at the right hand of God.

The church purported to take shape around Jesus' teaching. Yet, to accomplish the shift in focus from the *teaching* of Jesus to the *person* of Jesus, the church took the necessary step of gradually putting into Jesus' mouth sayings that Jesus himself almost certainly never spoke. Many of the sayings attributed to Jesus in the Gospels reflect beliefs of the Christian community *about* Jesus projected back into the mouth of the prophet/teacher.

The first two or three generations of believers were responsible for creating a body of writings that transformed the human Jesus into the future Son of Man, the Lord, the Redeemer, the divine Son of God. Still later generations of Christians collected twenty-seven of those Christian writings that had been produced during the period about 50 to 150 CE into what the church came to call the New Testament.

By the end of the second century the institutional church was taking shape. The church's ecclesiastical officials—bishops, elders, and deacons—were vested with or claimed for themselves the increased authority that was necessary for them to define for Christian communities the difference between what was correct teaching (or orthodoxy), and what was false or schismatic teaching (or heresy). The bishops also empowered themselves to identify those early Christian writings that, in their judgment, reflected what they claimed to be the apostolic teaching of the church. They claimed that teaching could be traced back to the earliest followers of Jesus and, therefore, presumably to Jesus himself. This anthology of books emerged as the heart of the Christian scriptures.

The church even assigned to its four *anonymous* gospels authorship by apostles or by disciples of apostles to secure the authoritative claim of apostolicity. The Gospels of Matthew and John were purported to have been written by eyewitnesses to the events; the Gospel of Mark by a disciple of Peter, and the Gospel of Luke by a disciple of Paul. Few scholars today accept the apostolic authorship of any of these otherwise anonymous gospels.

Toward the end of the second century, Irenaeus (ca. 140–ca. 202), bishop of Lyon, took steps to identify the core of a canon of authoritative Christian scriptures (a New Testament) on a par with the authoritative writings of the earliest church, the Jewish scriptures. By referring to the Jewish scriptures as the Old Testament or old covenant, the church was using terminology that expressed the Christian belief that these older Jewish writings were essentially inferior or incomplete when compared to the books of the New Testament (or new covenant). The Old Testament belonged to the old order, Judaism, which God had now replaced with the new order, the Body of Christ, the Christian church.[7]

Although there was little uniformity of belief and even less formal organization or ecclesiastical authority within and among Christian communities during the first six or seven decades of the church's history, the notion of a universal or Catholic Church began to emerge and take shape during the second century. The church in Rome gradually assumed for itself the position of primary authority within the universal church. Peter and Paul, major early figures in the movement, had died in Rome. Although neither was the actual founder of Roman Christianity, their significance to generations of Jesus' followers helped to validate the importance of the Christian Church in Rome. In addition, Rome was the seat of the empire, and by the beginning of the second century the Roman church was the largest in the Christian world. Because Roman Christianity claimed to stem from Peter and Paul, Christians, particularly in the West, looked to Rome as the preserver and representative of apostolic Christianity. Accordingly, the Roman bishop emerged as an authority not only in Rome, but increasingly so in churches in other cities in the Roman Empire, as well.

The authority of the Roman church was sealed in the first quarter of the fourth century by the conversion to Christianity of the Roman emperor Constantine, whose life spanned the years 280–337. In 312, at a time when the Roman Empire was in disarray, Constantine invaded Italy. On the eve of the battle for Rome, Constantine believed that he had seen in the heavens a vision of a cross and that God had spoken to him saying, "*in hoc signo vinces*" ("By this sign you will conquer"). Constantine was convinced that in 313 the Christian God had delivered to him at the Milvian Bridge the victory over Maxentius and had thereby entrusted Rome into his hands.

As a result of this victory, Constantine was now supreme ruler in the West. As a result of his vision, Constantine was committed to an alliance with the Christian church. From that day forward the emperor presumed that the Christian God would assure the unity and welfare of the Roman Empire. Shortly after his victory at Rome, Constantine, now emperor in the West, and his brother-in-law Licinius, emperor in the East, jointly promulgated the so-called Edict of Milan in early 313. This imperial decree granted Christians throughout the Roman Empire the freedom to practice their religion without threat of interference from the state.

---

7. The term "old testament" or "old covenant" is already alluded to in Hebrews 8:6–7: "But Jesus has now obtained a more excellent ministry, and to that degree he is the mediator of a better covenant, which has been enacted through better promises. For if that first covenant had been faultless, there would have been no need to look for a second one."

Eight years later in 321, Constantine issued a decree allowing Christian churches to inherit legacies from wealthy benefactors. In the same decree, he designated Sunday, the day of the Sun in the Roman calendar and the day of Jesus' resurrection for Christians, as a weekly holiday free from work. In addition, Constantine instituted a reform that assigned to the bishop of Rome the authority to resolve cases when both parties willingly agreed to the arrangement. Although Christianity continued for many years to be a minority religion in the Roman Empire, Constantine became increasingly involved in the affairs of the church, thereby further strengthening the church's influence. It was the emperor's policy to unite the Christian church to the Roman state, and he took the necessary steps to see to it that the marriage worked.

Constantine's brother-in-law Licinius continued to rule the Eastern Roman Empire until Constantine defeated him in 324 at Chrysopolis, across from Byzantium, and gained control of the East. The final struggle between the two emperors was caused, at least in part, by Licinius's mistreatment of Christians through a number of imperial measures. From 324 until his death in 337 Constantine ruled as sole emperor of the Roman Empire. To solidify further his authority in the East, Constantine built his new capital on the site of the thousand-year-old Greek colony of Byzantium, renaming it in 330 Constantinople, the city of Constantine.

Upon assuming leadership over the unified empire, Constantine found the Christian church embroiled in a divisive theological debate over the relationship of the Son of God to the Father. To address the matter, the emperor summoned the bishops of the universal church to a council in 325 in Nicaea in Asia Minor.[8] At that council Constantine, probably on the advice of the Spanish bishop Hosius, proposed the formula of *homoousia*, the consubstantiation of the Father and the Son. This first ecumenical or universal council of the church produced the Nicene Creed, a confession of faith that maintained that the Son was of the "same substance" as the Father (whatever that might mean!). This formula has served the subsequent history of the church as the definition of Christian orthodoxy on the question of the relationship of the Father and the Son.

Nicaea was the first universal council of the church. It was also unique in that the emperor himself not only attended but dominated the proceedings. The Arian enemies of the Nicene formula denied that the Father and the Son were of the same

---

8. Even earlier, in 313, a group in the North African church known as Donatists was at odds with the Roman church when they refused to accept Rome's appointment of Caecilian as bishop of Carthage. The North African group consecrated instead Majorinus, who was shortly thereafter succeeded by Donatus. Followers of Donatus, the Donatists, appealed to Constantine to settle the matter. The emperor initially referred the case to a commission of bishops, then to a synod of Italy and Gaul, but ultimately Constantine decided to hear the case himself in 316. At every step along the way the Donatists lost their case, whereupon they attacked their ecclesiastical opponents, and ultimately the state itself. What is noteworthy about this case is that an important precedent had already been set with the involvement of the emperor in the affairs of the church.

substance (*homoousia*) and maintained, instead, that the Son was rather of "like" or "similar substance" (*homoiousia*) with the Father.[9] By the time of Constantine's baptism on his deathbed in 337, the *homoiousia* party or the Arian opponents of the Nicene formula (*homoousia*) had gained the upper hand, but the Nicene formula ultimately prevailed in its definition of the relationship of the Son to the Father. This victory came, however, much later in 381 under Emperor Theodosius I at the Council of Constantinople. Theodosius I is also generally credited with stamping out the last vestiges of paganism in the Roman Empire and with putting an end to the Arian heresy. For his work, he became one of the few emperors usually referred to as "the Great."

The period from 313 (the Edict of Milan) to the fall of the Western Empire in 476 witnessed steady growth of the authority of the bishops of Rome. The Western Roman Empire fell to the Germanic Odoacer, who deposed the last emperor ruling from Rome. Nevertheless, by the end of the fourth century, the bishop of Rome had acquired still more authority, perhaps in part because there was virtually no challenge from a secular authority. Although the basis of the authority of the Roman church was deeply rooted in the fact that Rome had been the seat of the empire, that the Roman church was the wealthiest of all churches, and that Peter and Paul were buried in Rome, the preeminence of the bishop of Rome was based ultimately on the claim that its bishops were the successors of Peter, the first bishop of Rome, upon whom Jesus himself had established his church. As we argued in the introduction, not only is it questionable that Jesus actually spoke the words of Matthew 16:18–19; it is quite evident that these words reflect the teaching of one early Christian community, possibly Antioch where the Gospel of Matthew may have been written. Furthermore, even if it could be demonstrated that Jesus actually spoke these words during his lifetime, there is nothing in the text to suggest that Jesus was naming Peter as the first bishop of Rome, the first pope, and that Peter's successors would continue to serve in that role. That argument came into play only after Rome was already contending for primacy within the church.

By the end of the fourth century the authority of the Roman church was acknowledged almost universally in the West, and to some extent even in the East. However, Constantine's political decision to move his capital from Rome in the West to Constantinople in the East contributed to the tension over the claim to authority that already existed between Rome and Constantinople. By centralizing his empire in Constantinople, Constantine not only established imperial control of the Eastern church, but he also unintentionally allowed the authority of the bishop of Rome to grow unchecked in the West since there was no longer any prominent lay authority in Rome to challenge the pope's authority.

---

9. Some have remarked half-jokingly that the Council of Nicaea was a council of bishops that quibbled over an iota, the Greek letter *i*, because the difference between the Greek words *homoousia* (of the same [Greek *homo*] substance) and *homoiousia* (of similar or like [Greek *homoi*] substance) is in the absence or inclusion of an iota. Of course, the theological difference is enormous.

For seven centuries following Constantine's death, the church in the West, whose authority resided in Rome, and the church in the East, whose authority resided in Constantinople, vied for power, even as they remained essentially in communion. A glance at the struggle between East and West for authority and power indicates the depth of the issue and illustrates how this struggle led ultimately to the first major schism within the church.

Although the seeds of the division between Rome and Constantinople had already been planted in the fourth century, the first serious struggle for power between Eastern and Western Christianity was set in motion in 492 with the accession of Pope Gelasius in Rome. Early in his four-year reign, Gelasius decided to challenge Acacius, the patriarch of Constantinople, on the issue of Rome's claim to universal authority. Gelasius would concede to the East nothing that would compromise in any way the preeminent power and supremacy of Rome over the whole of Christianity. The pope persisted in claiming that Rome's primacy was derived not from an ecumenical council, but from Christ's divine institution of the Roman church. Gelasius maintained that Christ had conferred the primacy over the whole church upon Peter and thereafter upon his successors, the bishops of Rome. Rome was now interpreting the meaning of Jesus' words in Matthew 16 even more broadly to extend to the authority of the popes, who were, it claimed, the legitimate successors of Peter. Pope Gregory (the Great) repeated these same claims regarding Rome's supremacy over the universal church during his reign from 590 to 604.

Events of the eleventh century were in significant measure a repeat of these earlier struggles for ecclesiastical, if not political, power. In 1009 Pope Sergius of Rome wrote a confession of faith which incorporated the *filioque* in the creed, namely that the Holy Spirit proceeds "from the Father *and the Son* [*filioque* in Latin]." In response to this action, the church at Constantinople removed Pope Sergius's name and the name of the Roman church from its diptychs, the church tablets on which were written the names of sister churches and bishops officially recognized and liturgically commemorated. The Eastern formula for that portion of the creed was that the Holy Spirit proceeds "from the Father *by* the Son" instead of "from the Father *and* the Son [*filioque*]," hence Constantinople viewed the publication of Pope Sergius' confession of faith as still one more deliberate attempt by Rome to force the Eastern church to submit to the authority of the Roman bishop on a matter of theology.

A half century later, in 1054, a delegation from Rome, lead by Cardinal Hubert at the command of Pope Leo IX, traveled to Constantinople to establish union between the two churches, entirely on Rome's terms. The patriarch of Constantinople, Michael Cerularius, suspecting the political motives behind the visit, refused even to meet with the papal delegation. The visit ended with the Roman delegation excommunicating the Constantinopolitan patriarch, who was determined not only to establish his authority over other Eastern patriarchs but also to establish his independence from and equality with Rome. The official reasons for Hubert's denunciation and excommunication of Cerularius were the Eastern church's removal of the *filioque* from the creed, the Orthodox practice of married clergy, and the church's liturgical errors. Patriarch Michael Cerularius responded to Cardinal Hubert's action by excommunicating everyone responsible for the incident, and Cerularius, in turn, drew up a list of Roman abuses, including such differing liturgical practices in the Roman church as the use of unleavened rather than leavened bread for the celebration of the Eucharist, and baptism by one immersion in water instead of three. Thus began officially the great East-West schism, which persists to this day between Roman Catholic and Eastern Orthodox Christianity.[10]

Let there be no mistake. The church, especially the Roman church, was deeply involved in a struggle for power, both religious and political. Even in the so-called proto-orthodox period before the Council of Nicaea in 325, bishops vied for temporal power and often suppressed Christian communities with which they were in theological disagreement. By assuming the power to crush the views of others, by declaring some Christian writings as orthodox and others as heretical, bishops were major players in the Realpolitik of the church.

The Council of Nicaea in 325 was itself as much a political event as it was a theological one. Constantine was clearly using the church to enhance his own political power, even as the church was using the emperor to enhance its power within the empire. Out of this marriage of church and state came an imperial church, an uncomfortable and ultimately unhealthy wedding of religion and politics that has only recently led to a partial separation in some Western democracies.

It can be argued that Christianity was never meant to be an establishment religion. Christianity began as a protest movement, a peripheral cult within Judaism. A movement that originates by speaking out with a prophetic voice against an establishment religion or against an authority that merges religion and politics generally loses its prophetic voice once it gains temporal power. The thirst for power and authority easily seduces most peripheral cults into becoming powerful establishment religions. Christianity lost its heart and its soul when it embraced the position that temporal power was more important than adhering to and promoting the radical ethical teachings of its founding prophet.

So, too, the East/West schism was as much about power and politics as it was about theology, perhaps even more so. The real issue was whether Rome was willing to share power with Constantinople, which it was not; and whether Constantinople was willing to submit to Roman authority, which it was not.

Concurrent with the struggle for power between the Roman and Greek churches

---

10. The *Washington Post* reported on November 1, 2003 (p. B9), that "Roman Catholic and Orthodox Christian leaders in North America announced partial agreement on a doctrinal issue that has divided the two Christian branches for nearly 1,000 years." In a joint statement, the two groups affirmed the "normative and irrevocable dogmatic value" of the wording of the Constantinopolitan Creed of 381. The agreement recommends that Roman Catholics hereafter use the original text of the creed in worship (meaning Roman Catholics would drop the offending *filioque* [and the Son] from the creed) and cancel the anathema against Orthodox Christian usage issued by a council in 1274. The *Post* noted that these recommendations require Vatican approval. One giant step for ecumenism! But, a creed is still a creed!

was the conflict between the Roman and Irish churches. The issues were not theological, but focused primarily on the matter of ecclesiastical organization. The Irish church stemmed from Egyptian monasticism and was organized around monasteries rather than dioceses. The heads of land-owning communities, namely abbots and abbesses, exercised significant authority over bishops. Irish missionaries took their brand of Christianity to the British Isles, and converted many of the Germanic tribes, notably the Franks. In doing so, the Irish ran into Roman efforts, notably in the person of Pope Gregory I, to impose a hierarchical episcopal-papal structure throughout the church. In the twelfth century, Rome urged, or certainly approved, Anglo-Norman efforts to conquer Ireland. This encounter between Irish Christianity and Rome further supports my claim regarding the political quest for power within the church.

Before moving on to the next section, I would be remiss if I did not mention, however briefly, the Crusades of the eleventh, twelfth, and thirteenth centuries (1096 to 1296). These military expeditions undertaken by European Christians had as their stated objective the liberation of the Holy Land from the hands of Muslim infidels.

Even after Islam moved into Jerusalem in 637, European Christians continued to make pilgrimages to the holy sites. However, that became more difficult after the East-West schism of 1054 and even more difficult after the fall of Jerusalem to the Seljukian Turks in 1071.

Christians had always entertained the hope of recovering the holy places from the Muslim infidels, as the church generally referred to Islam. Furthermore, the gradual expulsion of Arabs from Spain and Sicily in the ninth century encouraged Christians in their hope to recover the Holy Land. The church had always understood that large areas of the Middle East had been lost to Islam at the expense of Christianity. By the times of the First Crusade (1066–1099), virtually all of Asia Minor (modern-day western Turkey) had fallen into the hands of the Islamic infidels.

The European Christians experienced modest victories or concessions during the two hundred years of the Crusades, capturing or controlling at times Antioch, Jerusalem, Nazareth, Bethlehem, Edessa, Byzantine Constantinople, and parts of Egypt, but the Christians were ultimately driven back, and the kingdom of Jerusalem passed once again into the hands of the Muslims. The Crusader misadventures were, of course, ultimately political events, efforts to extend the influence of the church to regions that Christianity had lost to Islam centuries earlier. They were about the extension of religious and political power.

A century and a half after the end of the last Crusade, an even greater loss for Christianity came with the fall of Constantinople. The capital of the Eastern Empire for more than a thousand years,[11] from its establishment by Constantine in 330, Constantinople fell to the Turks in 1453. Renamed Istanbul, the city served as the

---

11. There was a brief interruption in that period between 330 and 1453, when from 1204 to 1241 the Crusaders captured and held Constantinople and made it for a short period of time the capital of a Latin empire. It appeared, however briefly, that there could be a forced reunification of East and West.

Turkish capital until 1923, when, with the establishment of the Turkish Republic, the capital was transferred to Ankara.

When the stakes are high, lofty principles generally take a backseat to the quest for power.

THE RENAISSANCE AND THE REFORMATION

To a considerable extent the emergence of human reason as the primary criterion for truth had its origins in the driving forces behind the Renaissance and the Reformation. Beginning in the late fourteenth century in Italy and spreading through much of western Europe, the Renaissance revived an interest in antiquity, particularly in ancient Israel, ancient Egypt, ancient Mesopotamia, ancient Greece, and ancient Rome. This "rebirth" movement (the literal translation of the French word "Renaissance") brought a new attention to the languages, history, literature, art, architecture, philosophy, and religion of the ancient world. Renewed interest in the classics and in the ancient languages resulted in related critical work, including the preparation of editions of the classics, scriptures, and patristic writings. This effort was in place by 1400, and it was still in progress as late as 1700. Closely related to the interest in the classics was the development of the concepts of anachronism and historical periodization. Focus on the classics created a secular periodization of ancient, medieval, and new or modern that both paralleled and challenged the Christian teleological view that history has a definite and discernable purpose and is being directed by God toward a definite end. It was no longer clear that there was an overall design or purpose in history.

In addition to the new cosmology of Copernicus and others, there were also the challenges of the new geography and, with it, ethnography. The discovery of new worlds and new peoples beyond Europe raised fundamental questions about human nature and society. In *Utopia* (published in 1516), Sir Thomas More (1478–1535) posited an ideal non-Christian society (although it eagerly embraces Christianity) that had achieved a more peaceful and equitable social order than what existed in Christian Europe. In *Utopia*, More set out to critique the serious corruption of European civil life. Inspired by Plato's *Republic* and by the accounts of explorers such as Amerigo Vespucci and Christopher Columbus, More's work played a vital role in advancing the humanist awakening of the sixteenth century, which increasingly moved Europe away from the otherworldliness of medieval Christianity toward Renaissance secularism.

In other cases, writers focused on the "noble savage,"[12] a romantic notion of

---

12. The English poet and dramatist John Dryden (1631–1700) first used the phrase in 1672. The concept appears in many later works of the eighteenth and nineteenth centuries. It is associated especially with the philosophy of the French deist Jean-Jacques Rousseau (1712–1778) and with romanticism generally. Mary Shelley's (1797–1851) *Frankenstein* (1818) is one of the best-known examples of such stories in which the noble savage (the monster) is initially the embodiment of the ideal.

humankind free from the restraints of civilization. The noble savage, the quintessence of the uninhibited person, represented the idea that without the limitations of civilization, humankind is essentially good. This romantic idea of the noble savage did not mean that Europeans thought that the recently discovered indigenous peoples of Africa, Asia, the Middle East, and the Americas were their political and social equals. On the contrary, Europeans regarded them as fair game for exploitation, colonization, and even genocide. After all, they were not like us; they were not Christians; they were pagans, ripe for conversion to the one true religion.

The second great schism in the history of the church came almost five hundred years later than the East-West schism in the form of the Protestant Reformation. Despite challenges to the authority of the Roman church from Gallicanism beginning in thirteenth-century France, from John Wycliffe and the Lollards in late-fourteenth-century England, from Jan Hus and the Hussites in early-fifteenth-century Prague, and from other pre-Reformation movements in Europe, there was little expectation at the beginning of the sixteenth century that Germany or any other European country could successfully question the Roman Catholic Church's position of supreme leadership. Yet, an Augustinian monk named Martin Luther (1483–1546) joined the critics of the Roman Catholic Church's abuse of the sale of indulgences and threw the church into turmoil.

Building on the Renaissance's interest in the ancient world, the Reformation brought about a significant shift in the understanding of the seat of authority in Christian Europe. Until the time of the Protestant Reformation, the Roman Catholic Church served as the primary authority in the West. The teachings of the Roman Catholic Church were based to be sure on the Bible, but on the Bible as understood and interpreted by the fathers of the church and, most especially, by the church's successive representatives in Rome, the popes. Luther questioned the authority of the Roman Catholic Church and, in particular, the authority of the pope and shifted primary authority for all religious matters from the church to the holy scriptures.

Luther seems to have experienced something like a prophetic call sometime between 1512 and 1515 in what is usually called his *Turmerlebnis* (or "Tower Experience"). This experience came to Luther as a sudden revelation and convinced him of the truth of the Gospel, namely that justification comes by faith alone (*fide sola*), apart from works of the law. This phrase, which was apparently contained in his revelation, became the cornerstone of Luther's teaching and the slogan of his Reformation. Luther's strong emphasis on the all-pervading action of God in bringing about human salvation undermined both the importance of Christians performing good works and the role of human freedom or free will as an avenue or means to salvation.

In his polemic *An Open Letter to the Christian Nobility of the German Nation* (1520), and elsewhere throughout his later writings, Luther denied both the infallibility of the church's ecumenical councils and the primacy of the bishop of Rome, the pope. He exposed what he considered the absurdity of the church's claim that the pope alone is the singular authorized interpreter of the sacred scriptures. Rather, Luther claimed, everyone who is inspired with the spirit and the mind of Christ and who has the true faith has the right, the capability, and the responsibility to interpret the Bible. He assigned to the Bible primacy in all matters that had previously been referred to the Roman Catholic Church and, in particular, to the pope.

Luther made a direct appeal to the German princes to embrace his efforts to reform the church and called upon them to end their financial support of the Roman Catholic Church, its masses for the dead, its celibate clergy, its religious orders, its pilgrimages, and other ecclesiastical institutions and practices. Luther was trying to undermine the financial solvency of the Roman church. There was a particularly strong political overtone to Luther's appeal to the German princes in 1525 to check the insurrection of German peasants, which arose from the severe economic suffering of a large segment of the German peasantry. With Luther's backing for the cruel annihilation of the peasants, the rebellion was brutally suppressed, and the power of the Lutheran princes, upon whom Luther relied for protection and support, was strengthened.

When Luther assigned primary importance to the Bible, he, of course, did not have in mind the modern historical-critical method of examining and analyzing the Bible. He was claiming that not the Roman Catholic Church, not the Roman pope, but the Bible itself is the sole seat of ultimate authority, the vehicle through which the Holy Spirit works for his people. Luther was interested in the literal meaning of the scriptures. He assumed that the scriptures contain their own interpretation and that it is essential for individual Christians to be inspired by the spirit in order for them to come to the proper understanding of the meaning of the sacred texts. Luther put the Bible into the hands of the people by translating it into the vernacular German, a contribution that was largely responsible for the development of the modern German language.

With the Bible in the hands of the people, how could anyone distinguish between opposing interpretations by two individuals, both of whom claimed that their understanding of the text was what the Bible *really* meant? Luther believed that there should be no problem in understanding the scriptures, just as long as Christ remains the principal focus in the interpreter's endeavor. That requisite, of course, flies in the face of the modern historical-critical method. Yet, by putting the Bible into the hands of the people, Luther laid the groundwork for the subsequent development of biblical criticism. Now just about any literate person could read the biblical texts. Access had previously been limited to those few who were fluent in Hebrew, Greek, and Latin.

A slightly older contemporary of Martin Luther, the Dutch humanist Desiderius Erasmus (1466–1536) wrote *Enchiridion Militis Christiani* (*Manual of the Christian Soldier*) in 1501 and first published it in 1503. Erasmus was particularly critical of monasticism and of what he perceived to be egregious corruptions of the church, most specifically indulgences and the seemingly magical power of the relics of saints, whose authenticity he vigorously rejected. In his writings, Erasmus described the nature of true religion with observations and comments that were highly critical of the Roman Catholic Church.

Although Erasmus believed that divine wisdom reaches its perfection in Christ, he

directed his students to look also to the Greeks, to the Romans, and to other extrabib-
lical writings as legitimate sources for divine wisdom. Erasmus may actually have been
the first person to appeal to the use of reason in examining the writings of the Bible.

Although his writings, which included critical biblical texts, advanced a claim very
different from that of Luther, namely the importance of free will and human reason, both
of which were anathema to the Augustinian monk, Erasmus' critiques of the church
helped to prepare the way for Luther's Reformation. The first edition of Erasmus' *Col-
loquia*, usually regarded as his masterpiece, appeared in 1519. The audacity and inci-
siveness with which Erasmus handled the abuses of the Roman Catholic Church prepared men's minds for Luther's work. Although Erasmus was a severe critic of the
Catholic Church, his aversion to violence prevented him from joining the Protestant
Reformation, and he remained throughout his adult life an ordained priest and never left
the church. Ironically, following his death, the Roman Catholic Church placed onto its
index of forbidden books virtually all of Erasmus' writings.

The Protestant Reformation resulted in the destructive fragmentation of Latin
Christendom, even though it brought only limited divergence from the narrow orthodoxy of the Roman Catholic Church. The Reformation did, however, pave the way for
later transformation. For the leaders of the Reformation, the earth remained at the center
of their Ptolemaic universe. The sun, the moon, and the stars continued to revolve
around the earth. Catholics and Protestants alike knew positively that it was beyond the
firmament of the heaven in the sky that the Judeo-Christian God lived. The New Testament advanced that ancient Near Eastern worldview, and so, too, did the church
throughout most of the ensuing history of Christianity. Of course, it knew no better.

There were powerful political dynamics to both the Protestant Reformation and to
the Counter-Reformation. The latter was the Roman Catholic Church's effort at
renewal and revival in the aftermath of the success of Luther and other Protestant
Reformers. In addition, the Counter-Reformation was the result of forces within the
Roman Catholic Church that were also demanding major reform. Although there were
significant theological differences regarding definitions of doctrine, the means of salvation, the role of free will, and so forth, no one should underestimate the fact that
political power and claims to authority were always close to the center of the intrigues
and machinations that ensued in the struggle between Roman Catholics and Protestants and among Protestantism's proliferation of denominations from the time of the
Reformation into the twenty-first century. Power was once again the essential issue.

Perhaps the crowning moment in the quest for ultimate power and absolute
authority in Christianity's two-thousand-year history came in 1870 at the first Vatican Council. An assembly of nearly seven hundred bishops of the Roman Catholic
Church declared that the bishop of Rome, the pope, is infallible when he speaks ex
cathedra (i.e., when as the shepherd and teacher of *all Christians*, he defines a doctrine concerning faith or morals to be held by the *whole church*). The formal definition of this dogma of papal infallibility, as finally accepted by Vatican I, stated
clearly that the pope's definitions are "irreformable of themselves, and not from the
consent of the Church."

American Protestantism came up with its own absurd response to the Roman Catholic Church's outrageous claim of infallibility in a reactionary and regressive movement called Protestant fundamentalism. This authoritarian and repressive faction of various Protestant denominations emerged after World War I, especially in the United States. Fundamentalists rigidly uphold what they consider traditional Christian orthodoxy, most especially the literal inerrancy of the scriptures, but their agenda is as much about power as it is about religious orthodoxy. Roman Catholicism and fundamentalist Protestantism were both absolutist in their claims.

In 1925 the movement attracted international attention and ridicule when William Jennings Bryan (1860–1925), the leader of the American Democratic Party, assisted in the prosecution of a Tennessee schoolteacher, John Scopes, who was convicted of violating Tennessee state law by teaching the theory of biological evolution. Scopes was found guilty. The fundamentalists won that round, but their position was derided and scorned. The story of the Tennessee Monkey Trial has been dramatized as *Inherit the Wind*, both as a play and a film.

The fundamentalist movement assumed significance as a political lobby in the United States in the last quarter of the twentieth century, primarily in reaction to two decisions of the Supreme Court of the United States: *Murray v. Curlett*, which in 1963 barred government-sponsored reading of the Bible and recitation of the Lord's Prayer in public schools; and *Roe v. Wade*, which in 1973 legalized abortion on demand in the United States.

The Christian Coalition, a political lobby with fundamentalist beliefs and a right-wing political agenda, was founded in 1989 by Pat Robertson to give conservative Christians a political voice to counter these decisions of the Supreme Court and subsequent developments in the United States that flew in the face of their fundamentalist view of biblical Christianity. The Christian Coalition favors constitutional amendments to allow government-sponsored prayer in public schools, to ban abortion, and to limit marriage to one man and one woman; and it opposes such issues as what it calls special rights for gays and lesbians, affirmative action, and all forms of human cloning, including stem cell research. The Christian Coalition and allied organizations and lobbies have organized at the grassroots level to impose their own religious agenda on the United States in the face of the constitutional provision of a strict separation of church and state. The Christian Coalition and its allies are widely credited with helping to elect George W. Bush as president of the United States in November 2000 and again in 2004.

Perhaps the ultimate absurdity from these right-wing fundamentalists came in the form of a statement by Jerry Falwell on September 13, 2001, just two days after the terrorist attacks on the World Trade Center and the Pentagon. On a telecast of the *700 Club* with Pat Robertson, founding father of the Christian Coalition, Falwell said:

> The abortionists, the feminists, gays and lesbians who try to make that an acceptable lifestyle, the ACLU (American Civil Liberties Union), People For the American Way, I point my finger in their faces and say, "You let this happen."

To this statement Robertson basically added his own Amen!

To understand more clearly the desperation of both the 1870 Roman Catholic claim of papal infallibility and the twentieth-century Protestant fundamentalist claim of biblical inerrancy as dying gasps in the long list of Christian intrigues and machinations in the quest for power and ultimate authority, we turn our attention now to what many traditionalists regard as the enemy: the movement known as the Enlightenment, which elevated human reason to the position of the preeminent authority in the human search for truth.

Those details aside, the Protestant Reformation, the new cosmologies, geography, and ethnography are, in my view, all elements of challenges to the old order and the old powers, so that by the early seventeenth century, in the words of John Donne (1572–1631) in "The Anatomy of the World: The First Anniversary" (1611):

> And new philosophy calls all in doubt,
> The elements of fire is quite put out;
> . . . .
> 'Tis all in pieces, all coherence gone;
> All just supply, and all relation:
> Prince, subject, father, son are things forgot

The foundation of a new order had been laid. Old powers were about to give birth to a totally different kind of power: the power of human reason.

THE TRIUMPH OF REASON: THE ENLIGHTENMENT

Although the Italian Renaissance had revived briefly an interest in earlier Greek speculation about a heliocentric universe, most specifically the position proposed by Aristarchus of Samos (ca. 310–230 BCE), it was not until the time of the Polish astronomer Nicolaus Copernicus (1473–1543) that the notion began to take hold once again. Copernicus maintained that the sun and not the earth is at the center of our universe; and in so doing, he made a bold break with the accepted teaching of his time. In his masterpiece *The Revolution of Heavenly Spheres*, published shortly before his death in 1543, Copernicus set in motion the view that the earth was just one more planet and that the earth and the other planets revolve around the sun. His theory implied that the sun, the moon, the stars, and all of the planets are all in the heavens. With that shift in thinking, the contrast between heaven and earth gradually disappeared, and the modern concept of space began to emerge. The Copernican view of the universe threatened the church's foundational teaching about where God and the angels dwell. There was no longer a heavenly abode above, just the open and seemingly endless space of our universe.

The Danish astronomer Tyge (usually Latinized as Tycho) Brahe (1546–1601) rejected Copernicus' belief in a heliocentric universe, but he added mathematical precision to Copernicus' work. Brahe's observations of the positions and motions of the planets and the stars were more precise than any before his time. His onetime assistant, German mathematician Johannes Kepler (1571–1630), used Brahe's measurements to lend authority to Copernicus' heliocentric theory by providing the mathematical proofs required to establish an irrefutable mathematical foundation for the heliocentric theory. Specifically, Kepler's observations of the orbits of four of Jupiter's moons lent considerable support to Copernicus' theory. It was Kepler who placed astronomy solidly on its modern mathematical foundation. In fact, Kepler's three laws led him to the conclusion that the Creator was a geometer.[13]

The Italian astronomer and physicist Galileo Galilei (1564–1642) supported the view of a heliocentric universe. Galileo pointed his telescope to the heavens and was responsible for bringing still further attention and support to the work of Copernicus and his successors. Although challenged by the Roman Catholic Church and eventually condemned to death for his views, Galileo was able to save his life by recanting and withdrawing his "heretical" claim of a heliocentric universe. Although Galileo submitted to the enormous power of the Roman Catholic Church, it was too late: the cat was already out of the bag. In spite of the church's unquestioned authority in virtually all matters, science was beginning to work independently of the church and independently of the Bible.

The authority of both was substantially diminished by the Galileo controversy, even though the extent of the damage was not immediately understood. It was a shock to the common person that the earth was not the center of the universe and, therefore, that God might not be involved in the affairs of humankind in the way that the church and most people had always assumed. Ironically, it was not until December 28, 1991, more than three hundred fifty years after the church's condemnation of Galileo, that the Vatican officially admitted that the church had been wrong and that Galileo had been right. Too little, too late! Was the church actually exonerating Galileo or itself? Galileo, of course, needed no exoneration. The world had already known for centuries that the sun and not the earth was at the center of our solar system and that Galileo was one of the great geniuses of all time.

It was English physicist Sir Isaac Newton (1643–1727) who applied his bril-

---

13. Kepler's three laws were: (1) that the planets in our solar system move in elliptical orbits with the sun precisely at one focus of the ellipse; (2) that, if a line is drawn from a planet to the sun, that planet moves in an elliptical orbit with spreads that sweep out equal areas in equal times; and (3) that the interval of time of each planet's orbit is equal to the size of its mean orbital radius. Kepler understood that the mathematical motions of the planets represent the ultimate harmony and mathematical precision of the universe.

As an aside, in 1613 Kepler published in German a work on chronology and the year of Jesus' birth. He published an amplified version of that work in Latin a year later under the title *De Vero Anno quo Aeternus Dei Filius Humanam Naturam in Utero Benedictae Virginis Mariae Assumpsit* (*Concerning the True Year in which the Son of God assumed a Human Nature in the Uterus of the Blessed Virgin Mary*). In these works, Kepler demonstrated conclusively that the Christian calendar was in error by five years, and that Jesus had, therefore, been born in 4 BCE, a conclusion that is now almost universally accepted by New Testament scholars.

liance in mathematics, physics, optics, and astronomy to data previously advanced by Copernicus and Galileo. Many scientists and mathematicians consider Newton's *Philosophiae naturalis principia mathematica*, or *Principia* as it is usually known, to be the single most important scientific book ever written. Newton's conviction that there were natural, if not mathematical, explanations for everything that happened in the universe left little room for the personal God of the Judeo-Christian tradition, who, most believed, sat in the sky above the earth working his way within the world.[14] The mathematical models proposed by Copernicus, Brahe, Kepler, Galileo, and Newton substantially reduced the divine sphere of operation, effectively rendering God unnecessary as the Creator and Sustainer of the universe. The universe, so it appeared, was self-contained and perhaps even self-supporting.

Newton was probably the best representative of the synthesis of 150 years of work into a view of the physical world that was metaphorically extended into other areas as well.[15] The challenge to the church's apparent monopoly on truth came not only from the realm of science: mathematics, physics, and astronomy. It spilled over into other disciplines as well. The success of the new, more critical scientific method employed by Galileo, Copernicus, Kepler, and others generated confidence in the value of human reason as an essential element in the search for truth. The application of reason soon pervaded other areas of scholarship. The appeal of critically generated knowledge rather than knowledge that was based on received tradition or revelation, and especially tradition received from the Bible and the church, was welcome and became increasingly more influential. This critical spirit was at the center of the Enlightenment, whose motto was the command of Emmanuel Kant (1724–1804): *aude sapere* (dare to know).

New knowledge in the realms of history and geography began to question the authority of the Bible. In his *Methodus ad facilem historiarum cognitionem* (Method for the Easy Comprehension of History) (1566), French political writer Jean Bodin (1520–1596) laid the foundation of the philosophy of history, and Swiss humanist, poet, historian, physician, statesman, and early reformer Joachim Vadian (1484–1551) demanded that physical observation be used in writing geography.

Christian orthodoxy of the day demanded that believers set aside human reason whenever its results contradicted the teachings of the Bible or the church. The lines of battle were being drawn: there were apparently two independent and seemingly sometimes contradictory sources of truth: the Bible and the church on the one hand, and human reason on the other hand. The ensuing struggle for supremacy was inevitable. What should be the final court of appeal in those instances when the two authorities, faith and reason, appear to come into direct conflict? Should allegiance to the Christian faith, the church, and the holy scriptures outweigh and result in the dismissal or subordination of conclusions reached by human reason?

French philosopher René Descartes (1596–1650), one of the most important

---

14. Newton was also a devout Protestant who wrote on biblical chronologies.
15. Charles Darwin impacted the world in much the same way 250 years later.

philosophers of recent centuries, raised the notion of doubt to a universally valid principle in 1637 in his *Discourse on Method* and thereby changed philosophic, scientific, and historical thinking in ways that are still part of contemporary accepted wisdom. Descartes introduced three basic principles of inquiry:

1. Humankind, as a thinking subject, is at the center of all philosophical inquiry. Descartes' famous statement *cogito ergo sum* (I think, therefore I am) makes it clear that humankind is and must remain the focus of all human understanding.
2. Nothing should be accepted as true merely because it is in the tradition. Doubt everything except what is so evident that there can be no basis whatsoever for its doubt.
3. Reason is the sole criterion of truth.

Christian orthodoxy responded to Descartes dogmatically: reason should be subject and subordinate to the scriptures and the church, because fallen reason is no guide to knowledge. As a result of Descartes' insights and influence, reason has to this day become in scholarly circles the normative authority for truth, even over religion and over the church's sacred scriptures. Reason is also the norm in the scholarly pursuit of religious studies, whether it involves the philosophy of religion, biblical studies, comparative study of religion, sociology of religion, psychology of religion, or whatever other analytic method a scholar may use in examining the phenomenon of religion.

In his 1670 *Tractatus Theologico-Politicus*, Dutch Jewish philosopher Baruch (or Benedict) Spinoza (1632–1677) defended the right to philosophize in the face of religious or political interference, maintaining that truth cannot contradict itself. For Spinoza, the scriptures must be subject to and agree with human reason. Reason cannot be restrained by the religious sanctions of either the scriptures or the church. Spinoza's rules for biblical interpretation made it clear that scholars should study the Bible as they would study any other book with a clear, rational, and essentially independent and untheological mind. If the Bible is not rational, then its authority is seriously diminished.

Since the time of the Renaissance, scholars have applied literary criticism to the writings of antiquity. They have asked questions about the accuracy of ancient manuscripts, the sources of material, and the historical reliability of texts. In doing so, they were using methodologies that we now call textual criticism, source criticism, and historical criticism. French Oratorian priest Richard Simon (1638–1712) published in the last quarter of the seventeenth century a series of books in which he applied the principle of reason to the Bible. In doing so, he was the first scholar systematically to employ critical methods to biblical study and to question traditional teaching that had been handed down within the church for more than fifteen hundred years. Simon is the acknowledged father of the historical-critical study of the Bible. Predictably the Roman Catholic Church disciplined Simon for his impudence in applying a *profane* method to its *sacred* scriptures.

Simon's Protestant counterpart was Johann David Michaelis (1717–1791), who applied the tools of historical criticism to the New Testament without acknowledging the church's dogmatic presuppositions. Against the prevailing orthodoxy of his time, which embraced what we would today call the verbal inspiration of the Bible and its corollary, the inerrancy of the sacred scriptures, Michaelis found inconsistencies and contradictions in the Bible. Simon and Michaelis challenged independently the purported "history" in the Old and New Testaments. Following their leads, more and more scholars began to apply the historical method to the study of the scriptures and thereby treated the books of the Bible more and more like ordinary books from the ancient Near Eastern world. The process of secularization and objectification of the biblical texts had begun.

Politics had been decoupled from religion by the first great political philosopher of the Renaissance, Nicolo Machiavelli (1469–1527), whose treatise *The Prince* was written in 1513 and published after his death in 1532. This view of separating politics and religion was advanced more systematically by Thomas Hobbes (1588–1679), who argued that governments were needed in order to protect people from their own evil and their own selfishness. Hobbes maintained that the best government was one with the power of a leviathan, or great sea monster, hence the title of his most important work, *Leviathan* (1651). Hobbes believed in the need for absolute monarchy to provide the requisite leadership. Because people were interested in promoting only their own self-interests, Hobbes was skeptical about the viability and desirability of democracy.

The views of Machiavelli and Hobbes had definite distasteful elements. The political philosophy of John Locke (1632–1704) offered the American founding father and author of the Declaration of Independence Thomas Jefferson a more palatable formulation for the separation of church and state. Unlike Machiavelli and Hobbes, Locke's work is characterized by his strong opposition to authoritarianism, both on the level of the individual person, the absolute monarch, and on the level of institutions such as government and the church. Locke believed that it was essential for each individual to use reason in the search for truth and not simply rely upon the opinion of political or religious authorities.

Reason continued to triumph over revelation as the avenue to truth. It was increasingly important for religion to be essentially reasonable. People advocated tolerance in religion and opposed any form of compulsion in the area. Deism reigned.[16] Eighteenth-century Deists dealt freely with the Bible when in their minds it did not agree with human reason. *The* (President Thomas) *Jefferson Bible*, totally devoid of miracles, is just one example of the systematic application of reason to the biblical texts. It was in France that English and Scottish Deism blended with seventeenth-century rationalism to give rise to the Enlightenment. In Germany, scholars

---

16. Deism was the belief that God created the world but thereafter exercised no control over it or over the lives of people. The analogy of the watchmaker, who made the watch and then set it into perpetual motion, is sometimes used to explain Deism. Thomas Jefferson's civic deism was something of a commonplace among his class in Europe and America.

influenced by the principles of the Enlightenment (*Aufklärung*) used reason in their search for eternal truths contained in the scriptures. For those who accepted reason as the primary criterion of truth, it was always clear that although the scriptures may contain truth, they contain truth that can otherwise be discovered through the use of reason. Children of the Enlightenment believed that all truth is rational and that what is rational is capable of proof. One of the notable features of the Enlightenment and sometimes a point of pride was its cosmopolitan quality.

In the mid-nineteenth century, English biologist Charles Darwin (1809–1882) shook religious belief to its foundation by advancing his theory of biological evolution, which bridged the gap that separated subhuman from human life. Advances in geology and biology made it clear that the creation stories in Genesis were just that: "stories." As such, they were little more than myths, not unlike the creation myths in other religious traditions. The publication in 1859 of Darwin's *The Origin of Species* undermined fundamentally the religious understanding of the origin of human life: the belief that God had created Adam and Eve and placed them in the Garden of Eden. The consequences of Darwin's work led to the conviction that we humans are closely related to other primates and that the beginning of the universe was not even close to Bishop James Ussher's date of 4004 BCE. The universe's age should, instead, be measured in billions of years (13.7 billion is, I believe, the latest best estimate), and our own species, *Homo sapiens*, has apparently been around for about two hundred thousand years.

Austrian physician Sigmund Freud (1856–1939) probed the inner recesses of the human mind and forced us to look once again at religious belief as still one more function of human self-understanding. In his classic book *The Future of an Illusion*, Freud observed that, in all civilizations, religious beliefs are informed by three sources: (1) the beliefs of primal ancestors, (2) proofs handed down from those same primal ancestors, and (3) strict prohibition against raising any doubt about the authenticity of those beliefs. Freud observed that the only reason for the third point was the conscious effort to suppress any uncertainty regarding claims made on behalf of religious doctrines. Power was, once again, acknowledged to be a powerful factor in the realm of religion.

To Freud the psychical origin of religious beliefs is that they are the fulfillment of humankind's oldest and strongest wishes and are, as such, illusions, that is, false perceptions or beliefs that are not in agreement with the facts. Freud called a belief an illusion when wish fulfillment is a prominent factor in its motivation. Freud represented still one more devastating attack on conventional religious thinking. Like Copernicus and Galileo before them, Darwin and Freud have been and to this day still are castigated by most evangelical Christians.

The discoveries of Swiss psychologist Carl Gustav Jung (1875–1961) and German American mathematician Albert Einstein (1879–1955) pushed God even further into irrelevancy in a universe that can easily be understood as a self-sufficient closed system.

Perhaps the most recent challenge to the authority of religion from science and human reason came on February 28, 1953, when Francis Crick entered the Eagle

Pub in Cambridge, England, and announced that he and James Watson had "found the secret of life." The two men had built a model of deoxyribonucleic acid (DNA), the carrier of the genetic code and thus the key molecule of heredity, evolution, and developmental biology. Their discovery just over fifty years ago has transformed science, medicine, and much of modern life. DNA is a self-reproducing molecule that carries from one generation to the next the instructions for making all living things.

Nineteenth-century German philosopher Friedrich Nietzsche (1844–1900) challenged the very foundations of traditional Christianity. Although he was the first to make the public announcement, it was repeated again by theologians in the United States of America in the 1960s: God is dead! Could there be any doubt?

CONSEQUENCES

It is time to bring additional focus to this gallop through history and to sharpen the case for the quest for power, especially as it applies to the question of the future of Christianity.

Science and philosophy have together advanced reason as the primary mode for attaining truth and have, thereby, changed forever our understanding of the universe and of humankind. There is no turning back. The biblical view represented most clearly in the creation story in Genesis 1:1–2:4a is that of a flat earth, covered by a dome to which the sun, the moon, and the stars are attached. The waters of heaven are above that dome or firmament. In fact, it is the opening of the windows of that dome that results in the falling of rain or snow upon the earth below.

Beneath the earth are the waters upon which the earth rests and the underworld, basically a tunnel through which the sun travels on its nightly journey from the west, where it sets, to return to the east in time for the next sunrise.[17] The heavens are beyond the dome of the sky and serve as the permanent abode of God and his angels. This is the biblical cosmology, the image of the universe that has persisted in Judaism and Christianity for thousands of years. Let it be said in the full light of day that, despite the impact of the Enlightenment, millions of people, many of them American evangelical and fundamentalist Christians, still believe in the prescientific biblical cosmology. To do so is demonstrably absurd!

When the notion of this three-tiered or triple-decker universe came under attack, God's abode was also threatened. God was displaced; God was no longer "up there." For a time, I suppose, God was "out there," somewhere beyond the planets in the remote reaches of the universe, but that idea, too, had to give way to further advances in astronomy. The larger the universe became, the more problematic the geography of God and heaven. In addition, the revival of the notion that the earth is spherical and not flat raised a question regarding the geography of hell. Is hell somewhere in the liquid core of the earth? Is it there that the devil and his cronies reside?

---

17. Our language still assumes the biblical cosmology. We refer to sunrise and sunset as if it is the sun that is in motion around the earth.

It also became clear that the very concept of God was at stake. It is no longer possible to conceive of God as easily as a "person," or as "personal," especially when it is increasingly clear from both science and philosophy that as the extents of the universe are pushed back farther and farther toward infinity, there is no real *place* for God and, in addition, no real role or "job" for God in the new scheme.

More and more people suddenly realized that God is no longer necessary to explain the sunrise and sunset, the weather, birth and death, even the origin of life itself, or any other phenomena in nature. In fact, the impact of the new thinking effectively eliminated the possibility that there is room in the natural order for supernatural phenomena of any kind to intrude or intervene like a deus ex machina. There is no room for miracles: no partings of seas, no walkings on water, no virgin births, no resuscitated corpses.[18] Everything within the natural order without exception is within the purview of science and philosophy.

For two thousand years Christians have struggled as they have tried to understand the essence of their religion. That struggle has always had a powerful political dimension. That struggle has always involved a quest for power. It still does! But one thing is now clear: the struggle for power in Christianity and in all religions, for that matter, must now take a back seat, because that struggle has already been won by the power of human reason, which must now serve forever as the preeminent criterion for all truth. Although the battle still wages, the war has been won. Enlightenment principles can and must define our direction for the future of Christianity.

Perhaps it was an overstatement on the part of Nietzsche and the Death-of-God theologians to say that "*God* is dead," but it is certainly clear that the *concept of God* that had functioned meaningfully in the Judeo-Christian tradition for thousands of years is dying. And if the concept of God is dying, then what is the role and function of the Christian church? To try to revive the patient that is currently on life support but that has few, if any, vital signs? I think not!

---

18. For Deists the initial order of the universe may have been a "miracle," but not the miracle stories in the Bible. They were considered aberrations.

THE QUEST
FOR GOD

The atheist staring from his attic window is often nearer to God than the believer caught up in his own false image of God.

—Martin Buber

*I*n saying that "God is dead," we are, of course, actually saying that the popular "image" of God, the image of God as a superhuman being who *lives* somewhere above or beyond the earth; who *created* the universe; who *called* Abraham, Isaac, and Jacob; who *appointed* Moses to lead the people of Israel out of Egypt and Joshua to lead them into the promised land of Canaan; the God who *spoke* to the prophets and who *sent* his son, Jesus of Nazareth, into the world to preach, to suffer, and to die in order to redeem humankind from sin; the God who *orders* the summer and the winter, the sun and the rain, who *brings* earthquakes and famines— it is this God who is most assuredly dead. Or to be more accurate, it is rather this "concept" of God, this "image" of God that is dead and no longer functions meaningfully in this post-Enlightenment age in which we live.

We did not kill this God, and neither did our predecessors who brought us to where we are today: Copernicus, Galileo, Darwin, Freud, and the others. This concept of God was dead on arrival, even though it appears to have functioned for thousands of years in the prescientific age of humankind's adolescence. Our ancestors also believed that the world was flat, that the sun revolved around the earth, and that God created man out of the dust of the earth, but believing is never enough to make it so. Believing in the pre-Enlightenment concept of God does not bring that God to life or make that God real. For a variety of reasons, people have often been content to worship what we now know to have been an illusion.

In the introduction to this book, I mentioned that I like to believe that when Moses forbade the Israelites to make images of their god, he intended to include, as well, a prohibition against concepts or "mental images" of God. Of course, that is stretching the meaning of the story in the book of Exodus, but not by much. Is there, after all, a qualitative difference between an image of God carved from wood or stone, or molded of plaster or iron, and a mental image of God fashioned out of human imagination? The concept of God as a male deity who *created* the universe and who *called* one people out of all the peoples of the earth to be his own "chosen people" is, if you think about it, pure and unadulterated sexist tribalism and is as idolatrous as any carved statue that was meant to represent this rather limited tribal god. In fact, the concept of a god who *chooses* one nation, one people, at the expense of and above all other peoples is a primitive notion and is utterly offensive to modern reason. The verbs that I have italicized in both this paragraph and in the first paragraph of this chapter betray the degree to which we have been guilty of "imaging" God: He (obviously a male being) *lives, creates, appoints, speaks, sends, orders, brings, calls, chooses*—and that's just the hors d'oeuvre.

Neither do feminist theologians make a meaningful contribution to the discussion or an appropriate correction to our patriarchal biases when they speak of the female side of God or of God as a "she" rather than as a "he." Personally, I don't find prayers to "Our Father-Mother God" particularly edifying. Perhaps we should just refer to God as an "it." The personal pronouns "he" and "she" serve only to anthropomorphize God, to create God in our *human* image. How arrogant, how idolatrous of humankind to create God in *our own* image! The Greek philosopher Xenophanes (ca. 560 BCE–ca. 478 BCE) recognized more than two and a half millennia ago that men made gods in their own image; for example, the gods of the Ethiopians are black and snub-nosed; the gods of the Thracians have blue eyes and red hair (*fragment* 16). "If horses or oxen or lions had hands and could produce works of art," Xenophanes observed, "they, too, would represent the gods after their own fashion" (*fragment* 15).[19] Some of our precursors imagined God as a falcon, or an eagle, or a crocodile. Some saw God in nature, in the winds and the rains, or in the sun. Are these ancient images of God clearly inferior to our anthropomorphic image of God as Father, or Judge, or King? I think not! Images of gods quite obviously tell us more about the believer than about the gods who are the object of the believer's belief. In looking at people's concepts or "mental images" of their god, we learn more about the believers than we ever hope to learn about God him/her/itself.

When Moses commanded the people of Israel not to make any images of their god, he presumably understood the limitations of any image that deludes people into believing that an image affords a clear perception or picture of God, that the image presents some sort of "likeness" of God. It does not. Rather, it generally limits or reduces God. A concept is a human mental image, but it is still human and it is still an image, and it suffers the limitations of every image. It creates among believers

---

19. In the same fragment, Xenophanes also claimed that there was only one god—namely, the world. He believed that God is one eternal and incorporeal being and that in form God is of the same nature as the universe. God comprehends all things, is intelligent, and pervades all things but bears no resemblance to human nature, either in body or in mind. How enlightened of Xenophanes!

the false impression, the delusion, the lie that the image corresponds in some way to the reality of their god.

If our earlier outdated images of God are dead, what then, if anything, can we say about God? Or is God actually dead as well? Is God nothing more than the illusion that Sigmund Freud spoke of in *The Future of an Illusion*? We can probably never answer that question definitively, but I hope to explore a few avenues that may assist us in understanding better what, if anything, Moses and the prophets were speaking about when they spoke of God or of Yahweh.[20]

The word "God" is so encumbered with the outdated and misleading images advanced over the last three thousand or more years of Judaism and Christianity that I am tempted to say that we should probably just find another word, a word different from the word "God," once we get a better understanding of what it is that we are speaking about when we use the word. I'm inclined to reach for another word, a totally different word, but I will reserve judgment on that matter until the end of this chapter. Frankly, I rather like George Lucas's "The Force," especially when, in the *Star Wars* series, characters regularly greet one another by saying, "May the Force be with you." I rather prefer it to "God bless you." In fact, Lucas may be onto something significant. He may even be a closet Taoist!

MOSES AND THE EXODUS

According to the account in the book of Exodus, Moses was born in Egypt at about the time that the pharaoh (probably Ramses II) had ordered the execution of all Hebrew male babies. To save her son, Moses' mother placed the infant in a basket, which she set afloat on the Nile River. By chance Pharaoh's daughter found the child and raised him as her own son. Once an adult, Moses saw an Egyptian overseer beating a Hebrew slave, killed the overseer, and then fled to the land of Midian, probably in the Sinai Peninsula in modern-day Egypt.

As is the case with the birth and infancy stories of most ancient Near Eastern heroic figures, the story of Moses' origin is wrapped in myth and legend, so much so that we are not even sure whether Moses was actually Hebrew or Egyptian. In

---

20. Yahweh is the proper name by which Moses and the ancient Israelites called their god. The divine name was probably spoken by the people of Israel beginning with Moses in about 1290 BCE. Following the fall of Jerusalem and the destruction of King Solomon's Temple in 586 BCE and the ensuing deportation to Babylonia and the exile of 586–538 BCE, the name Yahweh fell into disuse. Thereafter, it was apparently forbidden to speak the divine name. In many English-language Bibles, in lieu of the personal name Yahweh, translators have the phrase "the LORD" with capital letters. When readers of the Bible see the words "the LORD," they ought to read these words as if the text said "Yahweh." The Jerusalem Bible is an excellent modern translation that actually uses the divine name Yahweh whenever it appears in the original Hebrew text. Moses certainly knew and used the divine name when he and his successors referred to Yahweh as the God of the Exodus.

spite of the effort of the anonymous author(s) of the book of Exodus to trace the name "Moses" (*mosheh*) to the Hebrew verb *mashah* meaning "to draw out of water,"[21] the name is almost certainly Egyptian and is found in combination form in such Egyptian names as Thut*mose* (a child of [the Egyptian god of wisdom] Thut) and Ra*meses* (a child of [the Egyptian sun god] Ra). But such details are of little consequence to the story and served primarily to entertain the storyteller's listeners and to focus special attention on the extraordinary man who had led the Hebrew slaves out of Egypt and into the freedom of the Sinai wilderness.

The core of the story of the Exodus, the escape from Egypt, is found in primitive form in an ancient couplet (two lines of poetry) called the Song of the Sea or the Song of Miriam, preserved in Exodus 15:20–21:

> Then the prophet Miriam, Aaron's sister, took a tambourine in her hand; and all the women went out after her with tambourines and with dancing. And Miriam sang to them:
>> Sing to the LORD [Yahweh], for he has triumphed gloriously;
>> horse and rider he has thrown into the sea.

The original Hebrew text of this poetic couplet is even more powerful than the English translation:

> *shiru leyahweh ki-ga'oh ga'ah*
> *sus werokebo ramah bayyam*

Listen to both the similar vowel sounds (assonance) and the wordplay (paronomasia) in the last two words of the first line—*ga'oh ga'ah*—of the original Hebrew, and the assonance in the last two words of the second line—*ramah bayyam*. Listen also to the many open vowel sounds in both lines. In these simple words in Exodus 15:21, we are probably listening to one of the earliest fragments of ancient Hebrew poetry. It is interesting that ancient tradition ascribes this couplet to Miriam and not to Moses, that it is Miriam and "all the women" who articulated the religious significance of the foundational event of Israel's history through ritual song and dance.

Although it was not properly understood until about 250 years ago, poetry comprises roughly one-third of the Hebrew Bible, the Christian Old Testament.[22] The principal feature of ancient Near Eastern poetry is parallelism, or the correspondence of thought in two consecutive lines of verse called a "couplet." In Exodus

---

21. The text of Exodus 2:10 is incorrect in its effort to connect the name Moses with the Hebrew verb *mashah*. The verb actually means "the one who draws out," and not "the one who is drawn out" (of water). Anyway, the Egyptian princess would certainly not have given her "adopted" child a Hebrew name, the language of the slave people, even in the unlikely event that she actually knew the Hebrew language.

22. The translators of the King James Bible did not understand the formal characteristics of Hebrew poetry. Accordingly, in spite of its admirable literary qualities, the King James Bible failed to capture the poetic quality of the original Hebrew poetry.

15:21, the phrase "Sing to Yahweh" introduces the two phrases that actually display the feature of parallelism. In Hebrew poetry the second line generally repeats, contrasts, or advances the idea set forth in the first line. In this case "he [Yahweh] has triumphed gloriously" is both repeated and advanced by the second line "horse and rider he [Yahweh] has thrown into the sea." Assonance appears in this couplet and in Hebrew poetry in general for its aesthetic quality.

Notice the simplicity of the story in the Song of Miriam. Sing to Yahweh, for it is he who has triumphed over the Egyptian oppressors. Yahweh has thrown the Egyptian soldiers, their chariots, and their horses into the sea. It appears that the Egyptian army got bogged down in the waters of the Sea of Reeds while they were pursuing Moses and the Hebrew slaves, and that the Hebrews, who were apparently on foot, were thereby able to reach their freedom on the other side of the water. The book of Exodus makes it clear that the escape of the Hebrew slaves from Egypt was, however, not simply an escape, at least not in the eyes of Moses and his sister Miriam. Indeed, it was actually not Moses who led the people of Israel out of Egypt, although quite apparently he did. It was Yahweh. The account interprets the escape from Egypt as an act of Israel's god Yahweh. Yahweh was the cause of the event, the leader of the escape, the author of the people's freedom. Through the Exodus, Yahweh brought Israel into existence.

In this simple couplet, we do not read about the waters rolling back and forming walls through which millions of Israelites passed in procession. Those legendary details are provided in later, more elaborate accounts elsewhere in the book of Exodus, in stories that are replete with legendary interviews between Moses and the Pharaoh, the ten plagues that preceded the escape, and other legendary features that highlight the significance of the Exodus. These legendary accounts celebrate the power of Yahweh and the importance of his prophet Moses, who served as Yahweh's mediator and presumably as the interpreter of what had transpired.

The unadulterated story of the Exodus in the Song of Miriam is much simpler and is quite profound in that simplicity. For reasons that are unclear, Moses apparently decided to lead a band of slaves out of Egypt. They were pursued by Pharaoh's army. When they came to the "sea," Moses evidently led the people into the marshy water, whose name in Hebrew is *yam suph*, or the "reed sea" (Exodus 10:19; 15:4; etc.), not the Red Sea as most English Bibles read and as most Christians believe. Another way to translate those words would be with the phrase "Papyrus Lake," a translation that would reflect more accurately the size and scale of the body of water that the people appear to have crossed—very possibly one of the lagoons in the northern Sinai Peninsula along the Mediterranean coast. The Red Sea is nowhere near the route of the Exodus. It is about a hundred miles south of the probable route of Moses and the Hebrew slaves. In any event, the slaves got to the other side of the "sea," whereas Pharaoh's charioteers were bogged down in the mud of the shallow marsh and presumably perished. Stated simply, the Hebrews escaped under Moses' leadership and inspiration. Yet the story is consistently told as if Yahweh, and not Moses, was the actual author of the event. Yahweh, not Moses, *delivered* the people from *slavery into freedom.* We likely have in this story Moses' interpretation of the escape as an act of Yahweh. In the simple couplet in the Song of Miriam in Exodus 15:21, we may actually have an eyewitness account and interpretation of that momentous event.

The traditional way of looking at this story is to read the entire account as if it were an actual historical event, complete with the built-in interpretation of Yahweh in the primary role as lead actor and with Moses in a supporting role as the instrument of Yahweh. Such a reading fails to take into account the requirement that the objective historian must peel away the interpretative mythological and legendary elements in the text.[23] At the core of the story there lies almost certainly an actual escape, an escape that must have seemed extraordinary to those who had, indeed, escaped. Most important in the words of the interpreter or the storyteller is the claim that Israel's god Yahweh was the author of that event, an interpretation that Moses himself may have provided at the time. It is, of course, not self-evident that the raw event, an escape, and the interpretation of the event as an act of Yahweh are one and the same thing. In fact, it is self-evident that they are not. Historical facts or events do not come with their built-in interpretations, especially interpretations that view such events as "acts of God." Someone else, the historian, the storyteller, or in this instance probably Moses himself, initially provided the primary interpretation of the event as an act of Yahweh. Moses told the people the *meaning* of what had happened. The Exodus was not an escape; it was a divine deliverance.

An account of that event in the morning-after edition of the Egyptian *Times* would certainly not have read: "Yahweh Delivered Hebrew Slaves into Freedom." It would more likely have read something like "Hebrew Slaves Escaped at Moses' Instigation." There was, of course, no Egyptian *Times*, and neither do we have any contemporary Egyptian account of what, at least to the Egyptians, was likely little more than a minor border incident involving a couple of hundred people. In fact, the story would probably not have made the paper had there been one. Think small!

But try to tell later generations of Israelites or contemporary Jews, who trace their origin to this event, that the Exodus was no more than a minor border incident, and they will tell you that this central event in their history marked the birth of their freedom. It provided them with their identity. So, too, most Americans are inclined to read the story of the arrival of the *Mayflower* at Plymouth Rock as a major event in American history, which it was—for Americans, that is. Important in the retelling of any story are the consequences of the original incident—what followed directly or indirectly as a result of the actual event. The Exodus was in a meaningful way the beginning of Israelite history. All Jews trace their origin back to that single simple event in about 1290 BCE, when a small band of Hebrew slaves under Moses' leadership escaped from the army of Pharaoh Ramses II by crossing a presumably small and shallow body of water in the northern Sinai Peninsula.

Now let us take this story one step further. What happens when we remove the

---

23. The *story* of the Exodus is at one level a "historicizing" of the ancient Near Eastern combat myth, an example of which is evident in the Babylonian creation story *Enuma Elish.*

word "Yahweh" or "God" from the account, as we must if we are to be faithful to our post-Enlightenment worldview which demands that we get rid of all "God-talk"? The story is about a transition from slavery into freedom and carries with it the "claim" that the transition from the one state to the other provided new meaning for those who participated in the event, as well as for those who continue to participate vicariously in that event. The Exodus is a story about human liberation, about human freedom, and the message of the story is clear: "It was a good thing for the Hebrew slaves to gain their freedom." Let's try again: "It was Good, it was Right for the Hebrew slaves to be free."

Writing the word "Good" with a capital *G* makes an even stronger, virtually absolute existential claim about the relevance of the Exodus event, as it imparts meaning to a substantial portion of the human race. The people who actually participated in the event in 1290 BCE claimed that the escape provided new meaning to their existence. In fact, it provided a new beginning to their existence. I intentionally substituted the word "Good" for "God" in this instance. The two words not only look similar, but they are in point of fact equivalent. Both words imply that there is "meaning" in the event that may not be inherent in the event itself. The meaning was afforded to those who shared in the event and to those who have continued to find meaning as they participate vicariously in the event many centuries after the fact.

Meaning was imparted not only to subsequent generations of Jews, but, as we shall see, to anyone who believes that the story states clearly that slavery is Evil (with a capital *E*) and that human freedom is Good (with a capital *G*). Perhaps a better way of restating the claim would be to say that "It was Right for the Hebrew slaves to be free." Or better yet, "It is Right for *all* people to be free. It is Wrong for *any* people to live in slavery." Does anyone doubt that? Yet it is not self-evident. It is rather a proclamation, a claim—to be sure a claim that for most people borders on being self-evident, even though Americans continued to keep slaves for almost two centuries until President Abraham Lincoln emancipated them in 1863.

THOMAS JEFFERSON AND THE DECLARATION OF INDEPENDENCE

Thomas Jefferson's language in the Declaration of Independence is helpful as we try to understand the full power of the claim found in the simple couplet in Exodus 15:21. In the Declaration of Independence, Jefferson wrote:

> We hold these Truths to be self-evident, that all Men are created equal, that they are endowed by their Creator with certain unalienable Rights, that among these are Life, Liberty, and the Pursuit of Happiness.

Like many of the founders of the United States, Thomas Jefferson was a Deist. He did not believe in the personal God of the Judeo-Christian tradition. He believed, rather, in a universe that was created by a "first cause," a universe that thereafter operated in a mechanical order in accordance with Newton's laws. Yet, in the Declaration of Independence, Jefferson was effectively restating the claim of the book of Exodus. Jefferson's language is packed with theological claims or their near equivalent. Notice:

1. The "We" in the passage are the signers of the Declaration of Independence;
2. "Hold these Truths" is a claim, a confessional statement by the "We"; Jefferson makes no attempt to prove "these Truths" or to establish them on the basis of human reason;
3. The claim of these Truths is rather "self-evident," there for all to behold and embrace;
4. The first of these self-evident Truths is that all people are created equal;[24]
5. The "unalienable rights" with which all people are endowed (by Jefferson's Deistic God) from the moment of birth are "Life, Liberty, and the Pursuit of Happiness."

Jefferson claimed unequivocally that all people are entitled to these rights simply by virtue of being born into the world, whether there is a God or no God, because the Creator in Jefferson's thought is not the God of Abraham, Isaac, and Jacob. Jefferson's Creator is the Cause, the Rational Principle, of the universe, something far more profound than the God of Moses and the Judeo-Christian tradition. In fact, Jefferson intentionally does not use the word "God" in this instance. The only use of the word "God" in the Declaration of Independence is in the preamble, where Jefferson wrote that the people have a right to "assume among the powers of the earth, the separate and equal station to which the Laws of Nature and of Nature's God entitle them." It is interesting that Jefferson mentions first "the Laws of Nature," and then secondly "and of Nature's God," probably as an equivalent.

It is my contention that the book of Exodus and Jefferson's Declaration of Independence are making the very same claim. It is the claim that human freedom is absolutely and unequivocally Right and that human oppression and slavery are absolutely and unequivocally Wrong, that people universally have an unalienable Right to Life, Liberty, and the Pursuit of Happiness.[25]

---

24. By "all Men are created equal," Jefferson, of course, meant all free white male landowners. Quite appropriately later generations of Americans have broadened Jefferson's original claim to include "all human beings," without bias.

25. British philosopher John Locke (1632–1704), who influenced Jefferson's thinking, detailed the rights to life, liberty, health, and property, which he understood as being part of the law of nature (a phrase that Jefferson presumably borrowed from Locke). It is the Golden Rule, interpreted in terms of natural rights. In *The Second Treatise of Government* (II, 6), Locke wrote: "The state of nature has a law of nature to govern it, which obliges everyone: and reason which is that law, teaches all mankind who will but consult it, that being all equal and independent, no one ought to harm another in his life, health, liberty or possessions."

These rights are not extended to people by kings, or governors, or congresses, or presidents. They reside rather within each and every individual from the moment of his or her birth. As in the story in the book of Exodus, Jefferson is making a claim: it is a claim that both Jefferson and the author of the book of Exodus regarded as self-evident.

This "self-evidence" is Jefferson's equivalent of "Yahweh" in the Song of Miriam. I contend that they are, in fact, one and the same thing, and that each term reflects a universal claim (Jefferson dares to refer to it as a universal "Truth") that is disclosed within the realm of human history to communities of believers who then express that claim in their foundational documents, whether in Exodus or in the Declaration. It is in the appropriation of this self-evident Truth that communities of believers are not only able but are compelled to proclaim that Truth. Like the words "Right" and "Good," "Truth" is still one more equivalent word for "God," the Absolute.

NEGRO SLAVES AND THEIR SPIRITUALS

It should be no surprise that this same "self-evident Truth" about the unalienable Right to Life, Liberty, and the Pursuit of Happiness was appropriated by still one more oppressed people, American Negro slaves, who in several of their spirituals made the connection between their own oppression and the exodus of the ancient Israelites. Perhaps the best-known example is the Negro spiritual "Go Down, Moses":

> When Israel was in Egypt's land,
> Let my people go!
> Oppressed so hard they could not stand,
> Let my people go!
> Chorus:
> Go down, Moses,
> Way down in Egypt's land.
> Tell old Pharaoh
> To let my people go!
>
> O let us all from bondage flee
> Let my people go!
> And let us all in Christ be free
> Let my people go!
> Chorus:
>
> You need not always weep and mourn
> Let my people go!
> And wear these slav'ry chains forlorn
> Let my people go!
> Chorus:

        Your foes shall not before you stand
        Let my people go!
        And you'll possess fair Canaan's land.
        Let my people go!
        Chorus:

Of the eleven stanzas of the original spiritual, I have quoted just four. The broad outline of the Exodus story is clear; the other seven stanzas provide additional details from the Exodus cycle.

    Having been introduced to Christianity by their white Christian slaveholders, Negro slaves in the period before emancipation drew inspiration from the story of the deliverance of the Hebrew slaves from oppression under Egypt's pharaoh. The Negro slaves believed that just as God had spoken to Moses and the Hebrew slaves in Egypt, that same God was now speaking to oppressed Negro slaves, who like the ancient Israelites would be delivered from slavery and eventually enter the promised land of human freedom.

    In all three instances, the Exodus from Egypt, the Declaration of Independence, and the Negro spiritual, the self-evident "Truth" of human freedom was revealed to an oppressed people. Out of their oppression they were able to see in their future the promised land of human freedom. The god of the Bible is a god who is disclosed in history. In fact, the Bible is sometimes characterized as a recitation of the acts of God's salvation history in behalf of his people, Israel. Stated differently, it is in their history that the people have discovered and appropriated certain "Truths." Sometimes the recollection, recitation, and appropriation of other people's stories of deliverance and human liberty can provide the inspiration or insight into certain existential truths of the human predicament, presumably because they say something universal about human nature and human aspirations. These stories speak loudly to the declaration of universal human rights, rights that transcend time and place. Fundamental among these rights are the Right of all People to be Free, the Right of all People to Life, to Liberty, and to the Pursuit of Happiness.

MOSES AND THE LAW

Let us look now at how the Israelites' new freedom resulted necessarily in the giving of the Law of Moses, the Ten Commandments. Clearly Moses and everyone else who escaped from Egypt understood that there could be no freedom without responsibility, that the other side of freedom is law. In fact, law is necessary to govern all relationships *among* free men and women, because there is a point where one person's freedom may impinge upon the freedom of other individuals. It is at that point, at that moment, that law necessarily comes into existence.

    Moses understood that need for law when he climbed Mount Sinai and received the Law. Whatever transpired on that mountain, Moses clearly believed that the Law was "given" to him. Whatever it was that Moses carved on those stone tablets, he was convinced that he was not the author of the Law. For Moses and his followers, just as Yahweh was the author of the people's freedom, so, too, was Yahweh the author of the Law (Exodus 20:1–17). The Law was the outward symbol of the agreement, the contract, the so-called covenant that Moses and the people of Israel subsequently contracted with Yahweh at the foot of Mount Sinai.

Evidence in the book of Exodus suggests that Moses first learned about Yahweh from his father-in-law, Jethro, who was the priest of Midian (Exodus 3:1). Moses' "call" and commission occurred in the Sinai wilderness, very likely on the sacred mountain where Jethro may have initially introduced Moses to Yahweh. The traditional site of Mount Sinai is in the central part of the Sinai Peninsula, the highest mountain in that wilderness region. In the story of his call, it is apparent that Moses did not know this god of Mount Sinai, because according to the account Moses asked the god his name (Exodus 3:13–16) and first learned the divine name "Yahweh." According to the story, upon returning to Egypt, Moses asked Pharaoh for permission to take the people of Israel to Yahweh's sacred mountain, which is described as being a three-day journey from the Nile Delta (Exodus 8:27).

The commandments that Moses delivered to the people at the foot of Mount Sinai are introduced by this prologue: "I am the LORD [Yahweh] your God, who brought you out of the land of Egypt, out of the house of bondage." These words of preamble tie Yahweh and the people once again to the Exodus event and now to the Law, the Ten Commandments that Moses received on Yahweh's sacred mountain.

There follow in the text of Exodus 20 the Ten Commandments, which fall into two distinct categories. The first three govern the relationship between the people of Israel and Yahweh. The fourth commandment is what I call the "swing" commandment: that is it can be understood as governing the relationship between Yahweh and the people of Israel and/or the relationship among the people of Israel. In fact, it does both. The last six commandments govern relationships among the people of the covenant. These laws clearly display an in-group ethic. They were intended to govern the relationship of Israelites to other Israelites rather than the relationship between the Israelites and other people. That distinction becomes clear just as soon as the Israelites come into contact with other people, whom they proceed to kill. Let us proceed to look more closely at the Ten Commandments:

1. *"You shall have no other gods before (or except) me"* (Exodus 20:3). This commandment is not, as many believe, an unequivocal statement of monotheism: namely, that there is one and only one god. It states rather that the people of Israel will worship only Yahweh to the exclusion of all other gods. This God of the Exodus, whose proper name is Yahweh, is now Israel's God, although there are, to be sure, other gods for other people. Scholars call this belief not monotheism, but henotheism, the worship of one god to the exclusion of all others. The implication of this first commandment is that the Hebrews, whom Yahweh delivered from slavery in Egypt, will worship no god except Yahweh, the author of their deliverance and the giver of their Law.

2. *"You shall not make for yourself an idol, whether in the form of anything that is in heaven above, or that is on the earth beneath, or that is in the water under the earth. You shall not bow down or worship them; for I the LORD [Yahweh] your God am a jealous God, punishing children for the iniquity of their parents, to the third and fourth generation of those who reject me, but showing steadfast love to the thousandth generation of those who love me and keep my commandment"* (Exodus 20:4–6). Christians have generally not taken this commandment seriously. For most of the history of Christianity, churches have been resplendent with statues and icons of God, angels, Jesus, saints, and others—things that are in heaven above, on the earth beneath, and in the water under the earth. Had Christians followed the second commandment rigorously, there would be no Christian art, as we know it.

3. *"You shall not make wrongful use of the name of the LORD [Yahweh] your God, for the LORD [Yahweh] will not acquit anyone who misuses his name"* (Exodus 20:7). The reference here applies to wrongful use of Yahweh's name, particularly in oaths. The people were enjoined not to use Yahweh's name wrongfully in a lying oath.

4. *"Remember the Sabbath day, and keep it holy. Six days you shall labor and do all your work. But the seventh day is a Sabbath to the LORD [Yahweh] your God; you shall not do any work—you, your son or your daughter, your male or female slave, your livestock, or the alien resident in your towns. For in six days the LORD [Yahweh] made heaven and earth, the sea, and all that is in them, but rested the seventh day; therefore the LORD [Yahweh] blessed the sabbath day and consecrated it"* (Exodus 20:8–11). This is the commandment that I called the "swing" commandment: it governs the relationship between the people of Israel and Yahweh, as do the first three commandments; and it governs, as well, the relationship among the people, as do the last six commandments. By observing the Sabbath, the people do as Yahweh did when he rested from creation on the seventh day. Ironically, apart from Seventh-day Adventists, Christians generally do not observe this commandment. The Sabbath, the seventh day, is Saturday. Indeed, Christians set aside this commandment when they began to observe Sunday, the day of the Sun, as the Lord's day, the day of Jesus' resurrection, in lieu of observing Saturday, the Sabbath. It is interesting to note that the commandment applies not only to the people of Israel and their families, but also to their slaves, their livestock, and to resident aliens in their midst.[26]

---

26. The version of this commandment in Deuteronomy 5:15 is interesting in the way in which it connects the observance of the Sabbath to the Exodus: "Remember that you were a slave in the land of Egypt, and that the LORD [Yahweh] your God brought you out from there with a mighty hand and an outstretched arm; therefore the LORD [Yahweh] your God commanded you to keep the sabbath day." The observance of the Sabbath seems to be a luxury of the people's newfound freedom. When they were slaves in Egypt, the Hebrews worked seven days a week.

5. *"Honor your father and your mother, so that your days may be long in the land the LORD [Yahweh] your God is giving you"* (Exodus 20:12). Respect of parents is of the utmost importance in virtually all traditional cultures. It is the foundation of the family.

6. *"You shall not murder"* (Exodus 20:13). The commandment is often translated erroneously as "You shall not kill," but this commandment was obviously not a prohibition against all killing, because Israelites regularly killed foreigners, people who were not part of the in-group. The commandment refers rather to intentional wrongful murder of fellow Israelites and, like the rest of commandments 4 to 10, applied only to the group.

7. *"You shall not commit adultery"* (Exodus 20:14). Adultery referred to intercourse between a married woman and any man other than her husband. Early Israelites practiced polygamy, so this commandment applied only to men who had intercourse with another man's wife. Since a man's wife was his property (see the tenth commandment), adultery was actually a violation of another man's property rights.

8. *"You shall not steal"* (Exodus 20:15). The commandment referred to people's possessions and may also have extended to kidnapping.

9. *"You shall not bear false witness against your neighbor"* (Exodus 20:16). Since witnesses both testify against and bring charges against someone, it was forbidden for anyone to be a lying witness against a fellow Israelite.

10. *"You shall not covet your neighbor's house; you shall not covet your neighbor's wife, or male slave, or female slave, or ox, or donkey, or anything that belongs to your neighbor"* (Exodus 20:17). The implication here is to desiring excessively something that belongs to another person to the point of contemplating theft. It is interesting that a man's wife is listed first, albeit along with the rest of a man's possessions. Wives belonged to their husbands.

In looking at the Ten Commandments, we need to answer the question of what they might mean to Christians today and how they function or should function in contemporary Christianity. This question is, I believe, directly related to our larger theme of the quest for God. It is especially interesting that Christians do not even attempt to observe all of the commandments, most especially the second (against images) and the fourth (to observe the Sabbath). In addition, the seventh commandment (against adultery) and the tenth (against coveting) do not apply equally to both sexes, and all of the commandments, in fact, originally applied only to the in-group. Even the most religious Christians do not pretend to follow the Ten Commandments literally in all of their implications. They have learned over the centuries to pick and choose among them.[27]

---

27. I find it ironic that fundamentalist Christians still lobby vehemently to have the Ten Commandments posted in public school classrooms, in courtrooms, and elsewhere. If they are so important, why are they not followed to the letter of the law by the very people who want them on view in public places?

Once we have removed the necessary God-talk from our vocabulary, because the concept of a personal transcendent God is no longer viable, what function, if any, do the Ten Commandments continue to serve in our churches, if not in society as a whole? I like to look at the Ten Commandments as a statement of the "moral imperative"; after establishing the relationship of the people to their god in the first three or four commandments, the rest of the commandments serve as a guide to what people should and should not do in their relationships with other people. The commandments are not a legal code of law so much as they are a guide or a roadmap that points us in a particular direction. As with any roadmap, we need to look the commandments over and make reasoned and responsible decisions with regard to which route to follow, and how to follow or not follow them. Of course, the commandments, and any law, should in our time clearly extend beyond just the in-group. Our code of ethics should govern our relationships with all people, not only our relationships with those who belong to our "tribe."

Making decisions that are reasonable as we live our lives in the full brightness of the Enlightenment, we need to understand that we cannot claim ultimate authority for our particular code of (religious) law as coming from some God who lives outside the universe and who is assumed to be the author of these commandments. There can be little doubt that, borrowing from early law codes, Moses was the actual author of the Ten Commandments, which he formulated in the aftermath of the Exodus to provide a framework for behavior among the newly liberated slaves. Do these commandments have any relevance for us more than three thousand years later? To what extent are the commandments *self-evident* and to what extent do the commandments need updating for the next millennium of Christianity's history? The Ten Commandments in the form published in Exodus 20 afford only minimal relevance to life in the twenty-first century.

An important question to ask in this context is how does the word "God" or the name "Yahweh" function in developing a contemporary code of social (or religious) ethics? How can we understand the "moral imperative" either in a religious or in a secular context, because ultimately all of our laws must be designed to govern relationships between or among people? Do the Ten Commandments supersede civil law? Obviously not! Do they complement it? Obviously not! Do they have any meaningful contemporary function in our society? Probably not, except as we understand them as still one more code of law from our ancient past. In fact, only two of the commandments find a place in our civil law, the commandments not to murder and not to steal. One hardly needs the Ten Commandments posted in a court of law to cover these two crimes. They appear universally in law codes in virtually every time and every place.

The God of Moses was, of course, much more than a framer of Israel's code of law. The God of Moses, the God of Israel and of Christianity, was a god of history. Moses saw Yahweh in the Exodus and in the covenant Law of Mount Sinai, and succeeding generations of Israelite prophets saw their god in the unfolding drama of Israel's history, both the good and the bad. Early Christianity, in continuity with tradition inherited from Judaism, saw God as well in a historical person, Jesus of Nazareth, and in the events associated with Jesus' life, death, and alleged resurrection.

As Christian philosophers and theologians appropriated the language, images, and concepts of Greek philosophy in order to understand in new contexts the God of ancient Israel and of early Christianity, that contact with Greco-Roman culture and philosophy led to an "enlargement" of the Christian concept of God. That biblical and Hellenistic concept of God is now dead.[28] It no longer functions meaningfully in a way that promotes a clear and rational understanding of the universe or a relevant contemporary understanding of the meaning of human existence.

If our traditional concept of God is dead, then we need to look elsewhere, especially if we are convinced that some of the universal Truths regarding the inviolability of human freedom and the need for universal law are viable for our own generation and into the foreseeable future. We need to discover in the ancient concept of God what was timely—that is, what belonged to a particular time and to a particular place—and try to extricate from that what, if anything, transcends time and place and is timeless and immutable. Once we have tackled that problem, we then need to ask whether we may need a new name for whatever it is that we believe lies at the foundation of the universe and ultimately provides meaning to human existence.

At the heart of this discussion is the question "With whom or with what was Moses in touch when he delivered the Hebrew slaves out of Egypt and when he delivered the Ten Commandments from Mount Sinai?" The traditional answer to that question is simple: Moses drew his inspiration from Israel's god Yahweh. Yahweh was the author of their freedom and the author of the Law. Moses was the prophet of Yahweh, the mediator or the messenger, the mouthpiece of Israel's living God.

Once we set aside that traditional but archaic and irrelevant answer as language that reflects a pre-Enlightenment understanding of the universe and a prerational understanding of human history, we are still faced with the dilemma of answering the who or the what question. Was Moses himself the author of the freedom of the Hebrew slaves and the author of the Sinai Law? Probably. Or was Moses in touch with someone or something deep within the recesses of his own inner being? Someone or something greater than Moses himself? Was Moses in touch with that self-evident Truth about which Thomas Jefferson spoke in the Declaration of Independence? Was that Truth nothing more than a conviction on Moses' or Jefferson's part, or does that Truth have a reality of its own?

Christianity maintains that this self-evident Truth does have a reality of its own. Paul Tillich pointed to the infinite center of human life, to the power or spirit that calls forth being in all living creatures. It was not the transcendental, external, personal God that Tillich directed us to, but rather an inner power or reality that, when encountered, opens humankind to the very meaning of human existence. Tillich tried to give this power, this spirit, this reality a name when he referred to it as "Ultimate Reality," or "The Ground of All Being," or "Being Itself." Tillich was convinced that

---

28. The Hellenistic concept of "God" may not be totally dead. The Stoic concept of the divine *Logos* is, in fact, very much like the Chinese Tao that I will discuss later in this chapter.

the old images of God, the old concepts of God, had to die before humankind could ever again use the word "God" meaningfully. Christians must learn to understand that this inner reality, this inner truth, this inner power is all that we can ever hope to be in contact with when we "listen to" or "speak to" whatever or whoever it is that we dare to call "God." As I stated earlier, it may even be necessary to get rid of the word "God," so as not to confuse traditional Christianity with the Christianity that must emerge in the new millennium.

INSIGHTS FROM TAOISM

If I am right in declaring that most of the effort to name and speak about God in Western religious thought has been an exercise in futility because the concept of a transcendental personal God is dead, then perhaps we should look outside our own Western religious tradition for new ways to approach that inner reality, that inner truth, that inner power that motivated Moses, Jesus, Jefferson, and others. Perhaps it may be time to look to the East for some help in understanding better who or what it is that humankind has called "God" throughout much of the recorded history of the Western world.

It is in that spirit that I now turn for help to China's ancient religious tradition called Taoism. The first great expression of philosophical Taoism is the poetic and terse writing known as the *Tao Te Ching* attributed traditionally to Lao-tzu, the anonymous "Old Sage" or "Master" or "Teacher," who lived during the first half of the sixth century BCE. His writing attempts to portray or express, but not describe, the nature of the Tao.

In the teaching of ancient Chinese religion and most specifically in the teaching of Lao-tzu, it is the cosmos or the totality of all that exists that deserves our focus and devotion rather than things or persons that arise out of that whole. Ancient Chinese thinkers were not content to frame a theory to account for the becoming, the being, and the passing away of single objects in our universe. They wished rather to account for the evident harmony and order they saw in nature as a whole. The concept they arrived at by way of an answer to that mystery was the Tao. The harmony and orderliness displayed in heaven and earth are, they said, the result of the cosmic presence of the Tao. In the *Tao Te Ching*, a collection of sayings of the Master (Lao-tzu) put together by disciples following his death, we read in the opening sentence, "The Tao that can be expressed is not the eternal Tao,"[29] that is, the Tao cannot be

---

29. From "Taoist Scriptures, The Tao-Te-King," chap. 1, in *The Bible of the World*, edited by Robert O. Ballou in collaboration with Friedrich Spielberg, and with the assistance and advice of Horace L. Friess (New York: Viking Press, 1939), p. 471. I have looked at a number of different translations of the *Tao Te Ching*, both in print and on the Internet. Not surprisingly, they vary considerably, sometimes to the extent that it is difficult to believe that you are reading the same chapter. Nevertheless, the same common thread runs through all of these translations, the indescribable profundity and elusiveness of the Tao. I have quoted from a translation that seems more intelligible to these Western ears.

adequately understood and certainly cannot be defined or described. Various passages suggest that the Tao pervades all reality and can be known only in silence and through experiences that transcend words.

The Tao is the ultimate reality on which everything else depends for its existence, but the Tao is not itself just one more existent thing. The Tao is rather prior to everything. It is, therefore, nameless, and to those of us who are accustomed to think only of entities or beings that we meet within the realm of space and time, the Tao is so very elusive, so far beyond our power to imagine and comprehend, that we are tempted to think that it is actually nothing at all. In some respects the Tao might be thought of as the governing principle of the universe.

The Tao is the prime source of creation and determines all things:

In its profundity it [the Tao] seems to be the origin of all things.
In its depth it seems ever to remain.
I do not know whose offspring it is;
But it looks like the predecessor of nature. (chapter 4)

The great Tao pervades everywhere, both on the left and on the right.
By it all things came into being, and it does not reject them. (chapter 34)

The Tao is the presence or power or absolute governing principle that is evident in the universe. It is also the Way (the literal meaning of the word "Tao") of living that human beings should follow in order to be in harmony with nature and the universe.

By adhering to the Tao of the past
You will master the existence of the present
And be able to know the origin of the past
This is called the clue of Tao. (chapter 14)

Accordingly, following the Tao is living in harmony with the governing principle or power that holds the universe together and that brings balance, harmony, kinship, and unity to everything in the universe.

In old times the perfect man of Tao was subtle, penetrating and so profound that he can hardly be understood. Because he cannot be understood, I shall endeavor to picture him:
    He is cautious, like one who crosses a stream in winter;
    He is hesitating, like one who fears his neighbors;
    He is modest, like one who is a guest;
    He is yielding, like ice that is going to melt;
    He is simple, like wood that is not yet wrought;
    He is vacant, like valleys that are hollow;
    He is dim, like water that is turbid. (chapter 15)

The Tao enters the realm of the historical and the phenomenal and in this form becomes accessible to human beings, so that they can "rest" in it, that is to say, live in accordance with it rather than trying to force it to obey their human wills. But for Lao-tzu, neither nature nor the material cosmos are the ultimate reality. Beyond the material universe there lies this impalpable and indescribable reality, what he called the Tao.

The appropriation of the Tao led Lao-tzu to renounce the striving, the ambition, and the self-seeking that characterizes so much of human life, particularly Western life. Instead, the natural harmony that Lao-tzu found in the Tao led him to live his life passively and unaggressively in simple harmony with nature. He believed that society would be harmonious only after humanity synchronized itself with nature and with the Tao, the mystical reality that underlies nature and the universe.

> He who attains Tao is everlasting.
> Though his body may decay he never perishes. (chapter 16)

In some respects Taoism, which seems to advocate passivity, and Judaism and Christianity, whose prophetic witnesses generally demand a call to action, seem to be at opposite extremes in what they advocate as appropriate behavior for their followers. One could, however, argue that Western appropriation of the Tao into the more Western concept of God might provide the necessary balance that we must incorporate into our personal lives and into the world around us. What I particularly like about Taoism is not its passivity, but rather its philosophical underpinning, its image or concept of "God," if you will. However, in saying this, it is essential to understand that the concept of the Tao is more elusive than the Judeo-Christian concept of God, and therefore quite alien to our way of thinking. In fact, it is totally elusive, because as soon as you think you have understood the Tao, that is the very moment when you have fallen into the trap of forgetting that "the Tao that can be expressed is not the eternal Tao." The true Tao cannot be spoken or truly understood.

I like to believe that Lao-tzu agrees with Moses who forbade making any images of God, which, as I have said before, should exclude erecting not only physical images, but conceptual images as well. For that very reason I find the Tao a particularly attractive concept to embrace and appropriate, as we attempt to rise above the Western concept of a personal transcendent, yet almost-human or anthropomorphic God. Looking sympathetically at a non-Western religious-philosophical tradition like Chinese Taoism may enable us more easily to relinquish the excess baggage that has been packed into the word "God" or the name "Yahweh," not only throughout the history of Christian theology, but even in the biblical texts, which are themselves problematic.

We Westerners should, however, probably avoid buying into religious Taoism's tendency to withdraw from and renounce the world; its worship of departed ancestors; its worship of natural phenomena such as mountains, rivers, and various kinds of animals; its rituals, sacrifices, and celebrations; and its belief in the Yin and the Yang, the two major Taoist principles that must be blended together harmoniously in life. I am, after all, not advocating that we become Taoists. Rather, I am proposing that we look at philosophical Taoism to help us develop a more profound, a more sophisticated, and a more relevant understanding of what we in the West have traditionally called "God."

I suspect that a thousand years from now we will sound more Taoist than Christian when we speak about God, when we speak about that which is at "the ground of all being," about that which is "the governing principle of the universe," about that which is the "moral imperative." I certainly hope so, for I think that reaching out in a totally new direction can be enormously helpful to Christian theology in overcoming the serious limitations of the Christian conception of God.

Perhaps the greatest value in appropriating aspects of Taoist philosophy into Christian thinking would be that we might be driven to consider more seriously Paul Tillich's inner Reality or inner Truth as an IT, rather than as a HE. We clearly need help in setting aside forever the transcendental personal God of traditional Christianity as we become involved more seriously in this quest for the God beyond God.

It could also be helpful to look at the ways in which some Christian mystics' idea of "the God beyond God" might possibly be compared to the Tao. That idea is found in the writings of Dionysius the Areopagite and reappears in modern theology in the writings of Paul Tillich, although Tillich cannot, of course, be considered a mystic. The Tao is not just the cosmos or nature; it is prior to them. Perhaps it is the "mother of creation." It is also eminently clear that the Tao is *not* a person and, therefore, *not God*, as that word is generally understood in the West. The Tao is nameless, formless, without any distinguishable characteristics. Somehow concealed in this elusive Ultimate is the power that moves the whole of our universe.

Westerners, including Christians, find this language elusive, difficult to comprehend, and even uncomfortable. I submit, however, that something like the Tao will, within the next thousand years, be closer to the Christian understanding of ultimate reality than the personal God in whom (or in which) Christians currently believe. I submit to you that Moses was right: our God is frankly too small.

INSIGHTS FROM MARTIN BUBER'S *I AND THOU*

Martin Buber's *I and Thou* (*Ich und Du*, 1923) advances a philosophy of personal dialogue that provides appropriate balance to the impersonal concept of the Tao that we considered above. In this deceptively small classic, Buber describes how personal dialogue defines the nature of reality. Human existence, he maintains, is defined by the way in which people engage in dialogue with other persons, with the world around us, and with God.

According to Buber, human beings adopt two very different attitudes or stances both in their relationships with other people and in their relationships with the world around them. One is the *I-Thou* (or *I-You*) relationship, and the other the *I-It* relationship. In an *I-Thou* relationship, a human being is aware of the connection or unity of being that is present when he or she is involved in a dialogue that engages another individual's total being. Such a subject-to-subject relationship involves closeness, mutuality, and reciprocity. It involves relating to another individual as a personal presence, and not as an object, a thing. The *I-Thou* relationship acknowledges that my being human is intertwined with other human beings. I am a human being only as I see myself in relationship to and with other human beings. An *I-Thou* relation is an encounter with Being itself because it is an ultimate relation that involves the whole being of both subjects as subjects.

An *I-It* relationship, on the other hand, implies detachment and distance from the other person and the treatment of the other person, not as another subject, but rather as an object, an It. In standing over and against the world in an *I-It* relationship, an individual seeks to analyze, to objectify, and to describe the world, not to engage it.

According to Buber, God is the Eternal Thou, the Thou who sustains eternally the *I-Thou* relation. Buber claims that in individual *I-Thou* relationships, we encounter the Eternal Thou who gives unity to all Being. God is the one *Thou* who never becomes an *It*. In the afterword to *I and Thou*, Buber asserts that "The close association of the relation to God with the relation to one's fellow-man . . . is my most essential concern." For Buber, "God's address to man penetrates the events in all our lives and all the events of the world around us, everything biographical and everything historical, and turns it into instruction, into demands for you and me." Buber promotes an ethic that does not exploit other people (or books, or works of art, or trees, or God) as objects of one's own personal experience. Rather, we need to learn how to understand everyone and everything around us as a *You* speaking to a *Me* and requiring a personal response.

In maintaining that life's deepest truth lies in human relationships, Buber identifies God as the "between-ness" that exists whenever one person engages another in an *I-Thou* relationship. Without an awareness of our own being and other people's being, God simply does not exist.

THE QUEST FOR GOD

In the course of this chapter, I hope to have engaged the reader in the simple, yet profound, exercise of looking for God in the universe, in history, in the world immediately around us, and in other people. To the extent that we can any longer speak about God at all, we can probably say that God is the meaning between humankind and the natural order and between one individual and another. God is "the moral imperative" that tells us how to act when we encounter and engage another individual, hopefully as a subject and not merely as still one more object. It is also in history, in everyday human encounters, in art, in poetry, in literature, in films, and in the written records of persons who have had prior meaningful encounters with God that we can hope to find God, who is the Ground of all Being.

Moses found God in the deliverance of the Hebrew slaves from bondage into freedom and in the Law that he delivered in an effort to define the boundaries between one Hebrew and another, once they had acquired their freedom and left their slavery behind them in Egypt. Jefferson found God in those self-evident Truths that all people are equal and have a Right to Life, Liberty, and the Pursuit of Happiness. It should be no surprise that the anonymous writer of the Negro spiritual "Go Down, Moses" found God in his or her own quest for emancipation from oppression. In each of these instances, people struck out to claim for themselves their freedom, their full humanity. It is in taking this step that they "found" God, the fountain of human freedom, the very source of Being.

Lao-tzu understood that the Tao is the prime source of creation and determines all things. He understood that the Tao is the presence or power or the absolute governing principle that is evident in the universe and in the Way of living that all people should follow in order to be in harmony with nature and the universe.

The common denominators in each illustration are humanity, the search for meaning, and the quest for human freedom. God stands at the center, but not as one more individual, however great, but rather as that which defines our very Being, that which is the very Ground or Foundation of all Being. Yet like the Tao, the true God cannot be spoken about or understood or defined, for just as soon as we try to give definition to God and erect an image or even a conceptual image of God, we are clearly guilty of idolatry.

We need to look to our own great religious past to find echoes of God's word. We also need to look selectively into other great religious traditions of the world for other echoes of or glimpses at God. We should probably be particularly wary in our own generation of people who claim to hear God's word. Like Moses in the story in Exodus 33:17–23, all that we ever see of God is God's back, and even then only after God has already passed us by.

Be relentless in the quest for the Tao, or the Force, or God. We need, however, to be particularly cautious because in giving Whoever or Whatever it is a name, we have already committed idolatry. Moses and Buber seem to have understood God as a *Thou*. Lao-tzu probably understood God as an *It*, although I am not entirely certain of that. I like to believe that the truth may lie somewhere between the two. Perhaps God is an *It* that we encounter in a personal way, suggesting to us thereby that *It* is actually a *Thou*.

Whatever it is that we encounter in the universe that affords us meaning is, after all, understood only from our side, the human side, of that encounter. Moses and Lao-tzu were right in warning us to approach this Ultimate Reality cautiously. We will, of course, never really know or understand the mystery of this governing principle that seems to hold together the universe and our humanity.

I call this chapter "The Quest for God," because it is just that: a lifelong quest. God is elusive. As soon as you think that you are onto something, like Lao-tzu and Moses, I assure you that you are not. Before starting on this quest, it is essential to let go of the excess baggage, the idolatry, that most of us bring to this quest.

Part 2
THE BIBLE

WHAT IS THE BIBLE?

$\mathcal{T}$he question of what the Bible is, and what it is not, is an enormously important issue for all Christians. A good deal depends on the significance the Bible holds in the lives of individual Christians and on the ways in which the Bible shapes the values and behavior of the particular denominations to which individual Christians belong.

In this chapter we will examine the collections of books that Jews and Christians call their Bible. We will consider the origins of these books and what Christians generally mean when they refer to these books as "inspired writings" or sacred scriptures. We will also take into account the implications of the secular method of historical investigation for the study of the world's religions generally, and for the study of the Bible specifically. In the following chapter we will then investigate some of the critical tools that scholars have developed and utilized in their scientific study of the Bible, more specifically the New Testament, and consider some of the implications of analytical study of the Bible for Christianity.

In light of this investigation, I propose to demonstrate, among other things, that a narrow fundamentalist interpretation of the Bible is not only unsuitable to the modern age, but that it is also inconsistent with the Christian church's understanding of the Bible throughout most of its history, and that it is also incompatible with the nature and character of the Bible itself. This will hopefully lay the foundation for understanding the need for modern historical investigation of the New Testament, with all of the implications that such study has for appreciating more clearly Jesus of Nazareth and his place in Christianity.

THE ORIGIN AND SCOPE OF THE BIBLE

So what exactly is this book that Christians call the Bible? Whatever else it may be, the Bible is not a book so much as it is an anthology or a collection of ancient books written roughly between two and three thousand years ago. The English word "Bible" is derived from the Old French word *bible*, which is based on the Latin word *biblia* and the Greek word βιβλία (*biblia*), meaning "books." The word originates from the ancient Canaanite or Phoenician city of Gebal, which was known to ancient Greeks as Byblos (hence the word "Bible"), a port about twenty miles north of Beirut and very possibly the city in which the first "books" were written.

The word "Bible" refers to the Christian scriptures, but the word is also used to refer to the scriptures of Judaism. When we refer to Christianity's canon of sacred scriptures, we need to understand that the Bible is a fixed collection of authoritative literature that the entire Christian community considers normative for its life and its faith.

The Hebrew Bible or the Christian Old Testament

The Jewish Bible or the Hebrew Bible, which Christians call their Old Testament, is actually a collection of twenty-four books (or originally scrolls), which in their English version constitute thirty-nine different books, as several books were sometimes contained on a single scroll in their original Hebrew form. Most of these books were originally written in Hebrew, but a few passages in the books of Ezra, Daniel, Jeremiah, and Genesis were originally written in Aramaic, a Semitic language closely related to Hebrew, and presumably the language that Jesus spoke.

The Hebrew Bible is traditionally divided into three sections:

1. **The Law** (Hebrew *Torah*): five books or scrolls—Genesis, Exodus, Leviticus, Numbers, and Deuteronomy. These books are sometimes referred to as the Pentateuch (Greek *penta* = five and *teuchos* = book) or the books of Moses, because authorship of these five books is traditionally attributed to Moses.
2. **The Prophets** (Hebrew *Nebi'im*): nine books or scrolls—The Former Prophets in four books or scrolls: namely Joshua, Judges, 1 and 2 Samuel, and 1 and 2 Kings;[30] and the Latter Prophets in five books or scrolls: namely Isaiah, Jeremiah, Ezekiel, Daniel, and the scroll of the twelve minor prophets (Hosea, Joel, Amos, Obadiah, Jonah, Micah, Nahum, Habakkuk, Zephaniah, Haggai, Zechariah, and Malachi).[31]

---

30. The books of 1 and 2 Samuel in the Hebrew Bible were written on a single scroll; so, too, were the books of 1 and 2 Kings written on a single scroll.

31. The twelve minor prophets, so called because of the shorter length of the books, not because these prophets were less important, were traditionally written on a single scroll. The major prophets, on the other hand, were so called not because they were more important than the minor prophets, but because these books were written on their own individual scrolls. Most scholars are convinced that the Isaiah scroll actually contains the work of three different

3. **The Writings** (Hebrew *Ketubim*): ten books or scrolls—Psalms, Job, Proverbs, Ruth, Song of Solomon, Ecclesiastes, Lamentations, Esther, Ezra-Nehemiah,[32] and 1 and 2 Chronicles.[33]

The process by which these books became canonical is long and complicated and beyond the scope of this work. Suffice it to say that before the fall of Jerusalem to the Romans in 70 CE and the consequent destruction of the second Jewish Temple, the scope and content of the Jewish canon seems to have been somewhat fluid, especially when it came to the books of the third division of the Hebrew Bible, the *Ketubim* or the Writings. The five books of the Law or the Torah were probably considered authoritative by about 450 BCE, and the books of the prophets by about 200 BCE.[34]

The third section, the Writings, achieved canonical status somewhat later. In fact, it was at the so-called Council of Jamnia, or Jabneh (ca. 90 CE), that the rabbis there assembled took measures to define the canon more precisely and more narrowly in favor of the twenty-four-book collection identified above.[35] These books ultimately emerged as the Hebrew Bible and served the earliest Christian communities as their Sacred Scriptures.

The New Testament

The Christian Bible consists of all of the books of the Hebrew Bible (called by Christians the Old Testament)[36] and the additional twenty-seven books of the New Testament, listed in their traditional order:

---

prophets: Isaiah of Jerusalem (chapters 1–39), an anonymous prophet generally known as Deutero-Isaiah or Second Isaiah (chapters 40–55), and an anonymous prophet known as Trito-Isaiah or Third Isaiah (chapters 56–66). The physical length of a biblical scroll, generally no more than about 22 to 24 feet, was a determining factor in how much could be written on it.

32. The books of Ezra and Nehemiah also shared a single scroll.

33. The books of 1 and 2 Chronicles also shared a single scroll.

34. Ecclesiasticus, or the Wisdom of Jesus ben Sirach, originally written in Jerusalem between 200 and 180 BCE and translated into Greek circa 132 BCE by the author's grandson, indicates in the prologue that the original author, the translator's grandfather, "devoted himself especially to the reading of the Law and the Prophets, and the other books of our ancestors." This passage bears clear testimony to the threefold division of the Jewish Scripture into Law, Prophets, and Writings, although the content of the third section (Writings) is less clear than that of the first two (the Law and the Prophets).

35. Although the view that the Torah or the Pentateuch achieved canonical status by about 450 BCE, the Prophets by 200 BCE, and the Writings at Jamnia by about 90 CE was widely accepted in the first half of the twentieth century, that view had to be modified with the discovery in 1948 of the Dead Sea Scrolls. Scholars now recognize that the Council of Jamnia (Jabneh) did not function as an authoritative Jewish council in the way in which later Christian councils functioned. The Council of Jamnia did not forever close the Jewish canon, at least regarding the books of the *Ketubim* or the Writings, with regard to which disagreement persisted.

36. The Roman Catholic and Eastern Orthodox Old Testament is based on a third-century BCE Alexandrian (Egyptian) translation of the Hebrew scriptures into Greek, commonly called

Four Gospels:
    Matthew
    Mark
    Luke
    John
The Acts of the Apostles
Thirteen letters attributed by tradition to the apostle Paul:
    Romans
    1 and 2 Corinthians
    Galatians
    Ephesians
    Philippians
    Colossians
    1 and 2 Thessalonians
    1 and 2 Timothy
    Titus
    Philemon
The so-called general epistles:
    Hebrews
    James
    1 and 2 Peter
    1, 2, and 3 John
    Jude
The Apocalypse or the Revelation of John

The New Testament evolved somewhat differently from the Hebrew Bible or the Old Testament. As was stated earlier, the Bible of the earliest Christian church during the first century of its existence was, in fact, the Jewish scriptures in the larger Greek version, the Septuagint, or LXX,[37] because Greek was the spoken and written language of most early Christians. There was, however, no distinctive collection of canonical Christian writings during the first century of the church's history.

the Septuagint (often abbreviated by the Roman numeral LXX or 70). The Septuagint contains all of the books of the Hebrew Bible and a number of additional writings: 1 Esdras, the Wisdom of Solomon, the Wisdom of Jesus ben Sirach (or Ecclesiasticus), Judith, Tobit, Baruch, the Letter of Jeremiah, the four books of Maccabees, and additions to the book of Daniel (namely Susanna, Bel and the Dragon, the Prayer of Azariah, and the Song of the Three Young Men), and Esther. Most Protestants, following the practice of Martin Luther, accept as their Old Testament only the books of the Hebrew Bible and not the so-called apocryphal or deutero-canonical books accepted by Roman Catholic and Eastern Orthodox Christians. Ironically, the original King James Bible of 1611 included the Old Testament Apocrypha. It was actually in the nineteenth century that Protestants came to include only the books of the Hebrew Bible in their Old Testament and to exclude the apocryphal or deutero-canonical books.

37. The use of LXX, the Roman numeral for 70, refers to the legend that the translation from Hebrew into Greek was done independently by seventy translators, whose individual translations were miraculously in total agreement.

By the middle of the first century, Christians had already begun to regard the words or the teachings of Jesus as a modifying factor in their study of the Hebrew Bible. The scriptures of early Christianity, which were the Hebrew scriptures, were studied by Christians in light of what the church remembered Jesus to have said and taught. For their understanding of Jesus' teachings, the earliest generations of Christians apparently relied on oral tradition that reported what Jesus had said, but gradually written collections of Jesus' teaching began to appear, first separately (as in the case of the hypothetical sayings document known as Q[38]), and somewhat later in early Christian gospels (Matthew, Mark, Luke, John, Thomas, etc.). Gradually these written gospels replaced the oral tradition of the earliest churches.

By the second half of the first century, Christians were also showing an interest in letters that Paul had written to individual churches that he had either founded or visited during his missionary journeys through the eastern Mediterranean world, primarily churches in modern-day Turkey, Greece, and Rome. It is interesting, indeed curious, that personal correspondence to specific churches came to be so highly regarded by Christians everywhere toward the end of the first century.

A New Testament was beginning to take shape to complement or to replace the sacred scriptures that Christian communities had inherited from Judaism. The development of that New Testament collection was complex and sometimes controversial. The earliest New Testament canonical list appeared circa 150 CE, when, in Rome, a church father named Marcion proposed a canon of sacred scriptures consisting only of his version of the Gospel of Luke and ten of Paul's letters, but no books of the Hebrew Bible. Marcion's canon was intended not to complement but rather to replace the Hebrew Bible. Although Marcion tried to divorce Judaism's daughter religion, Christianity, from its Jewish roots, his efforts failed in most Christian circles. Indeed, it was apparently in reaction against Marcion that other second-century Christian fathers, including Justin Martyr, Tatian, and several others, identified early Christian writings that were suitable for reading at services of worship *alongside* the books of the Hebrew Bible, *not in place of them*. These second-century fathers were effectively, if unwittingly, contributing to the process of establishing a New Testament of Christian books to complement the collection of Hebrew scriptures that had by this time largely fallen into place.

By the end of the second century, about twenty Christian "books" had achieved in most Christian communities an authoritative status that put them on a par with the books of the Hebrew Bible. The Christian books that were disputed even into the third and fourth centuries included: Hebrews, 2 Peter, 2 and 3 John, Jude, and the Revelation of John. In addition, several books not included in our final canonical collection of twenty-seven were sometimes included in local collections in individual or regional second-century churches: for example, the *Didache*, *1 Clement*, the *Apocalypse of Peter*, the *Shepherd of Hermas*, the *Gospel of Thomas*, the *Gospel of Peter*, *Barnabas*, the *Acts of Paul*, and others.

---

38. The case for the existence of the hypothetical source Q (the abbreviation for *Quelle*, the German word for "source") will be made in the next chapter.

The fates of Hebrews in Western churches and of the Revelation of John in Eastern churches were not resolved until the fourth century. The first mention of the twenty-seven books of our New Testament canon appeared in 367 CE in Athanasius' *Festal Letter*. Additionally, Jerome's translation of the same twenty-seven books into Latin, which he accomplished during the period circa 384–399 CE, came to be known as the Vulgate and exercised a considerable influence on the final collection. By the end of the fourth century, most Christian churches were in agreement on the boundaries of the canon of the New Testament.

Criteria for Inclusion in the New Testament Canon

Although no ecumenical (or universal) council of the ancient church defined the scope of the canon of the New Testament, several regional councils did. The Council of Laodicea in 363 maintained that there were twenty-six canonical books, omitting the Revelation of John; the Council of Hippo in 393 and the Council of Carthage in 397 both listed the twenty-seven books of our New Testament, even though they refuted the Pauline authorship of Hebrews. In reaching its decision on the scope of the New Testament canon, the church maintained that those documents that were suitable for consideration as Sacred Scriptures must be:

1. Apostolic, that is
    (a) written by an apostle of Jesus (e.g., the Gospels of Matthew and John, reputed to have been written respectively by Matthew and John, two of Jesus' twelve apostles; and the collection of Paul's letters); or
    (b) written by a disciple of an apostle (e.g., the Gospels of Mark and Luke, reputed to have been written respectively by Mark, a disciple of Peter; and Luke, a disciple of Paul; or
    (c) traceable to the earliest period of the church (e.g., Hebrews and the disputed catholic epistles, such as 2 Peter, 2 and 3 John, and Jude); or
2. Catholic, that is
    (a) in universal use throughout the church, or
    (b) broadly accessible to Christian churches in various regions, or
    (c) relevant to the church at large;
3. Orthodox (i.e., conforming to the church's correct teaching).[39]

---

39. The word "orthodoxy" is derived from two Greek words: *orthos*, meaning "correct," and *doxa*, meaning "opinion" or "teaching." Its opposite, "heresy," is derived from the Latin *haeresis*, meaning "a school of thought, either philosophical or religious" and the Greek *hairesis*, meaning "a selection, a school, a party, a division, a heresy." The implication of the word "heresy" is that it represents a school or faction or party that is deliberately at variance with clearly established or generally received views or doctrines. The issue is, of course, far more complicated than that. Heresies did not arise to serve as stubborn opponents of established Christianity's apostolic orthodoxy. Rather, certain tendencies in Christianity united to define orthodoxy in such as way as to suppress other opinions.

It is important to note that inspiration was *not* a criterion for canonicity in the early Christian church, because it was believed that inspiration characterized the entirety of the church's life.

It is evident that it was a human decision or a series of human decisions to identify as the church's sacred scriptures specific books from antiquity. Notwithstanding the claims religious communities have made to the contrary regarding the divine supervision that guided church fathers in their decisions, the evidence is clear. Divine inspiration must otherwise have worked differently in different communities.

The very fact that different Christians have different books in their canons of sacred scripture is sufficient proof that the Holy Spirit apparently worked differently for different denominations. Protestants generally number sixty-six books in their canon of sacred scriptures. Roman Catholic and Eastern Orthodox Christians include in their Bibles the same sixty-six books, plus additional books from what Protestants generally call the Apocrypha. The human factor is evident also inasmuch as it was a council of rabbis in Jamnia (in Palestine) in 90 CE and subsequent decisions of early Christian fathers and bishops in regional councils at Laodicea, Hippo, and Carthage that led to the establishment of what Christians have come to call the Bible or the canon of sacred scriptures.[40]

Stated simply, who authorized early Christian fathers in their decision to adopt the Septuagint as their Old Testament? And who inspired Christian fathers and bishops in their decisions to accept the twenty-seven books of the New Testament canon? The obvious and unequivocal answer is that the church fathers and bishops convinced their successors that they were inspired by the Holy Spirit in the decisions that lead them to identify the books of the sacred scriptures.

Who inspired Martin Luther when he dropped from his Old Testament the so-called apocryphal books found in the Septuagint but not contained in the Hebrew Bible? Once again, the simple answer is that successive generations of Protestants simply followed Luther's lead in this matter. Ironically, the King James Bible of 1611 included the apocryphal books, although modern editions of the King James Bible no longer follow the original version in this regard. And who authorized the rabbis assembled at Jamnia regarding the Hebrew canon? Like most such groups, including councils of the church, the assembled leaders simply claimed that authority for themselves or claimed that God had so authorized them through his Holy Spirit. Clear cases of circular reasoning!

WHAT DOES IT MEAN TO REFER TO THE BIBLE AS INSPIRED?

What do Jews and Christians mean when they refer to their collections of books as "canon"? Judaism and Christianity claim to have holy scriptures that are inspired by

---

40. The English word "canon" is also used to refer to the books of the Bible. The word is derived from Latin and Greek words meaning "rule" or "standard." For Christians, "canon" refers to the list of books of the Holy Scriptures accepted officially by the church as authoritative.

God. Traditionally, Christians view the canon as an authoritative collection of books and as a collection of authoritative books. But what exactly does that mean? Minimally it means that the books of the Bible themselves are trustworthy and that this particular collection of books is, in its totality, also trustworthy. But the issue is a bit more complicated.

To clarify the meaning of "biblical inspiration," it might be helpful to compare Islam's understanding of the Quran with Christianity's understanding of the Bible. For Muslims, the Quran is, purportedly, the record of direct revelations from God, the verbatim written record of God's revelations to his prophet Mohammed, and through Mohammed to faithful Muslim believers. For Muslims, the words of the Quran are, therefore, the actual words of God. There seems to be little room for interpretation or modernization in Islam's position on the matter of the Quran. Because of its understanding of the Quran, Islam has remained essentially a fundamentalist religion.

That is, of course, not what mainstream Christians understand when they speak of the Bible. For most Christians, the Bible is the *human* record of *human* responses to God's purported revelations. Unlike the Quran, which allegedly comes from Mohammed alone, the Bible comes from dozens of different human storytellers and writers over a period of almost two thousand years. Written texts of what were to become the books of the Bible were produced over a period of more than a thousand years from about 950 BCE to 150 CE. The Bible is, therefore, the record of dozens of persons' individual witnesses to their alleged encounters with what they call their god.

Although most Christians consider the Bible to be the word of God, by that they generally mean that the Bible is or contains the *Word of God* in the *words of humans*, a subtle but important distinction from what we find in Islam, where the Quran contains the very words of God. For both Jews and Christians, the books of the Bible are human responses and testimonies to God's revelations.

The traditional view of biblical inspiration claims that God or God's Holy Spirit inspired the individual authors of the books of the canon. It is difficult to know when and how the notion of inspired scripture originated, but when in about 458 (or 398) BCE Ezra returned to Jerusalem following the Babylonian Exile and brought with him the Torah (or the Law of Moses), those who heard him read the Torah recognized its authority:

7:73When the seventh month came—the people of Israel being settled in their towns—8:1all the people gathered together into the square before the Water Gate. They told the scribe Ezra to bring the book of the law of Moses, which the LORD [Yahweh] had given to Israel. 2Accordingly, the priest Ezra brought the law before the assembly, both men and women and all who could hear with understanding. This was on the first day of the seventh month. 3He read from it facing the square before the Water Gate from early morning until midday, in the presence of the men and women and those who could understand; and the ears of all the people were attentive to the book of the law. 4The scribe Ezra stood on a wooden platform that had been made for the purpose; and beside him stood Mattithiah, Shema, Anaiah, Uriah, Hilkiah, and Maaseiah on his right hand; and Pedaiah, Mishael, Malchijah,

Hashum, Hashbaddanah, Zechariah, and Meshullam on his left hand. 5And Ezra opened the book (i.e., unrolled the scroll) in the sight of all the people, for he was standing above all the people; *and when he opened it, all the people stood up.* (Nehemiah 7:73–8:5; italics mine)

The occasion for the reading of the law was apparently the completion of the new wall around the city of Jerusalem (ca. 458 or 398 BCE). Although the significance of Ezra's reading of the Mosaic Law is not entirely clear, it is evident that he and the people of Israel held this "book of the law of Moses" in reverence, because "when (Ezra) opened it, all the people stood up."

Several centuries later, at the end of the first century CE, in his work *Against Apion* 1.37–38, the Jewish historian Josephus noted that the authors of his sources, the twenty-two books of Jewish scripture, were prophets inspired by God:

It therefore naturally, or rather universally, follows (seeing that with us it is not open to everybody to write the records, and that there is no discrepancy in what is written; seeing that, on the contrary, the prophets alone had this privilege, obtaining their knowledge of the most remote and ancient history *through the inspiration which they owed to God*, and committing to writing a clear account of the events of their own time just as they occurred)—it follows, I say, that we do not possess myriads of inconsistent books, conflicting with each other. Our books, those *which are justly accredited*, are but two and twenty, and contain the record of all time.[41] (Italics mine)

And just slightly later than Josephus, the author of the New Testament book known as 2 Timothy wrote: "*All scripture is inspired by God* and is useful for teaching, for reproof, for correction, and for training in righteousness" (3:16; italics mine).[42]

Although Christians and Jews have claimed that God or the Holy Spirit inspired their sacred writings, it is not entirely clear what they understood by this "inspiration." Many Christians claim a much broader interpretation of divine inspiration than its limited application to the canon of sacred scriptures. For example, virtually all Christians assume that the Holy Spirit inspired the bishops at the early ecumenical councils of the

---

41. *Josephus*, trans. H. St. J. Thackeray, Loeb Classical Library (Cambridge, MA: Harvard University Press, 1961), pp. 178–79. Inasmuch as the Hebrew Bible in its final form contained twenty-four books, it is not clear which two books Josephus did not include in his list of inspired writings; Esther and Ecclesiastes are likely candidates.

42. See also John 11:49–52: "But one of them, Caiaphas, who was high priest that year, said to them, 'You know nothing at all! You do not understand that it is better for you to have one man die for the people than to have the whole nation destroyed.' *He did not say this on his own*, but being high priest that year *he prophesied* that Jesus was about to die for the nation and not for the nation only, but to gather into one the dispersed children of God" (italics mine). The author of the gospel assumes that God was guiding Caiaphas, albeit unwittingly on the part of the high priest, in his claim that Jesus was dying not only for the Jews but for all of humanity. The author of the Gospel of John is, of course, advancing the Christian claim that Jesus was a servant of God and that God was, accordingly, using the Jewish high priest Caiaphas as an instrument in the divine plan.

church when they produced the Nicene Creed's Trinitarian formula in 325 CE and the Chalcedonian formula in 451 CE that declared that Jesus is wholly human and wholly divine. Roman Catholics believe that inspiration guides the bishops at all ecumenical councils of the church and that the pope is inspired by the Holy Spirit when he speaks ex cathedra (from the chair of St. Peter) on matters of faith and morals.

The original sense of this claim that the books of the Bible are inspired appears to have been that the authors of these books were holy men, who in their works and in their words were inspired by God. When the prophets spoke, they spoke in the name of Yahweh: "Thus says Yahweh" is a common introduction to prophetic oracles in the Old Testament. "An oracle of Yahweh" is likewise a common ending to many prophetic oracles. But inspiration never meant that each and every word that the prophet spoke was inspired or, indeed, dictated by God. It likely meant that the prophets, as mediators of God, *heard* or sometimes *saw*[43] the word of God, which they then spoke in their own words in the oracles that they delivered to the people.

Nevertheless, the common view in many Protestant evangelical and fundamentalist circles, especially in the United States, is that the inspiration of the scriptures refers to the divine inspiration of the individual contributors, whose every word was delivered to them by God. This fundamentalist view of biblical inerrancy, word for word, and generally, for some peculiar, but totally unjustifiable, reason in the King James translation of the Bible, is very much like the view of Islamic orthodoxy on the inspiration of the Quran. This narrow view of the inerrancy of the Bible is not, however, the position of mainstream Catholic, Protestant, or Eastern Orthodox Christianity. The claim of the inerrancy of scripture in every word and in every detail is principally a phenomenon of twentieth-century American Protestant fundamentalism. It continues to persist into these opening years of the new millennium.

Whatever else it may be, the Bible is not a science manual; neither is it a history book, accurate and reliable in every detail. Yet that is what fundamentalists effectively demand by their literalist understanding of scriptural inspiration and biblical inerrancy. They read Genesis 1–3 as if it were an accurate, factual account of the creation of the universe and the origin of humankind. Hence they tend to reject outright many scientific theories, such as the big bang theory of the origin of the universe, and they dismiss as heresy Charles Darwin's views regarding human evolution from lower forms of life.[44]

---

43. The opening words of Amos are: "The words of Amos, who was among the shepherds of Tekoa, which he *saw* concerning Israel in the days of King Uzziah of Judah and in the days of King Jeroboam son of Joash of Israel, two years before the earthquake" (Amos 1:1; italics mine). See also Revelation 1:1–2: "The revelation of Jesus Christ, which God gave him to show his servants what must soon take place; he made it known by sending an angel to his servant John, who testified to the word of God and to the testimony of Jesus Christ, even to all that he *saw*" (italics mine).

44. Even President George W. Bush has stated that he does not "believe" in evolution, as if it were a matter of belief. Evolution is a well-established scientific theory; in fact, many scientists now simply call it a fact.

Rather evangelical fundamentalists advance a view of the Bible that imagines that God or the Holy Spirit spoke directly to, or more precisely dictated to, each individual writer the very words that each and every writer correctly heard, properly understood, and then faithfully transmitted orally and/or in written form as sacred scriptures. The final product was a Bible inerrant in every detail. How that translates into the inerrancy of the King James Version of the Bible remains a mystery to me. It should be clear, however, that there is nothing in either the Jewish or Christian scriptures to support this narrow fundamentalist view of biblical inspiration.

THE DILEMMA OF THE SECULAR METHOD

Our primary source for reconstructing the origins of Judaism and Christianity is, indeed, that very collection of writings that Jews and Christians refer to as the Bible, their holy writings. In recent centuries, scholars have appealed to the secular discipline of historical criticism to delve into these writings in order to reconstruct the history of ancient Israel and the beginnings of Christianity.

It is essential to understand that historical criticism of the Bible is a relatively new undertaking. The methodology, which is based on a secular understanding of history, emerged in Europe in the eighteenth century as a by-product of the Enlightenment. Although many ultraorthodox Jews and evangelical and fundamentalist Christians reject a secular approach to what they consider "sacred books," it is safe to say that the historical-critical method is universally accepted by responsible historians and that it has been embraced by mainstream Jewish and Christian denominations.

An example of the Roman Catholic Church's approval of the historical-critical method in relatively recent times is evident in the papal encyclical *Divino Afflante Spiritu*,[45] issued by Pope Pius XII on September 30, 1943. This encyclical rendered the historical-critical method as not only permissible for Roman Catholic scholars, but as "a duty" (§15) that is "not only necessary for the right understanding of the divinely-given writings, but is urgently demanded . . . " (§19).

The implications of applying this secular methodology to the study of the Bible continue to afford tension, however, both in Roman Catholicism and in many mainstream Protestant denominations. The encyclical itself recognizes the potential for that tension, although it does not appear to grasp fully or to speak meaningfully to the serious issues that remain unresolved when the historical-critical method is systematically and rigorously applied to the church's sacred writings. Allow me to cite a few passages from *Divino Afflante Spiritu* to illustrate the tension, which for more fundamentalist religious traditions might more appropriately be called the "conflict":

---

45. The full text of *Divino Afflante Spiritu* is available in English on the Internet on the Vatican's Web site: http://www.vatican.va/holy_father/pius_xii/encyclicals/documents/hf _p-xii_enc_30091943_divino-afflante-spiritu_en.html.

In our own time the Vatican Council [i.e., Vatican Council I in 1869–1870], with the object of condemning false doctrines regarding inspiration, declared that these same books [the books contained in the old Vulgate Latin edition] were to be regarded by the Church as sacred and canonical not because, having been composed by human industry, they were afterwards approved by her authority, not merely because they contain revelation, without error, but because, having been written under the inspiration of the Holy Spirit, they have God for their author, and as such were handed down to the Church herself (§1).

It is absolutely wrong and forbidden either to narrow inspiration to certain passages of Holy Scripture, or to admit that the sacred writer has erred, since divine inspiration not only is essentially incompatible with error but excludes and rejects it as absolutely and necessarily as it is impossible that God Himself, the supreme Truth, can utter that which is not true (§3).

. . . [T]here arose new and serious difficulties and questions from the wide-spread prejudices of rationalism and more especially from the discovery and investigation of the antiquities of the East (§4).

In claiming that God is the "author" of the books of the Bible, that these books are "without error," and that rationalism introduces "widespread prejudices" into the discussion, *Divino Afflante Spiritu* effectively subordinated all study of the Bible to the authority of the Roman Catholic Church. By definition, modern historical research appeals only to reason in its study of the data, not to any external human authority, such as a church or its leaders. Its methodology is totally secular.

The encyclical further states unequivocally that Catholic students of the Bible should be equipped with the scholarly tools necessary to "repel attacks against the divinely inspired books . . . in accordance with the mind of the Catholic Church" (§6). In addition, the encyclical maintains that the tools of modern historical criticism are "advantages which, not without a special design by Divine Providence, our age has acquired" and considers them "an inducement to interpreters of the Sacred Literature to make diligent use of this light, so abundantly given, to penetrate more deeply, explain more clearly and expound more lucidly the Divine Oracles" (§12).

Let me cite still one more paragraph from the encyclical to illustrate the dilemma of the historical-critical method for Roman Catholics, in particular, and for most mainstream Christians, in general:

But this state of things [questions or opinions raised by critics outside or hostile to Catholic doctrine] is no reason why the Catholic commentator, inspired by an active and ardent love of his subject and sincerely devoted to Holy Mother Church, should in any way be deterred from grappling again and again with these difficult problems, hitherto unsolved, not only that he may refute the objections of the adversaries, but also may attempt to find a satisfactory solution, which will be in full accord with the doctrine of the Church, in particular with the traditional teaching regarding the inerrancy of Sacred Scripture, and which will at the same time satisfy the indubitable conclusion of profane sciences (§46).

The dilemma is clear. *Divino Afflante Spiritu* assumes that there can be no conflict between the results of profane scientific investigation and the teachings of sacred scriptures, especially as interpreted by the church. Hence, Catholic scholars were bound by the 1943 encyclical to employ the profane methodology in the service of the teachings of the Catholic Church. It should be clear that theological conviction must come first, that the Catholic scholar is then expected to collect evidence and to build a case in a manner that supports and works within the confines of the church's predetermined theological convictions. The dilemma is that the conclusions are, in fact, decided before the research has even begun.

The Roman Catholic Church would, of course, never put it quite this bluntly, but this is the unavoidable implication of the church's view that human reason, correctly engaged, can never contradict the teachings of the church. For the unbiased scholar, however, the profane or secular method of historical investigation should seek no specific conclusion other than truth for its own sake, without any encumbrances or limits that have been laid out by any individual authority or by any particular church or religion. Reason alone and the impartial application of the historical-critical method must always be the sole basis for scholarly research. It is clear that the potential for tension or conflict is great in the application of this secular, scientific method of biblical research within the limits of any authoritative religious community, Roman Catholic, Southern Baptist, or otherwise.

The position set forth in *Divino Afflante Spiritu* needs to be reviewed in light of the more recent (August 15, 1990) *Apostolic Constitution of the Supreme Pontiff John Paul II on Catholic Universities*, commonly referred to as *Ex Corde Ecclesiae*.[46]

Not surprisingly, this more recent pronouncement of the Roman Catholic Church reflects the same tension found in the earlier encyclical. In its introduction, *Ex Corde Ecclesiae* states:

> A Catholic University's privileged task is to unite existentially by intellectual effort two orders of reality that too frequently tend to be placed in opposition as though they were antithetical: the search for truth, and the certainty of already knowing the fount of truth (§1).

This statement begs the question. Juxtaposing "the search for truth" and "the certainty of already knowing the fount of truth" presumes that reason and faith can never be in conflict, because reason ("the *search* for truth") is clearly subordinate to and inferior to faith ("the *certainty* of knowing the fount of truth"). *Search* implies an ongoing quest; *certainty* leaves little, if any, room for honest doubt. This tension is reflected later when the text states:

---

46. The full text of *Ex Corde Ecclesiae* is available in English on the Internet on the Vatican Web site at: http://www.vatican.va/holy_father/john_paul_ii/apost_constitutions/ documents/hf_jp-ii_apc_15081990_ex-corde-ecclesiae_en.html.

> It is in the context of the impartial search for truth that the relationship between faith and reason is brought to light and meaning. The invitation of Saint Augustine, *"Intellege ut credas; crede ut intellegas"* [understand in order that you might believe; believe in order that you might understand], is relevant to Catholic Universities that are called to explore courageously the riches of Revelation and of nature so that the united endeavor of intelligence and faith will enable people to come to the full measure of their humanity, created in the image and likeness of God, renewed even more marvelously, after sin, in Christ, and called to shine forth in the light of the Spirit (§5).

The section of this authoritative pronouncement on "The Identity of a Catholic University" further illustrates the dilemma, the tension, even more clearly:

> . . . every Catholic University, as *Catholic*, must have the following *essential chareristics*:
>   1. a Christian inspiration not only of individuals but of the university community as such;
>   2. a continuing reflection in the light of the Catholic faith upon the growing treasury of human knowledge, to which it seeks to contribute by its own research;
>   3. fidelity to the Christian message as it comes through the Church;
>   4. an inspirational commitment to the service of the people of God and of the human family in their pilgrimage to the transcendental goal which gives meaning to life (§13).

A tension or conflict is especially evident in such phrases as: *"a Christian inspiration . . . of the university community as such"* (1); *"in light of the Catholic faith"* (2); *"fidelity to the Christian message as it comes to us through the Church"* (3); and *"in their pilgrimage to the transcendental goal which gives meaning to life"* (4). Every paragraph in the statement of the essential characteristics of the Catholic University points to the tension, if not the conflict, between consecrating one's self "without reserve to *the cause of truth*" (§4) and dedicating one's self to "the research of all aspects of truth in their essential connection with the supreme Truth, who is God" (§4).

It simply cannot be presumed that the unconditional search for truth never leads to conclusions that conflict with the teachings of the Roman Catholic Church, or of any Christian church, or of any religion for that matter. The history of the church, both Catholic and Protestant, is strewn with efforts to suppress the advance of human learning and understanding. What happens when the *"impartial* search for truth" does lead a [Catholic] scholar at a Catholic University to conclusions that conflict with the teachings of Holy Mother Church? The case of Galileo comes immediately to mind. And can one be confident in the presumed *"united* endeavor of intelligence and faith," especially in a hierarchical religious structure like the Roman Catholic Church? History shouts a resounding "No!"

Most mainstream Protestant denominations have taken positions similar to these views of the Roman Catholic Church with regard to the application of the historical-critical method to the scriptures. What is particularly threatening to the most conservative or fundamentalist Christians and Jews, those who are far right of the mainstream, is that historical criticism of the Bible treats the biblical texts in the same manner in which it treats any works of ancient literature. Historians maintain, qua historians, that inasmuch as the Bible is qualitatively no different from other ancient literature, so, too, the method of studying the Bible scientifically can be no different.

We have witnessed in recent years ongoing efforts on the part of Christian fundamentalists to suppress the teaching in America's public schools of the big bang theory, which is the dominant scientific theory about the origin of the universe, and the theory of biological evolution, which is recognized as the binding force of all biological research. Yet, Copernicus, Darwin, Freud, and Marx are the collective antichrist of American fundamentalists, many of whom send their children to Christian schools or offer them home schooling in order to protect them from public schools that may be required by law to teach Darwinian evolution and the big bang theory.

Efforts on the part of Christian fundamentalists to have so-called creation science or, more recently, intelligent design taught in public schools as an alternative to biological evolution have consistently been set aside by the US Supreme Court. Creationism and intelligent design are not theories, and they are certainly not scientific. They are pre-Enlightenment religious beliefs or presuppositions that have outlived their usefulness. The use by the Religious Right of terms like creation science and the establishment of the so-called Center for Scientific Creation just do not cut it anymore. These movements are not only religious anachronisms, but they are also politically and even economically dangerous to the future of this nation, as they seek to take us and our children back to a time and a world that is no longer relevant. Their adherents consistently use their narrow-minded and generally intolerant backward-looking religion to combat scientific advancement, much as Wahabism does in Saudi Arabia.

A particular threat to some Christians, especially fundamentalist Christians, has been the implication of the historical-critical method, which requires scholars to look at the life and ministry of Jesus of Nazareth as they would look at the life of any individual who lived two thousand years ago. If applied rigorously, the historical-critical method does not allow the historian to hide behind the assumption that the Bible is qualitatively different from other ancient religious literature and is, therefore, exempt from the same rigorous scrutiny that scholars routinely apply to other ancient religious texts. Neither does it allow the historian, qua historian, to assume that Jesus of Nazareth was more than a man and that his life was, therefore, qualitatively different from other lives and is, as such, exempt from critical investigation. "No," say biblical scholars. Historians and scholars must apply the same secular rules of historical criticism and investigation to the Bible and to the life and ministry of Jesus as they apply to the study of any other literature or any other person.

Let us now turn our attention to some of the methods and specific tools that scholars have devised to help us to understand better the books of the New Testament, the life and ministry of Jesus of Nazareth, and the beginnings of Christianity.

Chapter 4

MODERN HISTORICAL CRITICISM OF THE NEW TESTAMENT

*I*n an earlier chapter we examined the ways in which the Renaissance and the Enlightenment gave rise to reason as the single most important criterion in the search for truth. It was inevitable that the principles that emerged to study and to understand better the universe, our own earth, and the history of humankind should and would eventually be applied to a study of the world's religions, the Bible, Jesus of Nazareth, and the history of Christianity.

The historical-critical method of studying the Bible, most specifically the study of the origin and development of ancient Israelite religion and the study of the life and ministry of Jesus, is based on the same secular methodology that originated in the wake of the Enlightenment. Historians routinely apply this secular methodology to study the history of ancient Greece, medieval Europe, nineteenth-century China, and modern America. Why would or should historians use a different methodology to study the history of ancient Israel or the origins of Christianity than they would use to study the history of modern Europe? Should we use different tools to study Confucius, Moses, Mohammed, and Jesus? Obviously not! The rules of historical investigation are the same whatever the subject matter at hand.

It was in the eighteenth century that historical criticism first found its way into the church and resulted by the end of that century in Herman Samuel Reimarus' *Fragmente eines Ungenannten* (*Fragments of an Unknown Writer*), published posthumously by Gotthold Ephraim Lessing between 1774 and 1778. Applying the secular methodology to the life of Jesus, Reimarus concluded that Jesus was a deluded eschatological visionary prophet who believed in the imminent end of history as we know it. Reimarus further maintained that the miracles of the New Testament should be explained or rationalized as natural phenomena and that Jesus' disciples stole his body and proclaimed his resurrection from the dead in order to provide a platform to propagate Christianity. It is no wonder that Reimarus did not publish his work during his lifetime, the consequences of which could well have been a heresy trial that would make the Scopes monkey trial of 1925 in Tennessee look like a day at the beach.

Whether we agree with Reimarus' specific conclusions or not is irrelevant. What is important, however, is that Reimarus made systematic use of the Enlightenment's seemingly radical methodology that reason or secular history is the only criterion by which a historian can credibly research and investigate the events surrounding the life and ministry of Jesus and the beginnings of Christianity. By employing that method, Reimarus sought to find the Jesus of history behind the Christ of the church's faith.

In the course of his study, Reimarus made it clear that many of the fundamental claims of Christianity fall outside the realm of historical reason and demand an alternative, a rational, explanation. In his reconstruction of the events surrounding Jesus' life, ministry, death, and resurrection, Reimarus made it clear that orthodox Christian theology has no historical foundation in spite of persistent efforts by the church for almost two thousand years to base Christian theology on historical certainty or, at least, historical probability. There is obviously no way to confirm as fact or to establish with any degree of certainty the "events" that appear to underpin some of the basic tenets of Christianity. Reimarus made it clear that there is no way for historians, qua historians, to deal with "miracles" or "resurrections." Such "events" fall outside the realm of historical reason and are faith claims, based not on history, Reimarus maintained, but based rather on a misunderstanding or misinterpretation of what actually happened.

Beginning with Reimarus, human reason and nonsupernatural historical investigation prevailed, undermining thereby the very foundation of orthodox Christianity's epistemology. The nearly eighteen-hundred-year effort to establish Christianity on the basis of sound historical certainty was deemed irrelevant, if not entirely dead. Reimarus and his intellectual heirs demonstrated conclusively that pure and unadulterated reason is the single tool by which we may draw on the New Testament to reconstruct the events that unfolded around the life and ministry of Jesus of Nazareth. Religious faith does not and cannot inform historical reason.

The intellectual revolution of the nineteenth century changed forever all thought and all study on just about every subject. Geology provided indisputable proof for the antiquity of the earth and of many animal species, including our own *Homo sapiens*, humankind.[47] By the end of the nineteenth century, evolutionary thought

---

47. I remember many years ago walking with a fundamentalist Christian friend of mine through one of the many gorges outside Aurora, New York, where I have lived for more than forty years. The area is rich in fossils. I bent down and picked up a piece of slate containing the fossil of some sort of shellfish and asked my friend how, based on his assumption that the world was only about six thousand years old, he could explain that prehistoric record of a creature that had lived in an ancient salt sea that had obviously covered this area eons ago. Without batting an eye, he answered that God had created the earth with the fossils already in place. In disbelief, I asked why God would do such a thing. Again, without batting an eye, he replied, "To test our faith." Instead of allowing the datum (the fossil of the shellfish) to speak

was commonplace not only in science but in the social sciences as well. The fierce debate that raged between religion and science throughout much of the nineteenth century died down toward the end of the century with science the clear, if not undisputed, victor.

The repercussions of that debate survive to the present in persistent and unrelenting efforts from the Evangelical Right, primarily in the United States, to regain lost territory. The war may be over, but the battle rages on. The truth of the matter is that no educated person can reasonably doubt that natural science and historical reason are the keys required to unlock an understanding of the origins of the universe and the descent of man from earlier forms of life. Yet tens of millions of Americans do deny just that. Likewise, historical reason alone is the key to understanding any and all events in past history, including the events surrounding the life and ministry of Jesus of Nazareth.

It is difficult to overestimate the importance of nineteenth-century scholarship for the contribution it made to the emerging critical methodology. Historical criticism became the only approved method of investigation and brought about a revolutionary change in the way in which the Bible was studied. The sacred scriptures, Jesus of Nazareth, and the two-thousand-year history of the Christian church had, so to speak, been secularized, and there was no turning back. The books of the Bible were no longer simply sacred scriptures; they were also very old documents that required secular study and analysis like every other ancient written source. Moreover, the Bible was no longer the undoubted single criterion for the writing of history. Rather the historical critical method was now the single undisputed criterion for understanding the Bible. The tables had been turned. Like Buddha, Confucius, Moses, and Mohammed, Jesus of Nazareth was clearly and unequivocally a man to be studied, to be analyzed, and to be questioned. The entire two-thousand-year history of Christianity required reexamination against the background of world history, primarily European history. It was clear that there could be no exemptions, no exceptions, no different rules, no different methodologies in the examination of the evidence simply because the subject of investigation was Jesus and Christianity.

People gradually came to understand that critically written historical analysis is not simply a retelling of Bible stories, an uncritical repetition of what the written sources already say. Historical analysis of the Bible produces, rather, an objective narrative based on what the sources say only after their competence, their reliability, and their intelligibility have been scrupulously and meticulously investigated, scru-

---

for itself, my friend had fit the datum (the fossil) into his preconceived religious belief that the account of creation in Genesis was fundamentally correct and that the earth was a mere six thousand years old. Given that he "knew" that the earth was a mere six thousand years old, my friend had to fit the datum (the fossil) into his preconception regarding the age of the earth. Hence, his preposterous explanation! I told my friend that I thought his God was perverse in creating evidence whose sole purpose was apparently to confuse and then test the faith of humankind. To this day he remains unconvinced. Our starting points were totally different; hence our conclusions were and still remain totally different.

tinized, analyzed, and probed. Like a prosecuting attorney in a courtroom, the historian of the New Testament rigorously cross-examines and questions each and every witness or piece of evidence to determine within the limits of historical reason what may actually have happened in the course of the life and ministry of Jesus. Biblical scholarship is analytical and objective because it uses all of the resources of the human mind to investigate all of the available sources. It is also systematic and methodical, because it has in mind the goal of reconstructing the past within the limits of historical reason.

The historical-critical method effectively excludes the biblical view of a personal god, who intervenes in human history, as an acceptable explanation for something that happened in the past. The rules of the game are clear: a supernatural, transcendent god cannot be advanced as the cause of or the explanation for any past, present, or future event. That is the one simple and unbreakable rule of writing history—even the history of religions, even the history of Christianity. Explanations can and must be sought only within the system of a closed universe. No exceptions allowed! The objective of all history is to put forward a body of acknowledged and reputable facts that answer the questions "What actually happened?" "When did it happen?" and "Why did it happen?" What, when, and why are the focus of historical investigation.

Quite obviously, history necessarily has a limited goal, which is what I mean when I speak about what we can know *within the limits of historical reason.* The historian cannot know all that there is to know about any subject or even about any single event, however limited the focus might be. The historian is clearly limited by the reliability of the sources and by the manner of interpreting the data. The goals of the biblical historian are the same as the goals of historians in general: to put forward a body of information arranged in a narrative that provides an account, an explanation, and an interpretation of the past.

Simply stated, historical criticism is a process for: (1) pulling together all possible witnesses to an event, both oral and written; (2) assessing the value of these witnesses with the help of every available critical tool; (3) linking all of the data into a single coherent and consistent arrangement; and (4) advancing a conclusion, together with all of its supporting evidence, in the form of a narrative. The art of collecting, evaluating, connecting, and presenting the evidence is what we call historical criticism. This process constitutes the writing of most history.

The good historian looks for every possible explanation for and interpretation of the significant data, looks at the facts in the light of various explanations and interpretations, and then eliminates the explanations and interpretations that fail to account adequately for the data. The explanation and interpretation of the data that best answers all of the questions and that deals best, most truthfully, and most directly with all of the data is generally the best possible explanation and interpretation. In drawing conclusions, the responsible historian presents a narrative explanation and interpretation with all of the supporting information.

Clearly the good historian is a person of honesty and integrity, with no personal agenda, and with an uncompromising passion for the truth for its own sake. The goal of history is quite simply to advance the truth about the past. In addition, because the writing of history does not have the objectivity and precision of the physical and mathematical sciences, historians must have balance and humility and not overstate their conclusions.

TOOLS OF NEW TESTAMENT CRITICISM

Fortunately, historians of the New Testament have some very distinctive and specialized tools or methodologies available to assist in reconstructing the past. The next section of this book deals with the quest for the historical Jesus and with the question of how a nonsupernatural Jesus can function in a Christianity relevant for the new millennium. To lay the foundation for that discussion in part 3, it is essential to introduce the reader to the critical reasoning and to some of the basic tools and methods that are currently available to both amateur and professional students of the New Testament as they engage in the search for the historical Jesus:[48]

1. Textual Criticism is the discipline that provides New Testament scholars with the tools required to establish the best and most accurate Greek text of the twenty-seven books of the New Testament. The discipline involves scrutinizing the ancient New Testament manuscript evidence against the background of contemporary literature from the world of classical antiquity to which the New Testament belongs. The objective is to reconstruct, as accurately as possible, the texts of the books of the New Testament in the forms they had when they left the hands of their original authors.

Textual criticism developed to assist scholars in reconstructing what they call the "autograph," the earliest or original text of each book. Regrettably, we do not have access to the autographs of any of the New Testament books. What we do have are, rather, copies of copies of copies, et cetera, of which, in the case of the New Testament, no two are identical. Scholars must, therefore, attempt to reconstruct the autograph from later imperfect and sometimes widely divergent manuscripts. By the way, this is a problem not only for the books of the New Testament but also for virtually all

---

48. It is, of course, impossible to do much more than introduce the reader briefly to the tools of analytic study of the New Testament, in this case primarily to some of the basic tools of gospel criticism. The literature is vast, and the diversity of opinion is sometimes quite narrow and sometimes very broad, depending on the issue. I hope here to do little more than to provide some small insight into a few of the methodological tools and to provide illustrations from the Gospels themselves of various methodologies. I hope thereby to keep the reading as uncomplicated and interesting as possible. What follows is sometimes subtle and very detailed, maybe even tedious, but I encourage the reader to work through this section slowly, following carefully the reasoning and the evidence. The reward will come in developing a minimal but respectable understanding of the methodologies that underlie scholarly efforts to understand better Jesus of Nazareth, who presumably stands at the center of Christianity.

ancient literature. The major difference is that there are many more manuscripts of New Testament books than there are of any other writings from classical antiquity.

It is relatively easy to speculate about how differences in the manuscript tradition may have developed. We know, for example, that during early Christian worship services someone may have read from a letter of Paul or from the Gospel of Mark. A visiting Christian might make or secure a copy of the relevant text to take to his home church, or one church might even take the initiative of sending a copy of a text to another church. The quality of the copy obviously depended on what an individual scribe intended in making that copy, but complete verbal accuracy does not appear to have ever been the most important consideration. The evidence indicates quite clearly that scribes virtually always made both accidental and deliberate changes in their manuscripts. Intentional alterations in the text range from rather innocuous efforts to improve the grammar and the style of the original to more serious theological alterations that were made to enhance or augment the understanding of Jesus or to advance a particular theological doctrine. It was in this manner that manuscripts of the individual books of the New Testament spread from church to church throughout the ancient Roman world, especially in the early decades of the history of Christianity.

It was almost certainly not until Christianity became the approved religion of the Roman Empire under Emperor Constantine in the early fourth century that "official" copies of the New Testament were made, but that was already more than 250 years after the writing of the autographs of most of the books. As it is, more than five thousand ancient manuscripts of New Testament books survive in the original Greek. There are, in addition, thousands of manuscripts of early translations from the original Greek into other ancient languages (Syriac, Latin, Coptic, Armenian, Georgian, Ethiopic, etc.) and numerous quotations or allusions to New Testament books in the writings of early church fathers. From this wealth of manuscripts, no two are identical. These are the data from which New Testament scholars have attempted to devise a method to reconstruct the autographs of the twenty-seven books of our canonical New Testament. To complicate the problem even further, with the exception of a few fragments, the earliest manuscripts date to about 200 CE, or more than a century after the autographs of most of the New Testament books were first written, and most of our surviving manuscripts are much later than that. Two of our most complete manuscripts date from about 350 CE.

Textual criticism of the Bible made great advances during the nineteenth century. Building upon the pioneering work of Erasmus in the sixteenth century, in 1831 Karl Lachmann produced in Germany the first truly critical text of the New Testament. A second edition of his work appeared in 1842–1850, together with an extensive critical apparatus and with suggestions on methodology. In the second half of the nineteenth century, German and English scholars wrote commentaries on virtually all of the books of the Bible, employing a methodology that was critical, linguistic, and historical, rather than a methodology designed to promote religious faith. These works were virtually all written by Christians for Christians to advance

Christianity. There was a striking naïveté among most of those scholars, who assumed that historical study of the Bible would serve to foster rather than to diminish the uniqueness of Christianity. That proved, of course, not to be the case.

To illustrate the importance of textual criticism, let us look at two passages in the Gospel of Mark to consider what scholars believe the autograph of the Gospel of Mark likely read, compared to what appears in most of our Bibles, most particularly in the widely used King James Version of 1611.

Mark 1:1. The first example is found in the opening words of the Gospel of Mark, actually in the title or so-called superscription, in Mark 1:1: "The beginning of the good news of Jesus Christ, the Son of God." In recent translations there is often a footnote to this verse saying something like "some ancient authorities lack the words 'the Son of God.'" A more honest footnote would say that most textual critics agree that the words "the Son of God" did not appear in the autograph of Mark but that they were added by later scribes to enhance the image of Jesus by advancing or by making more specific the doctrine of Jesus' divine sonship. Although several early manuscripts have the phrase "the Son of God," it is not found in many of the most important manuscript witnesses.

In addition, it is frankly much easier to explain why an early scribe might have added the phrase "the Son of God" than it is to explain why an early scribe would have deleted it. So why not simply print in our English translations of Mark 1:1 what most textual critics believe was the original text: "The beginning of the good news of Jesus Christ"? Period! It puzzles me that contemporary translations of the New Testament still tend to avoid tampering with what has been the traditional reading since the appearance of the often authoritative but, critically speaking, inferior King James Version, even when it is clear to scholars that the text they are printing in modern translation was almost certainly not the text of the autograph. Quite frankly, this practice is outright dishonest, but it persists in many otherwise excellent modern editions.

Mark 6:3. A second example appears in Mark 6:3, a passage that reports that some people, upon hearing Jesus preach in the synagogue in Nazareth, expressed amazement at his teaching and said, in the words of most English translations, something like: "Is not this the carpenter, the son of Mary and the brother of James and Joses and Judas and Simon, and are not his sisters here with us?" A footnote to this passage often states something like: "Other ancient authorities read: 'Is this not the son of the carpenter and of Mary, etc.?'" Once again, textual critics agree that what is in the footnote in some Bibles was probably in the autograph of the Gospel of Mark. The concern with this verse is that the probable original text of Mark 6:3 implies that both Joseph *and* Mary were Jesus' biological parents. Unthinkable! Most likely, later copyists deliberately changed the text because it contradicted the later teaching of Matthew and Luke that Joseph was not Jesus' father and that Jesus was, in fact, born of a virgin.

Interestingly, this passage in Mark 6:3 raises another theological problem for Christians who believe in the perpetual virginity of Mary. The text refers specifically to Jesus' siblings, at least six in number: four named brothers—James, Joses, Judas, and Simon—and at least two and possibly more unnamed sisters. The church's belief in the *perpetual* virginity of Mary appears to have originated in the middle of the second century, possibly with the writing of the *Protevangelium of James*, but apparently did not result in changes to the reference to Jesus' brothers and sisters in this text of Mark's gospel.

Instead of tampering with this portion of the text, the church explained this passage in one of two ways: either the six or more other children were actually Jesus' more distant relatives (perhaps cousins) rather than his biological brothers and sisters, or they were Joseph's children from a previous marriage. Of course, there is no credible evidence to support either explanation. Both are rather feeble efforts to explain the data in light of a prior theological commitment to belief in Mary's perpetual virginity.

The meaning of the text of Mark 6:3 is clear: Jesus had several brothers and sisters, all of whom were, like him, the children of Mary and Joseph. This opinion is also supported by the text of Luke 2:7, which reports that Mary "gave birth to her *firstborn* son [Jesus] and wrapped him in bands of cloth, etc." *Firstborn* clearly implies that Mary bore other children. It would be quite unusual to refer to an *only* child as a *firstborn* child. Jesus was apparently the eldest of Mary and Joseph's seven (or more) children.

With respect to this verse, once again theological orthodoxy in the form of modified manuscripts has relegated the generally accepted text of the autograph to a footnote in many modern translations. More conservative or traditional translations like the King James Version and the New International Version do not even include the footnote. It is interesting that the parallel to Mark 6:3 in Matthew 13:55 reads: "Is this not the carpenter's son? Is not his mother called Mary?" And the parallel text in Luke 4:22 reads: "Is not this Joseph's son?" It is difficult to explain why Matthew and Luke would have identified Joseph as Jesus' father in this passage if they had not found this detail in the manuscripts of Mark to which they had access.[49] In addition, a related passage in John 6:42 reads: "Is not this Jesus, the son of Joseph, whose father and mother we know?"

Hopefully these two illustrations indicate the importance of textual criticism in providing scholars with the tools needed to reconstruct the autograph of the Gospel of Mark, as well as the autographs of the other twenty-six books of the New Testament. These two examples should give Christians food for thought as they use this information in their quest for the historical Jesus. It is obviously essential to have available to scholars and laypersons alike translations of the New Testament free from theological bias and consistently as close as possible to the autographs that came from the pens of the original authors.

2. Philological Study is the discipline that endeavors to determine the intended meaning of a text at the time it was first written. Lexicography, grammar, and the study of related foreign languages and of related texts are all essential elements in promoting a better understanding of the books of the New Testament. All of the books of the New Testament were written originally in Koine (or common) Greek, now a dead language, although an antecedent of modern Greek.

---

49. Later in this chapter I will present the evidence to show that the authors of the Gospels of Matthew and Luke almost certainly used the Gospel of Mark as one of their primary sources.

I propose to introduce here a single example of the importance of philological study for an understanding of the Bible. Although the example appears in the Gospel of Matthew, it reaches back into the Old Testament to a passage in Isaiah 7:14. The text of Isaiah 7:14 in the New Revised Standard Version of the Bible reads:

> Therefore, the Lord himself will give you a sign. Look, a young woman is with child and shall bear a son, and shall name him Immanuel.

A footnote to the text indicates that the Greek translation of this passage identifies the future mother not as a "young woman," but as a "virgin."[50] In fact, that footnote is likely there because the King James Bible and many subsequent versions have translated this passage in Isaiah 7:14 thus:

> Therefore the Lord himself shall give you a sign; Behold, a virgin shall conceive, and bear a son, and shall call his name Immanuel.

The passage in Isaiah has traditionally been understood by Christians as an Old Testament proof-text in which Isaiah prophesied more than seven hundred years before the event of Jesus' birth by the virgin Mary. The author of the Gospel of Matthew quoted Isaiah as evidence that Jesus' birth by the virgin Mary was the fulfillment of Isaiah's prophecy. Matthew, however, was using not the Hebrew original of Isaiah but rather the Greek (mis)translation of this passage when he wrote:

> Look, the virgin shall conceive and bear a son, and they shall name him Emmanuel. (Matthew 1:23).

So what exactly did Isaiah say and mean when he spoke these words in the eighth century BCE? It is here that philological study comes into play. The setting of the passage in Isaiah 7 is the political events in the southern kingdom of Judah in 734 BCE. Isaiah was apparently trying to persuade Judah's King Ahaz not to capitulate to Assyria in his effort to prevent an attack on his kingdom by the northern coalition of Syria and Samaria (Northern Israel). To encourage King Ahaz to accept his advice, Isaiah invited the king to ask him for a sign. When Ahaz refused Isaiah's request, the prophet offered the sign that "the young woman [Hebrew 'almâ] is pregnant and about to give birth to a son; she will give him the name Immanuel." By the time the child is five or six years old, Isaiah said, the land of the threatening Syrian-Samarian alliance would be laid waste; the threat to Ahaz and to his kingdom of Judah would be removed.

Although it is not clear who the young woman or her son were, it is clear that

---

50. Jewish scholars living in Alexandria, Egypt, between 250 and 150 BCE translated the Hebrew Bible into Greek for the benefit of Jews whose families had been living in Egypt for several centuries. These Jews no longer understood their scriptures in the original Hebrew, hence the need for the Greek translation.

the passage does not and cannot refer to the virgin Mary and Jesus. For the sign to have had any meaning to King Ahaz, Isaiah must have been referring to a young woman already known to both the prophet and the king and to a birth that would take place within a few months. After all, the young woman was already pregnant. The meaning of the passage in Isaiah 7:14 is clear to scholars who have studied the text in the original Hebrew. Jesus' birth to Mary more than seven hundred years in the future would obviously have had no significance to King Ahaz and could not have served as a meaningful sign to him in 734 BCE.

Clearly the translators of the King James Bible assumed the validity of the link between Isaiah 7:14 and Matthew 1:23, because the translation of the passage in Isaiah in the King James Version (and in most subsequent conservative Christian translations) was influenced by the use of the Greek work *parthenos* (virgin), the third-century BCE Septuagint's (mis)translation of Isaiah's Hebrew word *'almâ* (young woman). It is one thing to note that the author of the Gospel of Matthew apparently knew the book of Isaiah not in the original Hebrew, but rather in the Greek translation. It is quite another thing to use Matthew's version of the Septuagint Greek's (mis)translation to render into English the text of Isaiah 7:14. Yet that is exactly what happened in the King James Version.

Philological study has made it clear that Isaiah was speaking about a pregnant young woman (Hebrew *'almâ*), not about a virgin (Hebrew *bĕthûlah*). It is also evident that the pregnant woman about whom Isaiah was speaking was obviously not a virgin. Yet, the translators of the King James Bible were determined to connect the text of Isaiah to the text of Matthew in order to reinforce Matthew's claim that Isaiah was referring to Mary and Jesus.

What is important in modern translations, however, is to translate into English as accurately as possible the meaning of the original text in *its own context*. Adding the footnote in the Revised Standard Version that the Greek text says "virgin" is misleading and only adds to the confusion. Simply stated, the author of the Gospel of Matthew made a mistake in quoting Isaiah as a proof-text for the virgin birth. The mistake resulted from the fact that he used not the original Hebrew text of the book of Isaiah, which was clear on the matter, but that he used instead a Greek (mis)translation of Isaiah, the Septuagint. The author of the Gospel of Matthew may not have been able to read the text of Isaiah in the original Hebrew, so we cannot assign blame entirely to him. But we can assign blame to translators who can read Hebrew and who continue to perpetuate the error. Modern translators have sometimes been reluctant to suggest the simple truth that Isaiah was not referring to Mary and Jesus.

The following table illustrates the ways in which various translations of the Bible have rendered into English the Hebrew word *'almâ*:[51]

51. In addition to the translations listed in the chart, the Web site www.biblegateway .com lists numerous additional, presumably evangelical-approved, translations, which yield the following results: New American Standard Bible (NASB): "a virgin"; The Message (MSG): "a girl who is presently a virgin"; Amplified Bible (AMP): "the young woman who is unmarried and a virgin"; New Living Translation (NLT): "the virgin"; English Standard

Bible Translation	Date	Character	Translation of *'almâ*
Douay-Rheims Bible	1609	Translated from Vulgate	virgin
King James Version	1611	Authorized Protestant	virgin
Revised Standard Version	1946	Revision of KJV	young woman
Jerusalem Bible	1966	Roman Catholic	maiden
New International Version	1978	Evangelical Christian	virgin
Anchor Bible Commentary	2000	Nondenominational	young woman

Clearly, the study of lexicography, grammar, and the meaning of the words in related foreign languages has made it clear what this passage in Isaiah does and does not say. Although scholars have not been able to identify either the young woman or her son in Isaiah 7:14, it is clear that the author of the Gospel of Matthew unwittingly misused this passage as a proof-text for Jesus' birth from a virgin because he was relying on the Greek (mis)translation. In fact, it is very likely that the passage in Isaiah 7:14 in the Greek (mis)translation is the sole basis for the church's belief that Jesus was born of a virgin. As we have already seen, even in the New Testament itself there are passages that assume that Mary and Joseph were both Jesus' biological parents.

3. Literary Criticism is the discipline that examines the literary and compositional devices and methods used by authors to organize and compose their thoughts and beliefs in order to present them in written and/or spoken forms. The books of the New Testament had literary prototypes or models in the ancient world, and these established forms or genres influenced the early Christians who wrote not only our canonical books but also the sources that lie behind many of the canonical books.

Very few of the books of the New Testament are the product of a single author. Most underwent several stages in the course of their composition, and literary criticism attempts to uncover the layers of the compositional process. In the earliest church, oral tradition met many if not most of the needs of the church. But as the

---

Version (ESV): "the virgin"; Contemporary English Version (CEV): "a virgin"; New King James Version (NKJV): "the virgin"; 21st Century King James Version (KJ21): "a virgin"; American Standard Version (ASV): "a virgin"; Young's Literal Translation (YLT): "the Virgin"; Darby Translation (DARBY): "the virgin"; New International Version–UK (NIV-UK): "the virgin." A footnote to the CEV, in an attempt to be scholarly, clearly betrays its prejudice: "In this context the difficult Hebrew word did not imply a virgin birth. However, in the Greek translation made about 200 (BCE) and used by many early Christians, the word *parthenos* had a double meaning. While the translator [of the Septuagint] took it to mean 'young woman,' Matthew understood it to mean 'virgin' and quoted the passage (Matthew 1:23) because it was the appropriate description of Mary, the mother of Jesus." It is evident that in each and every one of these instances, the translation is colored by evangelical orthodox bias, not by scholarly philological study.

church began to generate written documents to serve the needs of early Christian communities, the authors adapted existing genres to express the needs of the church. There are four basic genres among the writings of the New Testament: gospels, acts, letters, and an apocalypse.

Gospels. Although many scholars have argued that the author of the Gospel of Mark created the literary genre called "gospel," more recently New Testament scholars have identified important similarities between the canonical gospels and Greco-Roman biographies and have recognized that the Gospels of Matthew, Mark, Luke, and John are a particular kind of Greco-Roman biography with distinctive qualities that stem from their Christian character.

Unlike modern biographies, which collect factual data about a person's life into a chronological framework, Greco-Roman biographies were more concerned with portraying a person's qualities and character traits than with reporting what had actually happened in that person's life. Typically ancient biography focused on aspects of a person's nature, primarily to inform readers or listeners about what kind of person he or she was and to encourage others to behave similarly. Typically, Greco-Roman biographies attempted to show how great this individual was.

History. The Acts of the Apostles, the second volume of the work Luke-Acts, is similar to other histories fashioned in antiquity. Like most ancient historians, the author of Acts created for his book a number of speeches that he attributed to Peter and Paul, the two principal characters of the book. And like other ancient historians, the author of Acts strove not so much for historical accuracy as he did for similarity and plausibility. The author of Acts wrote a general history tracing developments in early Christianity following Jesus' death down to the time of the book's composition, focusing on the spread of Christianity from its birthplace in Jerusalem to Rome, the seat of the Empire.

Letters. More than half of the books of the New Testament are epistles or letters. An epistle is a piece of public or private correspondence sent through the ancient equivalent of modern-day mail. In the ancient world, this generally meant sending someone to hand deliver a letter, or entrusting someone traveling in the right direction to deliver the correspondence. In antiquity, letters generally began by identifying the sender of the correspondence, followed by the name of the person or persons being addressed, and a greeting at the outset. These opening remarks were then followed by the body of the letter.

Apocalyse. The apocalypse or the revelation was a book that described the coming of the end-time as that was disclosed or unveiled to a prophet in a vision. Apocalypses were often characterized by pseudonymity, symbolic imagery, numerology, and the expectation of an imminent cosmic cataclysm through which God would destroy the existing ruling powers of evil and raise the righteous to life in a messianic kingdom.

It is important to recognize that the books of our canonical New Testament, when examined in the context of their own time, imitate known forms or genres from the ancient Greco-Roman world. Nothing is more important to historical criticism of the Bible than looking at the biblical material in its own historical and literary context.

4. Source Criticism is the discipline that studies the sources, both oral and written, that an author may have had access to and used. Most specifically, in this regard, is a study of the so-called synoptic problem, the study of the literary relationship among the Gospels of Matthew, Mark, and Luke. Since the eighteenth century scholars have recognized that there is a clear literary relationship among these three gospels, because they contain parallel material, often in the exact same or very similar words, in a similar narrative framework, and with stories often in the same sequence.

The principal considerations that establish that Mark is the earliest of the synoptic Gospels and that Matthew and Luke made use of Mark are:[52]

1. Matthew reproduces 90 percent and Luke 15 percent of the subject matter of Mark in language that is largely identical with Mark's language (the argument from content).
2. In those passages found in all three gospels, either Matthew or Luke or both are almost always in close verbal agreement with Mark. Matthew and Luke almost never agree together against Mark (the argument from wording).
3. The order of stories in Mark is clearly the more original and is, in general, supported by both Matthew and Luke. Where either one departs from the Markan order, the other is usually found supporting Mark's order (the argument from order or arrangement).
4. Matthew and Luke improve upon and refine Mark's language, style, and grammar (the argument from editorial improvement).
5. The way in which Markan and non-Markan material is distributed throughout Matthew and Luke suggests that the authors of Matthew and Luke were working with Mark independently and were incorporating into the Markan outline material from other sources.

The chart below reproduces the account of Jesus' healing of Peter's mother-in law, a story that appears in all three of the synoptic Gospels. Words that are found in both Matthew and Mark are underlined, and words that are found in both Mark and Luke are printed in italics. Some words in Mark will obviously be both underlined and italicized, meaning that they are found in all three gospels.

---

52. Burnett Hillman Streeter, "The Priority of Mark," *The Four Gospels: A Study of Origins* (London: Macmillan and Co., 1924), pp. 157–69, 195–97. Reprinted in Arthur J. Bellinzoni, ed., *The Two-Source Hypothesis: A Critical Appraisal* (Macon, GA: Mercer University Press, 1985), pp. 23–36; additional arguments both for and against the priority of Mark can be found in this collection of essays. Suffice it to say that the overwhelming consensus of contemporary New Testament scholarship is that Mark wrote first and was used by both Matthew and Luke.

Matthew 8:14–15	Mark 1:29–30	Luke 4:18–19
And	*And* immediately *he left the synagogue,* *and* <u>*entered*</u> <u>*the house of*</u> *Simon* and Andrew, with James and John.	*And he* arose and *left the synagogue,* *and* *entered* *the house of Simon*
when Jesus <u>entered</u> <u>the house of</u> Peter,		
he saw		
his <u>mother-in-law</u> <u>lying sick</u> <u>with a fever;</u>	*Now Simon's* <u>*mother-in-law*</u> <u>lay sick</u> <u>*with a fever,*</u> *and immediately they* told *him* of *her.*	*Now Simon's mother-in-law* was ill *with a* high *fever,* *and they* besought *him* for *her.*
<u>he</u> touched <u>her hand</u>	*And <u>he</u>* came and took <u>her</u> by the <u>hand</u> *and* lifted her up,	*And he* stood over her *and* rebuked *the fever*
<u>and the fever left her,</u> and <u>she</u> rose <u>and</u> served him.	<u>*and the fever left her*</u>; <u>*and*</u> <u>*she served them.*</u>	*and* it *left her*; and *immediately she* rose *and* *served them.*
total words: 32 words underlined: 23 % underlined: 72%	total words: 55 words underlined: 23 % underlined: 42% words in italics: 34 % words in italics: 62% words either underlined or italicized or both: 38 % words either underlined or italicized or both: 69%	total words: 48 words in italics: 34 % words in italics: 71%

What exactly does the above chart illustrate? First, there is clearly a literary relationship among the three gospels, requiring that they be looked at together, and necessitating an explanation. The English texts of Matthew and Mark share twenty-three words either exactly or nearly exactly and almost always in the same order. Mark and Luke share thirty-four words either exactly or nearly exactly the same and almost always in the same order. As we have already noted, most scholars have concluded that Mark is the earliest of the three synoptic Gospels and that it served as a source for both Matthew and Luke.

Assuming that Mark is the earliest of the three gospels, scholars have also noted that Matthew and Luke not only followed Mark's gospel very closely, but both Matthew and Luke also abbreviated Mark, possibly to make room for additional material in their gospels. The example above is typical of passages found in all three gospels, the so-called triple tradition. In addition, there are passages in the double tradition as well, material found only in Matthew and Mark, and material found only in Mark and Luke. The close literary relationship appears, as we might expect, in these passages in the double tradition as well.

In addition to the material for which Mark is the presumed source for Matthew or Luke or both, there are about two hundred verses, mostly sayings material, that are similar in both Matthew and Luke but that are not found in Mark. There are only three possible explanations for the strong verbal agreement of these two hundred verses: (1) either Matthew used Luke, or (2) Luke used Matthew, or (3) both independently used a common source. The suggestion that Matthew used Luke or that Luke used Matthew breaks down for two reasons: (1) following the temptation story at the beginning of the Gospels, there is not a single instance in which Matthew and Luke agree in inserting the same saying at the same point in the Markan outline, and (2) sometimes Luke and sometimes Matthew appears to reproduce a saying in what appears to be the more original form. Both of these observations do, however, make sense if Matthew and Luke were using the same source independently and were separately incorporating sayings from this source into the framework of Mark. Scholars have referred to this hypothetical source as Q for *Quelle*, the German word for "source."[53]

In the chart below we see one such example of material that is presumed to come from the Q source. The material seems to be a collection of sayings of Jesus on anxiety. The material appears in very similar form in both Matthew and Luke. Words that are found in both gospels are underlined.

Matthew 6:25–34	Luke 12:22–32
	And he said to his disciples,
"Therefore I tell you,	"Therefore I tell you,
do not be anxious about your life,	do not be anxious about your life,
what you shall eat or what you shall drink,	what you shall eat,
nor about your body,	nor about your body,
what you shall put on.	What you shall put on.
Is not life more than food,	For life is more than food,
and the body more than clothing?	and the body more than clothing.
Look at the birds of the air: they neither	Consider the ravens: they neither
sow nor reap	sow nor reap, they have neither
nor gather into barns,	storehouse nor barn,
and yet your heavenly Father feeds them.	and yet God feeds them.
Are you not of more value than	Of how much more value are you than
they?	the birds!
And which of you by being anxious	And which of you by being anxious
can add one cubit to his life span?	can add a cubit to his span of life?
	If then you are not as able to do as
	small a thing as that,
And why are you anxious about clothing?	why are you anxious about the rest?
Consider the lilies of the field,	Consider the lilies
how they grow; they neither toil nor spin;	how they grow; they neither toil nor spin;

53. See Streeter, "The Priority of Mark," pp. 182–86, reprinted in Bellinzoni, *The Two-Source Hypothesis*, pp. 221–25. Other arguments both for and against the hypothetical source Q are contained in Bellinzoni, *The Two-Source Hypothesis*, pp. 227–433.

yet I tell you, even Solomon
in all his glory
was not arrayed like one of these.
But if God so clothes the grass of the field,
which today is alive and
tomorrow is thrown into the oven,
will he not much more clothe you,
O men of little faith?
Therefore, do not be anxious, saying,
'What shall we eat?' or
'What shall we drink?' or
'What shall we wear?'
For the Gentiles seek
all these things;
and your heavenly Father
knows that you need them all,
But seek first his kingdom
and his righteousness,
and all these things shall be yours as well.
Therefore do not be anxious
about tomorrow,
for tomorrow will be anxious for itself.
Let the day's own trouble
be sufficient for the day."

total words: 236
words underlined: 152
% words underlined: 64%

yet I tell you, even Solomon
in all his glory
was not arrayed like one of these.
But if God so clothes the grass
which is alive in the field today and
tomorrow is thrown into the oven,
how much more will he clothe you,
O men of little faith!
And do not seek
what you are to eat
and what you are to drink,
nor be of anxious mind.
For the nations of the world seek
these things;
and your Father
knows that you need them.
Instead, seek his kingdom,

And these things shall be yours as well.
Fear not, little flock,
for it is your Father's good pleasure
to give you the kingdom."

total words: 235
words underlined: 152
% words underlined: 65%

In addition to the material that Matthew and Luke drew from Mark and from the sayings source Q, there is material that appears only in Matthew (often identified as coming from a source called M) and material that appears only in Luke (often identified as coming from a source called L). Although the existence of M and L is more problematic than the case for Q, a diagram of the so-called four-source hypothesis of the synoptic Gospels looks like this:

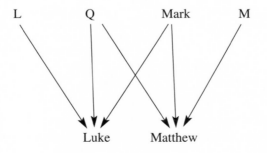

The principal contribution of literary and source criticism has been to show conclusively that the authors of our gospels used literary genres that were common in classical antiquity and that they made use of written sources in composing their own gospels. The proposed solution to the synoptic problem casts considerable light on the manner in which our gospel writers collected, edited, and presented existing tradition in written form to early Christian communities.

5. Form Criticism is the discipline that reaches behind the written sources of our gospels in an effort to reconstruct the earlier oral tradition, which it then identifies, classifies, and relates to its presumed sociological setting in the life of early Christian communities.

Form Criticism of the New Testament, a fundamental discipline in biblical studies, was initiated by Martin Dibelius' *Die Formgeschichte des Evangeliums* [*From Tradition to Gospel*] (1919), Rudolf Bultmann's *Die Geschichte der synoptischen Tradition* [*The History of the Synoptic Tradition*] (1921), and Vincent Taylor's *The Formation of the Gospel Tradition* (1933). Form critics assume: (1) that before there were written gospels or even written sources of gospels, there was a period of oral tradition in the early church; (2) that with the exception of the Passion narrative,[54] narrative and sayings material circulated independently as single stories or detached units of tradition; (3) that the material can be classified according to certain identifiable forms; (4) that the vital factors that gave rise to these forms can be found in the practical needs and interests of early Christian communities; (5) that the material of the tradition has no biographical, chronological, or geographical value; and (6) that the original forms of the tradition can be recovered and its history traced by discovering the laws of oral tradition.

Scholars have observed that, especially in the Gospel of Mark, individual stories often begin with the word "and," little more than an awkward connective intended to link the story to the preceding story (see footnote 55, p. 104). This observation led to the conclusion that each story in the synoptic Gospels or each pericope, as scholars came to call them, may have been a freestanding unit of tradition during the period of oral transmission. This insight led scholars to the conclusion that the author of the Gospel of Mark may have collected individual units of oral tradition, individual stories, to use them as building blocks when he incorporated them into his gospel. These individual units of oral tradition appear to survive in Mark (as well as

---

54. The Passion narrative refers to the accounts in the latter chapters of the Gospels recounting the stories of Jesus' entry into Jerusalem, his arrest, trial, crucifixion, death, and resurrection. Although not all scholars agree, the Passion narrative may have assumed oral and even written form early in the church's history, perhaps decades before its appearance in the Gospel of Mark. As Christians remembered and possibly rehearsed annually the events leading up to Jesus' death and resurrection, particularly during the week preceding the celebration of Easter, they may have developed a liturgy for the commemoration of the days leading up to Jesus' crucifixion and their celebration of his resurrection. In this manner, a Passion narrative, whether written or oral, may have emerged in the years immediately following Jesus' death.

in Matthew and Luke) as the individual pericopes (or units of tradition) that are the components of the gospel.

Scholars noticed that the material in the Gospel of Mark, as well as material in the Gospels of Matthew and Luke, tended to fall into five different literary "forms": pronouncement stories, miracle stories, parables, sayings material, and legends (or stories about Jesus).

Pronouncement Stories are short stories generally involving a controversy or discussion in which an opponent of Jesus asks him a question or poses a problem. Following an exchange, a saying or pronouncement of Jesus resolves the issue. Many of these stories were likely composed around a traditional saying of Jesus; hence the framework for the saying may sometimes be a creation of the Christian community rather than an integral part of the story itself. An excellent example of a pronouncement story is the passage in Mark 12:13–17, a story copied and reworked in Matthew 22:15–22 and in Luke 20:20–26. In its presumed oldest form in Mark, the story reads:

> 13Then they sent to him some Pharisees and some Herodians to trap him in what he said. 14And they came and said to him, "Teacher, we know that you are sincere, and show deference to no one; for you do not regard people with partiality, but teach the way of God in accordance with the truth. Is it lawful to pay taxes to the emperor or not? 15Should we pay them, or should we not?" But knowing their hypocrisy, he said to them, "Why are you putting me to the test? Bring me a denarius and let me see it." 16And they brought one. Then he said to them, "Whose head is this, and whose title?" They answered, "The emperor's." 17Jesus said to them, "Give to the emperor the things that are the emperor's, and to God the things that are God's." And they were utterly amazed at him.

There are some interesting features to this story (or pericope). The opening word "then"[55] is nothing more than a connective that Mark used to link this story, to be sure very loosely, to the preceding story. It does not mean that this was the "event" in Jesus' life that followed immediately upon the "event" reported in the previous story (or pericope), the parable of the wicked tenants. In fact, in Matthew's gospel the preceding pericope is the parable of the wedding banquet. Luke, on the other hand, follows Mark's sequence.

The "they" in verse 13 is no one, in particular. It has no real antecedent, even if the reader looks into the preceding pericopes. It is, rather, Mark's way of setting the stage for the new story. There follows then the dialogue or controversy in which Jesus' enemies, some Pharisees and Herodians, try to trap him. The point of the story

---

55. The word here is actually *kai*, the Greek word "and." Mark uses the conjunction "and" tirelessly to connect the individual pericopes or stories in his gospel (see, e.g., Mark 1:7; 1:9; 1:12; 1:16; 1:21; 1:23; 1:29; 1:35; 1:39; 2:1; 2:13; and so on throughout the body of his gospel. Although the King James Version slavishly translates these "ands," most modern translations (regrettably) omit the "ands," or for stylistic reasons change them to some other word, thereby masking the situation.

is contained in Jesus' pronouncement at the end of the pericope: "Give to the emperor the things that are the emperor's, and to God the things that are God's." Very possibly this pronouncement circulated as an isolated saying, and the oral tradition of the early church provided the narrative framework. In other words, even if we could be certain that we are reading an authentic saying of Jesus, we cannot be certain that the saying was spoken under the circumstances provided in Mark's story. Mark rounds out the pericope with the closing editorial words: "And they were utterly amazed at him." It would be naïve to think that with these words Mark is describing what actually happened following Jesus' delivery of the pronouncement. Rather, what we are seeing in our discussion of this pericope is how Mark took a unit of oral tradition and incorporated it stylistically into his gospel between two other units of tradition.

Miracle Stories, too, follow a traditional form. There is generally a description of a disorder, followed by an actual healing, followed by the amazement of the crowd. There is an excellent example of a miracle story in Mark 1:40–45, a story copied and reworked in Matthew 8:1–4 and in Luke 5:12–16. In its presumed oldest form in Mark, the story reads:

> 40A leper came to him begging him, and kneeling said to him, "If you choose, you may make me clean." 41Moved by pity, Jesus stretched out his hand and touched him, and said to him, "I do choose. Be made clean!" 42Immediately the leprosy left him, and he was made clean. 43After sternly warning him he sent him away at once, 44saying to him, "See that you say nothing to anyone; but go, show yourself to the priest, and offer him for your cleansing what Moses commanded, as a testimony to them." 45But he went out and began to confirm it freely, and to spread the word, so that Jesus could no longer go into a town openly, but stayed out in the country; and people came from every quarter.

Although it is not clear from this English translation of the story, this pericope in the original Greek (and in the KJV) begins characteristically with the word "and," the typical Markan manner of connecting pericopes. In Mark, the previous story is a description of Jesus' preaching tour through Galilee. In Matthew, the preceding section contains a series of warnings by Jesus; in Luke, it is Jesus' call of his first disciples. Notice how Matthew and Luke both digress from Mark's order or outline, but they do so differently, just as we would expect if they were working independently of each other.

When we read a miracle story in the Gospels, it is essential to realize that we are not reading an account of a *miracle* that Jesus performed, but that we are rather reading a *miracle story* from the early church, a story whose purpose, as part of the missionary propaganda of the early church, was to intensify and reinforce belief in Jesus. The distinction between "miracle" and "miracle story" is fundamental. It is essential to read miracle stories as stories whose origin and development are understood best in the context of the early church, not in the context of the life and ministry of the historical Jesus of Nazareth. Having said that, it is, however, not impossible that this particular miracle story had its origin in the context of something that Jesus actually said and did. In this case, we may be dealing with an actual situation in which Jesus, as was characteristic of him, refused to discriminate between people who were ritually clean and people who were ritually unclean (such as women, sinners, lepers, etc.). There were very likely occasions in the course of Jesus' ministry when he might have declared lepers to be ritually "clean." It is an easy step to see how the church's oral tradition might have turned such a story into a story in which the leper was actually cleansed or physically healed of leprosy.

Parables were a common form of teaching through illustration in Jewish circles in Jesus' time. The Gospel parables are stories that Jesus told to illustrate some detail or truth, generally about the imminent coming of God's rule. In the parables, Jesus usually compared God's rule to something that his audience would easily understand, often using images from agriculture. Most of the parables begin with the phrase, "The Kingdom of God (or God's rule) is like . . . ."

There is an excellent example of a parable in Mark 4:26–29, the only parable in Mark's gospel without a parallel in either Matthew or Luke. The text of Mark reads:

> 26He also said, "The kingdom of God is as if someone would scatter seed on the ground, 27and would sleep and rise night and day, and the seed would sprout and grow, he does not know how. 28The earth produces of itself, first the stalk, then the head, then the full grain in the head. 29But when the grain is ripe, at once he goes in with his sickle, because the harvest has come.

The parables are often difficult to understand because the reader is not hearing them in their original physical setting and historical context, where the meaning would have been evident to those present. However, it appears that this parable is one of many so-called parables of growth that Jesus delivered to illustrate that God's rule was already growing on earth whenever anyone did God's will. Verse 29 appears to speak to the imminent end of history as we know it and the arrival of the end-time that would usher in God's judgment and God's rule.

Sayings Material generally refers to individual sayings or to clusters of sayings attributed to Jesus. There is a good example of such a sayings cluster in Mark 4:21–25. This material is found intact in Luke 8:16–18, but it has been scattered throughout the Gospel of Matthew, where it is found in Matthew 5:15; 10:26; 7:2; and 13:12.

The text of Mark reads:

> 21He said to them, "Is a lamp brought in to be put under a bushel basket, or under the bed, and not on the lampstand? 22For there is nothing hidden, except to be disclosed; nor is anything secret, except to come to light. 23Let anyone with ears to hear listen!" 24And he said to them, "Pay attention to what you hear; the measure you give will be the measure you get, and still more will be given you. 25For to those who have, more will be given; and from those who have nothing, even what they have will be taken away."

As the author of the Gospel of Matthew apparently perceived, these sayings in Mark 4:21–25 are distinct and unrelated and could hardly have been delivered by Jesus in this sequence on a single occasion. Rather in their present form, they are connected by key words: *lamp* in verse 21 and *light* in verse 22, *hear* in verses 23 and 24, and *more* and *given* in verses 24 and 25. These sayings were probably remembered in this order in the oral tradition by means of these key words and were apparently heard in this cluster and arrangement by the author of the Gospel of Mark or were known through a written source available to the author of Mark.

Legends (or **Stories about Jesus**) are stories that purport to relate an event in the life of Jesus by surrounding that event with amazing, wondrous, or even super-natural details. Many of these legends appear to be "biographical" in detail, but the miraculous elements in these stories reveal their legendary character. The birth and infancy narratives in Matthew and Luke; the story of Jesus' baptism in Matthew, Mark, and Luke; the transfiguration of Jesus in Matthew, Mark, and Luke; and the resurrection appearances, especially in Matthew and Luke, are all legends, whose purpose is clearly to augment the portrait of Jesus.

There are no formal characteristics to these legends about Jesus. The legends noted above are all very well known, so I have not reproduced here the biblical texts of any of the legends about Jesus.

6. Redaction Criticism is the discipline that studies the contribution of the editor or redactor who composed, using both oral and written sources, the final literary work available to us in the various books of the New Testament.

Whereas form criticism concentrates on the preexisting oral tradition that served as the building blocks of the Gospels of Matthew, Mark, and Luke, redaction criticism focuses on the ways in which the individual authors made use of the oral and written traditions which they inherited and then reshaped into their own literary compositions. Redaction criticism focuses on the fact that the evangelists were not so much authors as they were editors or redactors of earlier oral and written material.

One way to look at the authors of the Gospels of Matthew and Luke as redactors is to look at the ways in which they changed their Markan source when they incorporated material from Mark into their own gospels. It is relatively easy to assess a gospel's theological emphasis or bias when you can see the way in which an author or redactor edited an existing written source. Returning to the passage we discussed above in presenting the two-source (or four-source) hypothesis, we can see how Matthew and Luke modified Mark.

In the chart below we have reproduced once again the account of Jesus' healing of Peter's mother-in-law, a story that appears in all three of the synoptic Gospels. Words that are found in both Matthew and Mark are underlined, and words that are found in both Mark and Luke are printed in italics. Some words in Mark are both underlined and italicized, meaning that they are found in all three gospels.

Matthew 8:14–15	**Mark 1:29–30**	**Luke 4:18–19**
And	*And* immediately *he left the synagogue,*	*And he* arose and *left the synagogue,*
when Jesus <u>entered</u> <u>the house of</u> Peter,	*and* <u>*entered*</u> <u>*the house of*</u> Simon and Andrew, with James and John.	*and* entered *the house of* Simon
he saw his <u>mother-in-law</u> <u>lying sick</u> <u>with a fever;</u>	*Now Simon's* <u>*mother-in-law*</u> <u>lay sick</u> <u>*with a fever,*</u> *and immediately they* told *him* of *her.*	*Now Simon's mother-in-law* was ill *with a* high *fever,* *and they* besought *him* for *her.*
<u>he</u> touched <u>her hand</u>	*And* <u>*he*</u> came and took <u>her</u> by the <u>hand</u> *and* lifted her up,	*And he* stood over her *and* rebuked *the fever*
<u>and the fever left her,</u> and <u>she</u> rose <u>and</u> served him.	<u>*and the fever left her*</u>; <u>*and*</u> *she served them.*	*and* it *left her*; and *immediately she* rose *and served them.*

Assuming that the author of the Gospel of Matthew used Mark as his source for this story, material in Matthew that is *not* underlined reflects ways in which Matthew edited his Markan source. It is equally important to observe that Matthew has omitted material found in his Markan source. Likewise Luke edited his Markan source and consciously chose not to include certain details found in Mark. The changes in Matthew and Luke are what interest redaction critics. Some of the omissions may be for no reason other than tightening up what some scholars have described as Mark's diffuse style; some changes may be for the purpose of clarification; and some changes may reflect a conscious effort to address particular theological concerns of the evangelist. Obviously, little can be learned by looking at the editorial changes in a single pericope of only a couple of verses, but a great deal can and has been learned about the redaction process by applying this exercise to the synoptic Gospels in their entirety.

CONCLUSIONS

Not all New Testament scholars agree on every detail as to what constitutes the text of the autograph of the Gospel of Mark, on the exact meaning of every word in the Greek text of the Gospel of Matthew, on whether the Gospels of the New Testament are influenced by Greco-Roman biographies, on details of the literary relationship among the synoptic Gospels, on the exact form that the tradition assumed during the period of oral transmission, or on what exactly the author of the Gospel of Matthew intended to do in editing the Gospel of Mark as he was incorporating it and other written and/or oral material into his own literary creation. Nevertheless, scholars do agree on the method and methodologies that constitute historical criticism of the New Testament. Scholars are also in general agreement that traditions about Jesus took shape within the early church; that these traditions circulated orally in brief stories or units of tradition; that the oral tradition appears to have taken shape in a rather limited number of literary forms; that the tradition survived primarily not for its biographical value but because it served the needs of early Christian communities; that the Gospel of Mark was probably the first of the synoptic Gospels; that Mark was built upon units of oral tradition and possibly some written sources available to the author; and that Matthew and Luke made use of Mark, a sayings source (Q), and other written and oral sources in composing their own gospels.

More problematic, however, is the question of the degree to which the pericopes in the synoptic Gospels of Matthew, Mark, and Luke reflect the life, ministry, and teachings of Jesus of Nazareth or, rather, the confessional belief of the early church that Jesus was God's agent in history, God's Messiah, God's Son. Do the stories in the synoptic Gospels teach us more about the historical Jesus or more about what the first and second generations of Christians believed about Jesus? We shall examine that troublesome question in greater detail in part 3.

One thing is eminently clear: the New Testament is an important source for any reconstruction of the life and ministry of Jesus and the beginnings of Christianity. However, in undertaking such a task, scholars must make use of all of the critical resources available to them as they attempt to present a balanced and unbiased reconstruction of that history.

Because the New Testament is an important resource for understanding the religious beliefs of those who stood at the center of Christian beginnings, we may know more about what these early Christians believed than we do about the details of the earlier history that lies behind their beliefs. And, whatever else, the New Testament puts us into close contact with what those early Christian writers believed to be their god and what they believed was the relationship of their god to Jesus of Nazareth.

So, what exactly is the Bible? It is obviously different things to different people. Minimally, the Hebrew Bible is a collection of twenty-four books written by Jews between about 950 and 150 BCE. The Christian Bible is a collection of sixty-six books (or more if you are Roman Catholic or Eastern Orthodox), written by Jews and Christians over a period of just over one thousand years between about 950 BCE and 150 CE. These books are considered authoritative by Jews and Christians in their respective communities.

The Jewish Bible (the Christian Old Testament) contains the record of what ancient Israelites understood as their encounter with their god Yahweh. That story begins with a primordial history that contains the myth of the creation of the universe and the stories of the fall of Adam and Eve in the Garden of Eden, the great flood, and some other purported "events" of Israel's prehistory.

The primordial history is followed by the call of the patriarchs, Israel's ancestors, Abraham, Isaac, and Jacob (also called Israel). The focal point of Israel's history is, however, the story of Moses and the deliverance of the people of Israel from slavery in Egypt and the establishment of the covenant or special contract that served as the contractual bond between Israel and its god Yahweh.

Following the Moses cycle, the story continues with the conquest and entrenchment of the land of Canaan, the land that Jews believe their god Yahweh promised to them, and the story of the subsequent conquest of Israel by several of its neighbors: the Assyrians, Babylonians, Persians, Greeks, and Romans. It is a story of victory and defeat, establishment and exile. At each step along the way, Israel understood history not as the simple unfolding of historical events, but rather as religious history, Yahweh's acts in behalf of his chosen people, Israel.

In this anthology of books, the Jewish Bible contains, as well, books that record the teachings of some of Israel's greatest prophets, teachers of wisdom, and apocalyptists. The prophets were mediators between Yahweh and his people and delivered oracles containing the word of Yahweh as addressed to specific historical events or social conditions. The prophets were mouthpieces of Yahweh, who spoke his word to his people. Teachers of wisdom reflected on more existential questions, such as the meaning of life and the meaning of evil, and reflected on how to live a life in accordance with divine wisdom. The wisdom movement reflects contact with religious and philosophical traditions outside Israel. Apocalyptists announced the end of history, as we know it, and the future establishment of God's rule on earth.

Christians accepted into their canon these books of Jewish scripture and added a collection of twenty-seven books of their own, the New Testament. This New Testament (or New Covenant) focuses on the life and ministry of Jesus of Nazareth and contains the record of the establishment of the Christian church. It also includes personal letters from Paul and others to early Christian communities, and the vision of a Christian apocalyptic prophet, who recorded his own personal vision of the end-time.

Although we have laid out some of the tools that help scholars better reconstruct Hebrew and Christian beginnings, we have said little about the significance of the books that constitute the Jewish and Christian scriptures. This is, of course, a matter on which Christians and non-Christians differ, and on which Christians frequently disagree with other Christians.

For fundamentalist Christians, these books are the inerrant word of God, perfect and free from error in every detail. These books are God's word to humanity, binding on every religious Christian, who will be saved if he or she follows the call to accept Jesus of Nazareth as his or her personal savior and lives in accordance with the teachings of the holy scriptures. We have sought in this and previous chapters to indicate that this evangelical fundamentalist view is not only mistaken and irrelevant in this modern age, but that it is inconsistent with the church's understanding of the Bible during the long history of Christianity.

More liberal Christians view the Bible as the inspired Word of God, written in the words of men. That is to say that the writers were inspired individuals, who recorded their own "vision" of God in their own words. Accordingly, the actual words of the Bible are not inspired; it is rather the substance or spirit of the Bible's teaching that is inspired by the one true God. Such a view allows for the use of historical-criticism of the Bible, even if that is sometimes constrained by the teachings of the church, as we have already observed in our examination of the situation within Roman Catholicism. Certain core teachings appear to be inviolable for Christians, most specifically the belief in one God and in his Son, Jesus of Nazareth, whom Christians call the Christ, or the Messiah.

Historical criticism of the Bible reflects a secular approach to the literature under investigation and implies that the conclusions reached should depend only on the objective data, the evidence, and should not reflect the personal religious beliefs of the scholar assessing the data. Religious belief, or lack thereof, should have nothing whatsoever to do with the manner in which scholars do their research and reach their conclusions. The work of the historian of the New Testament is neither to advance Christianity nor to attack it, but rather to advance our knowledge about the life and ministry of Jesus and the origins and development of the early church. This task is best accomplished by examining all of the evidence, the data, within its own literary, historical, cultural, religious, and sociological contexts. One should not be able to read the work of a New Testament scholar and know that the scholar is Roman Catholic or Jewish, Unitarian or agnostic, Orthodox or atheist. New Testament scholarship should be neutral and governed by the canons of historical investigation, not by the canons of individual religious denominations.

Part 3
JESUS

Chapter 5
ACCORDING TO
THE SCRIPTURES

he Gospel of Luke is the only gospel that tells the story of the appearance of the resurrected Jesus to two of his apostles on the road to Emmaus. Several interesting and important motifs flow through this story; however, in this chapter I intend to focus on the theme of stories about Jesus that the early Christian community understood as fulfilling the Hebrew scriptures, the church's Old Testament. It is worth quoting this story in Luke 24:13–35 in its entirety:

> 13Now on that same day two of them were going to a village called Emmaus, about seven miles from Jerusalem, 14and talking with each other about all these things that had happened. 15While they were talking and discussing, Jesus himself came near and went with them, 16but their eyes were kept from recognizing him. 17And he said to them, "What are you discussing with each other while you walk along?" They stood still, looking sad. 18Then one of them, whose name was Cleopas, answered him, "Are you the only stranger in Jerusalem who does not know the things that have taken place there in these days?" 19He asked them, "What things?" They replied, "The things about Jesus of Nazareth, who was a prophet mighty in deed and word before God and all the people, 20and how our chief priests and leaders handed him over to be condemned to death and crucified him. 21But we had hoped that he was the one to redeem Israel. Yes, and besides all this, it is now the third day since these things took place. 22Moreover, some women of our group astounded us. They were at the tomb early this morning, 23and when they did not find his body there, they came back and told us that they had indeed seen a vision of angels who said that he was alive. 24Some of those who were with us went to the tomb and found it just as the women had said; but they did not see him." 25Then he said to them, "Oh, how foolish you are, and how slow of heart to believe all that the prophets have declared! 26Was it not necessary that the Messiah should suffer these things and then enter into his glory?" 27Then beginning with Moses and all the prophets, he interpreted to them the things about himself in all the scriptures.
>
> 28As they came near the village to which they were going, he walked ahead as

if he were going on. 29But they urged him strongly, saying, "Stay with us, because it is almost evening and the day is now nearly over." So he went in to stay with them. 30When he was at the table with them, he took bread, blessed and broke it, and gave it to them. 31Then their eyes were opened, and they recognized him; and he vanished from their sight. 32They said to each other, "Were not our hearts burning within us while he was talking to us on the road, while he was opening the scriptures to us?" 33That same hour they got up and returned to Jerusalem; and they found the eleven and their companions gathered together. 34They were saying, "The Lord has risen indeed, and he has appeared to Simon!" 35Then they told what had happened on the road, and how he had been made known to them in the breaking of the bread.

In this story, the risen Lord appeared, seemingly in human form, to two of his disciples, who did not recognize him. The two men proceeded to tell the resurrected Jesus about what had recently transpired concerning his arrest, crucifixion, and death and reported the testimony of some women who had a vision of angels who told them that Jesus was alive. The risen Christ then chided the two men for their slowness to believe. Then, beginning with Moses and the prophets, the risen Lord interpreted to the two disciples the things concerning him in the Jewish scriptures. Later, while they were eating with the risen Lord, the two men finally recognized Jesus in the Eucharistic meal he was sharing with them, at which point he disappeared from their sight.

The story of Jesus' appearance on the road to Emmaus makes it clear to the reader (listener)[56] that the risen Lord is known to the church in the breaking of the bread, the Eucharistic meal. Although the two men knew and recognized Jesus as the risen Lord, his physical presence was no longer manifest once the believers recognized him "in the breaking of the bread" (v. 35). According to the story, as soon as the disciples recognized the risen Christ, he disappeared. The author of the Gospel of Luke is reminding the Christian community that it is in the communal meal of the bread and wine that the church knows its Lord, even though Jesus is no longer physically present with them. Christ will be present with the church now and henceforth not visibly, but rather only in the bread and wine. They will recognize him not by seeing him with their eyes but rather by knowing him through the eyes of faith in the celebration of the Eucharistic meal. It is here that Jesus is manifest to the church—and it is at this point in the story that Jesus vanishes.

Another critical theme of this story is evident in verse 25 ("Oh, how foolish you are, and how slow you are to believe *all that the prophets have declared!*"); in verse 27 (Then *beginning with Moses and all the prophets, he interpreted to them the things about himself in all the scriptures*); and again in verse 32 ("Were not our hearts burning within us . . . *while he was opening the scriptures to us?*"). These verses make it clear that the church believed that it was the risen Lord himself who first disclosed to his disciples through the Jewish scriptures the meaning of his life,

---

56. Few in the early Christian community would have actually "read" the Gospels. More likely, someone read the Gospels aloud to the community during worship services.

death, and resurrection. The meaning of these events was apparently not clear to Jesus' disciples during his lifetime. It was divulged to them only after his death through their reading of the Jewish scriptures.[57] However, this story makes it clear that they believed that the meaning of Jesus' life, death, and resurrection had been unveiled through the power and inspiration of none other than the risen Lord. It was the risen Christ himself who in this story instructed his disciples in the interpretation of the Jewish scriptures. The significance of what Moses and the prophets pro-claimed *to the church* about Jesus of Nazareth is evident in Luke's words "Was it not necessary that the Messiah should suffer these things and then enter his glory?" (v. 26). Although Luke provides no specific references to the Law and the prophets in this particular story, he does so elsewhere in his gospel. For example, in Luke 7:27, in a reference to John the Baptist, Luke writes:

> This is the one about whom it is written:
> "See, I am sending my messenger ahead of you,
> who will prepare your way before you."

The scriptural text that Luke cites in this instance is Malachi 3:1.

This powerful story of Jesus' appearance on the road to Emmaus is an important key to assist us in unlocking the mystery of how Jesus' followers, who deserted him in his final hours, came later to understand his death as a victory rather than as a defeat. The Gospels report that the disciples deserted Jesus, beginning apparently with Judas' betrayal (Mark 14:10–11; Matthew 26:14–16; Luke 22:3–6; and John 13:2), followed by Peter's denial (Mark 14:66–72; Matthew 26:69–75; Luke 22:56–62; and John 18:25–27). It appears that Jesus' disciples all fled before his death. There is no mention of any of them at his crucifixion. Some of his women fol-lowers are referred to as having been present at the Crucifixion; Mark 15:40 mentions Mary Magdalene, Mary the mother of James the younger and of Joses, and Salome; Matthew 27:56 names Mary Magdalene, Mary the mother of James and Joseph, and the mother of the sons of Zebedee; Luke 23:49 mentions the women who had come with Jesus from Galilee but gives no names;[58] and John 19:25–26 refers to Jesus'

---

57. It is interesting in this regard to note the passage in the Gospel of John concerning Jesus' cleansing of the Temple (John 2:13–22). In this version of the story, the Jews ask Jesus for a sign after he drove from the Temple the money changers and those selling animals for sacrifice. Jesus answers the Jews by saying: "Destroy this temple, and in three days I will raise it up," to which they respond, "This temple has been under construction for forty-six years, and will you raise it up in three days?" We are then told by the evangelist that Jesus was speaking of the temple of his body, an allusion to his forthcoming resurrection. The story in John concludes: "*After he was raised from the dead*, his disciples remembered that he had said this; and *they believed the scripture* and the word that Jesus had spoken" (John 2:22).

58. Luke may have in mind those women mentioned in 8:2–3 (Mary Magdalene, Joanna the wife of Herod's steward Chuza, Susanna, and "many others who provided for them out of their resources") and in 24:10 (Mary Magdalene, Joanna, Mary the mother of James, and "the other women with them").

mother (although not by name), his mother's sister (also not by name), Mary the wife of Clopas, and Mary Magdalene, and to the mysterious and otherwise nameless beloved disciple (often identified in Christian tradition, probably erroneously, as John). Mark 15:42–47, Matthew 27:57–61, Luke 23:50–56, and John19:38–42 all mention Joseph of Arimathea as the man who buried Jesus, although only Matthew (27:57) and John (19:38) identify Joseph as a disciple of Jesus.

Neither were Jesus' disciples at the tomb on the third day after the Crucifixion for the Resurrection, even though Jesus is represented in three of the Gospels as having three times predicted in some detail the events leading up to his deliverance to the Gentiles, suffering, death, and resurrection: first in Mark 8:31–33, Matthew 16:21–23, Luke 9:22; second in Mark 9:30–32, Matthew 17:22–23, Luke 9:43b–45; and third in Mark 10:32–34, Matthew 20:17–19, Luke 18:31–34. It is difficult, if not impossible, to imagine why the apostles were not at the tomb that Easter morning if Jesus had three times predicted in such detail the events leading up to his demise. A much more likely scenario is that the disciples all deserted Jesus before his death, presumably out of fear, disillusionment, and despair.

The early Christian community subsequently explained the problematic events of Jesus' last days in light of their subsequent reading of the Jewish scriptures *following Jesus' death*, and Jesus' three predictions of his passion developed in the Christian community at an even later date to indicate clearly that Jesus knew in detail what lay ahead of him, even if his disciples did not fully understand what Jesus was trying to tell them. Jesus' followers clearly unlocked retrospectively and through a search of the Jewish scriptures the meaning of what had appeared to them earlier as the victory of the Jews and Romans over their prophetic leader.

This interpretation is further reinforced in the following story in Luke 24:36–49, in which following his appearance to the men on the road to Emmaus, Jesus appeared to his disciples in Jerusalem. The critical portion of this story for our purposes is found in Jesus' words to his disciples in Luke 24:44–47:

> 44Then he said to them, "These are my words that I spoke to you while I was still with you—that everything written about me in the law of Moses, the prophets, and the psalms must be fulfilled." 45Then he opened their minds to understanding the scriptures, 46and he said to them, "Thus it is written, that the Messiah is to suffer and to rise from the dead on the third day, 47and that repentance and forgiveness of sins is to be proclaimed in his name to all nations, beginning from Jerusalem.

Although these two stories are found only in the Gospel of Luke, which was probably written sometime around 85 CE, more than fifty years after Jesus' death, the practice of interpreting the life and ministry, and especially the death and resurrection, of Jesus in light of the Hebrew scriptures clearly dates to the earliest period in the life of the Christian community. Evidence for it is found decades earlier than the writing of the Gospel of Luke in the letters of Paul, as well as in traditional material incorporated into Luke's other book, the Acts of the Apostles.

In 1 Corinthians 15:3–8, Paul wrote to the church at Corinth what he had obviously received as tradition much earlier than the actual writing of this letter about 54 CE:[59]

> 3For I handed on to you as of first importance what I in turn had received: that Christ died for our sins *in accordance with the scriptures*, 4and that he was buried, and that he was raised on the third day *in accordance with the scriptures*, 5and that he appeared to Cephas, then to the twelve. 6Then he appeared to more than five hundred brothers and sisters, most of whom are still alive, though some have died. 7Then he appeared to James, then to all the apostles. 8Last of all, as to one untimely born, he appeared also to me.

Paul made it clear in his letter to the Corinthian Christians that he had earlier received a tradition and was passing it on to them, namely that in two instances (see the italics above), Jesus' death and resurrection, the Hebrew scriptures provided the key to an understanding of those events. Jesus' death and resurrection both unfolded *in accordance with the scriptures*. I submit that the meaning of these events was imparted to the church *following* Jesus' death and only after Jesus' followers began to look into their sacred writings for an understanding of what they could not otherwise make sense of or understand. Paul subsequently received that tradition and passed it on to the Corinthian community at the time of his initial visit to and the establishment of the Christian church in that city.

Jesus' death must initially have appeared to be a defeat at the hands of the Jews and the Romans. How could God have abandoned their leader, their prophet, and rendered meaningless all that Jesus had taught and represented to them? The answer to that puzzling question was revealed to them only in their subsequent reading of the Hebrew scriptures, and so they began to tell the story of Jesus' life, death, and resurrection *in accordance with the scriptures*. The death of Jesus *for our sins* apparently occurred in fulfillment of Isaiah 53:4–6, 9–12:

> 4 Surely he has borne our infirmities
> and carried our diseases;
> yet we accounted him stricken,
> struck down by God, and afflicted.
> 5 But he was wounded for our transgressions,
> crushed for our iniquities;
> upon him was the punishment that made us whole,

---

59. The chronology of Paul's career and hence the dating of events in the life of the early Christian community are based on the so-called Gallio inscription. An inscription at Delphi in Greece allows scholars to date Gallio's proconsulate in Corinth to the period of about 51–53 CE and may indicate that Paul established the church at Corinth during that period. The relevant New Testament passage in this regard is Acts 18:12: "But when Gallio was proconsul of Achaia, the Jews made a united attack on Paul and brought him before the tribunal." Paul probably wrote his letter to the Corinthian Christians from Ephesus several years after founding the community. Hence, the suggested date of about 54 CE.

and by his bruises we are healed.
6 All we like sheep have gone astray;
we have all turned to our own way,
and the LORD has laid on him
the iniquity of us all. . . .
9 They made his grave with the wicked
and his tomb with the rich,
although he had done no violence
and there was no deceit in his mouth.
10 Yet it was the will of the LORD to crush him with pain.
When you make his life an offering for sin,
he shall see his offspring, and shall prolong his days;
through him the will of the LORD shall prosper.
11 Out of anguish he shall see light;
he shall find satisfaction through his knowledge.
The righteous one, my servant, shall make many righteous,
and he shall bear their iniquities.
12 Therefore I will allot him a portion with the great,
and he shall divide the spoil with the strong;
because he poured out himself to death,
and was numbered with the transgressors;
yet he bore the sin of many,
and made intercessions for the transgressors.

Jesus' resurrection *on the third day* occurred in fulfillment of Hosea 6:2:

After two days he will revive us;
on the third day he will raise us up,
that we may live before him.

However improbable we may consider the connection between these verses in Isaiah
and Hosea and events surrounding Jesus' death, what is important is that early Christians clearly made that connection.

Let us now look at the account of Jesus' crucifixion in the Gospel of Mark. It is
evident in this narrative that the author of this gospel (or an earlier source available to
him) reported the final moments of Jesus' life with the Hebrew scriptures very much
in mind in the reporting of every detail. Compare the text of Mark's gospel in the left-
hand column with material in the Hebrew scriptures in the right-hand column that was,
I maintain, clearly available and evident to Mark or to Mark's source:

Mark 15:21–32   **Jewish scriptures**

21They compelled a passer-by, who
was coming in from the country, to
carry his cross; it was Simon of Cyrene,
the father of Alexander and Rufus.

22Then they brought Jesus to the place
called Golgatha (which means the
place of a skull),

23And they offered him wine mixed
with myrrh; but he did not take it.

Proverbs 31:6 Give strong drink
to one who is perishing, and wine
to those in bitter distress.
Psalms 69:21 They gave me poison for
food, and for my thirst they gave me
vinegar to drink.

24And they crucified him, and divided
his clothes among them, casting lots
to decide what each should take.

Psalms 22:18 They divide my
clothes among themselves, and
for my clothing they cast lots.

25And it was nine o'clock in the morning
when they crucified him.

26The inscription of the charge against
him read, "The King of the Jews."

27And with him they crucified two bandits,
one on his right and one on his left.

[28And the scripture was fulfilled that says,
"And he was counted among the lawless."]

[This verse is not found in our
best manuscripts and was added to Mark
later from Luke 22:37.]

29Those who passed by derided him,
shaking their heads and saying, "Aha!
You who would destroy the temple and
build it in three days,

30save yourself, and come down from the cross!"

Psalms 22:7 All who see me
mock at me; they make mouths at
me, they shake their heads.
Psalms 109:25 I am the object of
scorn to my accusers; when
they see me, they shake their
heads.
Lamentations 2:15 All who pass
along the way clap their hands at
you; they hiss and wag their
heads at daughter Jerusalem.

31In the same way the chief priests,
along with the scribes, were also mocking
him among themselves and saying,
"He saved others; he cannot save himself.

Wisdom 2:17–18 Let us see if
his words are true, and let us test
what will happen at the end
of his life; for if the righteous man is
God's child, he
will help him and will deliver

32Let the Messiah, the King of Israel, come down from the cross now, so that we may see and believe." Those who were crucified with him also taunted him.

him from the hands of his adversaries.

Psalms 22:8 "Commit your cause to the LORD; let him deliver— let him rescue the one in whom he delights!"

In the text of Mark 15:21–32 as quoted above, only verses 21–22 and 25–27 have no apparent parallel or source of inspiration in the Hebrew scriptures. Hence, the only material that is not motivated or colored in any way by biblical "proof-texts" is that Simon of Cyrene helped to carry Jesus' cross to the site of execution at Golgatha, that the crucifixion took place at nine in the morning, and that there was an inscription on the cross that read "The King of the Jews." We cannot be certain that these details are historically reliable simply because there are no apparent sources of inspiration for them in the Hebrew scriptures, but we should be extremely cautious about claiming as historical Mark's remaining details, which appear to be inspired or colored largely by a reading of the Hebrew scriptures.

There was apparently a brief foundation story behind Mark or his source to which a good deal of legendary tradition attached itself. Although it is impossible to determine exactly what is historical in this story and what is legendary, there can be little doubt that the story in its present form has been put together with the help of building blocks from the Hebrew scriptures, texts that the early Christian church identified and assembled to impart meaning to Jesus' otherwise seemingly meaningless death. Some important questions for consideration are these:

To what extent have passages from the Hebrew scriptures colored the accounts as we currently have them in the Gospel of Mark?

To what extent did events surrounding Jesus' crucifixion simply evoke memories of passages in the Hebrew scriptures?

To what extent are these stories simply the product of early Christian piety or mythmaking?

There can be no question that the Hebrew scriptures colored the way in which Mark and his successors presented details in this account of Jesus' crucifixion. It is more difficult to determine whether there is historical memory at the heart of some of the details or whether Mark (or his source) provided details primarily or even exclusively from the reading of the Hebrew scriptures.

Critical in the table above is the fact that five of the allusions to Hebrew scriptures are to passages in Psalms, and three of those five allusions are to verses in Psalm 22, a clear favorite of the early Christian church. We need in this regard to recall the words of the risen Lord in Luke 24:44: "These are my words that I spoke to you while

I was still with you—that everything written about me in the law of Moses, the prophets, *and the psalms* must be fulfilled" (italics mine). The frequent use of Psalms and, in particular, of Psalm 22 is suspicious. I am convinced that Paul had in mind exactly such a process of searching in the Hebrew scriptures for "proof-texts," when he recited the early tradition that "Christ died for our sins *in accordance with the scriptures*" (1 Corinthians 15:3). Indeed, as I mentioned above, the material in this verse in 1 Corinthians 15 is clearly pre-Pauline, since Paul states clearly that he was passing on to the Corinthian Christians what he had received earlier.

Traditionally, the church has pointed to these same passages in the Hebrew scriptures and the New Testament and has used them to demonstrate that these Old Testament "prophecies" were *fulfilled* in the life and ministry of Jesus. These examples of prophecy and fulfillment are generally regarded by the church as "proof positive" of Jesus' divine origin and messiahship.

I am now turning that spurious argument on its head and claiming that "events" in the gospel stories have been colored, if not invented, by consulting passages from the Hebrew scriptures. In fact, the story of Jesus' death in Mark 15 was built upon passages from the Hebrew scriptures to such an extent that it is no longer possible to say much more about Jesus' death than that he was crucified by the Romans at a place called Golgatha and that a certain Simon of Cyrene may have helped to carry his cross. Even the inscription on the cross may be an irony to illustrate that the Romans were right in identifying Jesus as "King of the Jews," a title that Jesus certainly never claimed for himself, the story of the triumphal entry in Mark 11:1–11 notwithstanding.

Let us now look at a couple of passages concerning Jesus' resurrection from what appears to be the earliest Christian tradition. This exercise is especially important, inasmuch as Paul claimed in 1 Corinthians 15:4 that Christ "was raised on the third day *in accordance with the scriptures.*"

Two passages in Acts and a passage in Paul's Letter to the Romans provide important clues to the belief of the earliest Christian communities before Matthew, Mark, Luke, and John developed elaborate and, indeed, contradictory accounts of the Resurrection. Acts 2:14–36 purports to report Peter's address to the crowd immediately following Pentecost. The tradition is surely not a verbatim stenographic account of Peter's speech, but it is very likely a primitive statement of the early church's preached message. Peter has this to say about Jesus:

> 22"You that are Israelites, listen to what I have to say: Jesus of Nazareth, a man attested to you by God with deeds of power, wonders, and signs that God did through him among you, as you yourselves know—23this man, handed over to you *according to the definite plan and foreknowledge of God*, you crucified and killed by the hands of those outside the law, 24But God raised him up, having freed him from death, because it was impossible for him to be held in its power. 25For David said concerning him,
> 'I saw the Lord always before me,
> for he is at my right hand so that I will not be shaken;

26 therefore my heart was glad, and my tongue rejoiced;
   moreover my flesh will live in hope.
27 For you will not abandon my soul to Hades,
   or let your Holy One experience corruption.
28 You have made known to me the ways of life;
   you will make me full of gladness with your presence.'
29 "Fellow Israelites, I may say to you confidentially of our ancestor David that he both died and was buried, and his tomb is with us to this day. 30Since he was a prophet, he knew that God had sworn with an oath to him that he would put one of his descendants on the throne. 31*Foreseeing this*, David spoke of the resurrection of the Messiah, saying,
   'He was not abandoned to Hades,
   nor did his flesh experience corruption.'
32 This Jesus God raised up, and of that all of us are witnesses. 33Being therefore exalted at the right hand of God, and having received from the Father the promise of the Holy Spirit, he has poured out this that you both see and hear. 34For David did not ascend into the heavens, but he himself says,
   'The Lord said to my Lord,
   "Sit at my right hand, 35until I make your enemies your footstool."'
36 Therefore let the entire house of Israel know with certainty that God has made him both Lord and Messiah, this Jesus whom you crucified." (Italics mine)

This passage contains a number of interesting features that support my thesis that some of the early Christian communities' tradition was built on perceived proof-texts from the Hebrew scriptures. The words "according to the definite plan and foreknowledge of God" in verse 23 and "foreseeing this" in verse 31, as well as the proof-texts themselves cited in Acts 2:25–28 (= Psalms 16:8–11), Acts 2:31 (= Psalms 16:10), and Acts 2:34–35 (= Psalms 110:1), attest to the way in which the early church apparently built its message—the good news or gospel about Jesus the Messiah—around passages from the Hebrew scriptures. There is, in addition, verse 30: "Since he was a prophet, he knew that *God had sworn with an oath* to him that he *would put one of his descendants on his throne*"; the italicized words in this verse recall Psalms 132:11: The LORD *swore to David a sure oath* from which he will not turn back: "*One of the sons of your body I will set on your throne*" (italics mine).

In this passage in Acts 2 the handing of Jesus over to the Jews (v. 23), Jesus' role as Son of David (vv. 30–31), Jesus' exaltation to God's right hand (vv. 25–28 and v. 35), and Jesus' resurrection (v. 31) are clearly based on a search of the Hebrew scriptures for passages that might give meaning to Jesus' apparently unexpected and, therefore, presumably otherwise meaningless demise. According to this passage in Acts 2, these events all occurred as part of a divine plan recorded clearly in advance in Israel's sacred books. Notice that the author initially introduced Jesus in Peter's speech as "a man *attested to you by God with deeds of power, wonders, and signs that God did through him*." Notice also that Jesus did not rise from the dead; *God raised him* from the dead. Everything in this speech indicates that what has transpired in the life, death, and resurrection of Jesus was part of God's plan and was foretold in Israel's sacred writings. As in the case of Mark 15, which we examined above, it is interesting that in the case of this passage in Acts 2, all four of the Old Testament passages cited are from Psalms. Remember Luke 24:44: "everything written about me in the law of Moses, the prophets, *and the psalms* must be fulfilled" (italics mine).

A particularly important insight into the earliest church's understanding of Jesus' resurrection is afforded in Acts 2:36, which states that "God *has made* him both Lord (Greek = *kyrios*) and Messiah (Greek = *christos*), this Jesus whom you crucified" (italics mine). The implication of this claim could not be clearer. God *made* Jesus Lord and Messiah *following* his death, apparently by delivering him from death and exalting him to his right hand to a position of honor and authority. Notice that in these verses in Acts there is no resuscitated corpse, no physical resurrection appearances. This so-called "exaltation theology" may be the earliest and most primitive understanding of what "happened" to Jesus *after* his death: God delivered Jesus from death (Hades) (v. 27) and directed him to sit at his right hand in heaven (v. 34), thereby naming this Jesus, whom the Jews had crucified and put to death, "Lord and Messiah" (v. 36, cf. also 2:23–24). By exalting Jesus to his right hand, God vindicated Jesus and reversed and undid what might appear to be the victory of the Jews and Romans over Jesus in putting him to death. God was saying yes to Jesus, when the world (the Jews and Romans) had said no. This exaltation theology contrasts with Luke's own theology in the Gospel of Luke, and, therefore, likely reflects the most primitive teaching of the church regarding what *happened* to Jesus following his death.

Further evidence of this early teaching can be found in Acts. 3:15 ("and you killed the Author of life, whom *God raised* from the dead") and Acts 4:10–11 (10"Let it be known to all of you, and to all the people of Israel, that this man is standing before you in good health by the name of Jesus of Nazareth, whom you crucified, whom *God raised* from the dead. 11This Jesus is 'the stone that was rejected by you, the builders; it has become the cornerstone'" [= Psalms 118:22]). Notice once again that the book of Psalms was a particularly popular source of proof-texts for the early Christian church.

Paul, the earliest writer of books (letters) in our canonical New Testament, was obviously familiar with the same primitive exaltation theology that we found in Peter's speech in Acts. In fact, this exaltation theology was apparently current long before the composition of the four canonical gospels (ca. 70–100 CE), in which we find the much later accounts of the empty tomb and physical appearances of the risen Lord to eyewitnesses. The opening words of Paul's Letter to the Romans, written circa 58 CE, proves the point:

> 1Paul, a servant of Jesus Christ, called to be an apostle, set apart for the gospel of God, 2*which he promised beforehand through his prophets in the holy scriptures*, 3the gospel concerning his Son, who was descended from David according to the flesh 4and *was declared to be Son of God with power according to the spirit of holiness by resurrection from the dead*, Jesus Christ our Lord, 5through whom we have received grace and apostleship to bring about the obedience of faith among all the

Gentiles for the sake of his name, including yourselves who are called to belong to
Jesus Christ. (Italics mine)

As in the passages previously cited, Paul appeals in this instance to the promises of
the prophets in the Hebrew scriptures (v. 2) as the basis of the church's gospel. He
is apparently referring to the church's earliest preached message when he speaks of
"the gospel of God" (v. 1). It is likely that this formula in verses 1–3 was formulated
before Paul appropriated it here in his letter to the Romans. As we have already
observed in Acts, Paul makes it clear that it was by virtue of Jesus' resurrection from
the dead that he was *declared* to be Son of God (v. 4; italics mine). Jesus' Sonship,
Messiahship, Lordship *were conferred on him* by God *after* his death. This important detail provides critical insight into how we should and should not understand
Jesus' life and ministry, and how we should and should not read the Gospels.

Our four Gospels were clearly built on the same kind of reading of the Hebrew
scriptures in early Christian communities, as we have already shown in some detail
in the account of Jesus' death in Mark 15. Most scholars consider the Gospel of
Mark to be the earliest of the written gospels and to have served as a source for the
Gospels of Matthew and Luke.[60] Let us, therefore, look first at Mark and then subsequently at the other Gospels to see how our four canonical gospels fit into the picture we have begun to paint.

Most Christians have in their minds a picture of Jesus based primarily on the
theology and general framework of the Gospel of John with stories from the Gospels
of Matthew, Mark, and Luke fit into that Johannine framework. The truth is far more
complicated. As we have already seen, there is actually a direct literary relationship
among three of the four Gospels, since Matthew and Luke apparently both used
Mark independently as one of their sources in the writing of their own gospels. In
addition, the authors of Matthew and Luke apparently had access to a second
common source, traditionally called Q (an abbreviation for the German word *Quelle*
or "source"). In addition, the authors of the Gospels of Matthew and Luke also had
access to their own special material, whether written or oral, traditionally known as
special-Matthew (or M) and special-Luke (or L).

The author of the Gospel of John may not have known any of the other written
gospels, but he clearly used some of the same traditions in the creation of his gospel. The
popular picture of the four evangelists independently writing their gospels under the
inspiration of the Holy Spirit may still be the belief of many evangelical fundamentalist
Christians, but no reputable New Testament scholar would be guilty of such naïveté.

The Gospel of Mark, our earliest gospel, written about 68 CE, begins with John
the Baptist's proclamation of "a baptism of repentance for the forgiveness of sins"

---

60. The overwhelming majority of New Testament scholars believe that the Gospel of
Mark was written first and that it served as one of the sources for the Gospels of Matthew and
Luke. The arguments for and against the priority of Mark are available in Arthur J. Bellinzoni,
ed., *The Two-Source Hypothesis: A Critical Appraisal* (Macon, GA: Mercer University Press,
1985) and have been presented in summary form in the previous chapter.

(Mark 1:4) and the baptism of Jesus (1:9–11). There are no birth narratives in Mark; neither are there any accounts of resurrection appearances. Mark ends with the women's discovery of the empty tomb and their flight from the tomb in fear (16:8).

The gospel begins by introducing John the Baptist with a citation from the Jewish scriptures (Mark 1:2–4):

> ₂As it is written in the prophet Isaiah,
> "See, I am sending my messenger ahead of you,
> who will prepare your way;
> ₃the voice of one crying in the wilderness:
> 'Prepare the way of the Lord,
> make his paths straight,'"
> ₄John the baptizer appeared in the wilderness, proclaiming a baptism of repentance for the forgiveness of sins.

For Mark, John is the forerunner of Jesus, the one who proclaimed Jesus' coming. Yet even the forerunner was clearly part of God's plan, so he, too, must be introduced with a citation from the Hebrew scriptures. Although Mark identifies the citation as coming from the prophet Isaiah (the first time we have had a quotation's source positively identified), Mark is wrong in citing this text as coming from Isaiah. It is rather a composite quotation and draws upon three very different verses in the Old Testament:

1. **Malachi 3:1** See, *I am sending my messenger to prepare the way before me*, and the Lord whom you seek will suddenly come to his temple.
2. **Exodus 23:20** *I am going to send an angel in front of you*, to guard you on your way and *to bring you to a place that I have prepared*.
3. **Isaiah 40:3** A voice cries out:
   "In the wilderness prepare the way of the LORD,
   make straight in the desert a highway for our God."

The fact that the author of the Gospel of Mark at least in part misidentifies the source of his quotation(s) may suggest that he himself did not have access to biblical manuscripts and that he might rather be quoting from a collection of passages that early Christian scribes had researched and identified in the Hebrew scriptures and written down in a brief, readily accessible document, a collection of proof-texts to support their claims about Jesus. Be that as it may, the point I am underscoring here is that the Hebrew scriptures set the stage once again for an important "event": this time it was Jesus' baptism.

In his account of Jesus' baptism, Mark reports that Jesus went from Nazareth to the area of the Jordan River where John was preaching, apparently in order to be baptized. Mark does not recognize the problem involved in Jesus' submitting to John's "baptism of repentance for the forgiveness of sins" (v. 4). The implication in Mark's gospel is that in submitting to John's baptism, Jesus was himself a sinner and perhaps even a follower, a disciple, of John. This position is reinforced with the information that, in the Gospel of Mark, Jesus began his own ministry only after the arrest of John the Baptist (Mark 1:14 "Now after John was arrested, Jesus came to Galilee, proclaiming the good news of God and saying, 'The time is fulfilled, and the kingdom of God has come near; repent, and believe in the good news'").

Matthew apparently recognized the problem in Mark's text and so, in writing his own gospel, modified Mark's text by adding the words: "John would have prevented him, saying, 'I need to be baptized by you, and do you come to me?'" (Matthew 3:14). Returning to the account of Jesus' baptism in the Gospel of Mark, just as Jesus was emerging from the waters of the Jordan, "he saw the heaven torn apart and the Spirit descending like a dove on him" (Mark 1:10). Mark continues, "And a voice came from heaven, 'You are my Son, the Beloved; with you I am well pleased'" (Mark 1:11). The divine approval combines elements from Psalms 2:7 and Isaiah 42:1:

Psalms 2:7   I will tell of the decree of the LORD:
He said to me, you are my son;
today I have begotten you.

Isaiah 42:1   *Here is my servant, whom I uphold,*
My chosen, in whom my soul delights;
I have put my spirit upon him;
he will bring forth justice to the nations.

From this story two points emerge. First, like other material we have examined, the author of the Gospel of Mark built the story of Jesus' baptism around two texts from the Hebrew scriptures, Isaiah and Psalms (cf. Luke 24:44's words: "everything written about me in the law of Moses, the prophets, and psalms must be fulfilled"). Second, Mark appears to trace Jesus' divine Sonship not from his exaltation/resurrection, as we saw in passages in Acts and Romans, but rather from Jesus' baptism. Apparently nothing before the baptism was known to the author of the Gospel of Mark, because the baptism and the voice from heaven are the defining moment in Jesus' life in this gospel. At his baptism Jesus was *adopted* as God's son and, following John's arrest, began his own public ministry (Mark 1:14).

The authors of the Gospels of Matthew and Luke go one step further than Mark in tracing Jesus' Messiahship/Sonship/Lordship back to his birth. The first two chapters of Matthew contain no fewer than five proof-texts that serve as a basis for details in Matthew's story.

1. Jesus' birth from a virgin (Matthew 1:18–21) took place to fulfill a prophecy in Isaiah 7:14 (see Matthew 1:23):

Matthew 1:23   *Look, the virgin shall conceive and bear a son,*
and they shall name him Emmanuel.

Isaiah 7:14   *Look, the young woman*[61]
is with child and shall bear a son,
and shall name him Immanuel.

2. Jesus is reported to have been born in Bethlehem of Judea (Matthew 2:5) to fulfill a prophecy that combines material from Micah 5:2 and 2 Samuel 5:2 (see Matthew 2:6):

Matthew 2:5–6   They told him, "In Bethlehem of Judea; for so it has been written by the prophet:
'And you, *Bethlehem*, in the land of Judah
are by no means least along the rulers of Judah;
for from you shall come a ruler
who is to shepherd my people Israel.'"

Micah 5:2   But you, O *Bethleham* of Ephrathah
who are one of the little clans of Judah,
from you shall come forth for me one who is to rule in
Israel
whose origin is from old, from ancient days.

2 Samuel 5:2   The LORD said to you: *It is you who shall be shepherd of*
my people Israel, you who shall be ruler over Israel.

3. The flight of Joseph, Mary, and the infant Jesus to Egypt (Matthew 2:13–15) fulfills a prophecy in Hosea 11:1 (see Matthew 2:15):

Matthew 2:15   *Out of Egypt have I called my son.*

Hosea 11:1   When Israel was a child, I loved him, and *out of Egypt I*
called him my son.

4. The massacre of the children (Matthew 2:16) fulfills a prophecy in Jeremiah 31:15 (see Matthew 2:17):

Matthew 2:17   Then was fulfilled what had been spoken through the prophet Jeremiah:

---

61. The Greek text of Isaiah that the author of the Gospel of Matthew would have had access to would have read "virgin" in 7:14 rather than "young woman." The original Hebrew reads "young woman," but it was mistranslated into the Greek as "virgin." Hence, Matthew is here dependent on a mistranslation in his use or misuse of this passage as a "proof-text." This argument was made in more detail in the previous chapter.

> *"A voice was heard in Ramah,*
>> *wailing and loud lamentation,*
> *Rachel weeping for her children;*
>> *she refused to be consoled, because they are no more.*

Jeremiah 31:15 Thus says the LORD:
> *A voice is heard from Ramah,*
> *lamentation and bitter weeping.*
> *Rachel is weeping for her children;*
> *she refuses to be comforted for her children,*
> *because they are no more.*

5. The fifth and last of the proof-texts is problematic. Following the flight to Egypt and the massacre of the children, Joseph, Mary, and Jesus returned not to Bethlehem, the place of his birth and the family's apparent home, but rather to Nazareth in Galilee, "so that what was spoken through the prophets might be fulfilled, 'He will be called a Nazorean" (Matthew 2:23). The problem is that no text in the Hebrew scriptures corresponds to this apparent quotation. It is not clear what text the author of the Gospel of Matthew had in mind.

What is clear, however, from this discussion of Matthew's birth narrative is that many of the themes in this story were built on Old Testament passages: Jesus' birth from a virgin (1:18–21), the site of Jesus' birth in Bethlehem (2:5–6), the flight to Egypt (2:13–15), the massacre of the children (2:16–18), and the relocation of the family to Nazareth (2:23). It is easy to see how the Hebrew scriptures contributed to the Gospel of Matthew's development of a legendary tradition surrounding Jesus' birth. If the apparently legendary information based on Matthew's (or the early church's) reading of the Hebrew scriptures is bracketed, the story reveals only the barest outline of Jesus' origin:

1. Jesus' parents were Joseph and Mary (in fact, the Gospel of John refers to Jesus twice as the "son of Joseph"). (See also, John 1:45: "Philip found Nathaniel and said to him, 'We have found him about whom Moses in the law and also the prophets wrote, Jesus son of Joseph from Nazareth'"; and John 6:42: "They were saying, 'Is not this Jesus, the son of Joseph, whose father and mother we know?'").
2. Jesus was born in Nazareth (he is always referred to as Jesus of Nazareth, never as Jesus of Bethlehem).

Apparently there was no flight to Egypt; the story in Matthew models Jesus after Moses, who led the people of Israel out of Egypt during the time of the Exodus. Neither, apparently, was there a massacre of the children, as reported in Matthew; the story once again models Jesus after Moses in Exodus 1:22; 11:4–6, when, according to the tradition, before the Exodus of the Hebrews from Egypt, Pharaoh ordered the massacre of every boy born to the Hebrews.

Despite its dubious historicity, the story of Jesus' birth does, however, accomplish an important purpose in the Gospel of Matthew. It not only provides a story in fulfillment of the Hebrew scriptures, but it also traces Jesus' Sonship not to his resurrection/exaltation (as in Acts and Paul) nor to Jesus' baptism (as in Mark), but rather to Mary's conception by the Holy Spirit (when "she was found to be with child from the Holy Spirit" [Matthew 1:18]). In these passages we are witnessing in the church's writings a gradual move to a "higher" Christology, a more developed interpretation of the person of Jesus. We now find that Jesus was not only designated Son of God by virtue of his resurrection from the dead (Acts and Paul), or designated Son of God at his baptism (Mark), but he was conceived miraculously by the power of God.

Like the Gospel of Matthew, the Gospel of Luke also has a birth narrative, but it is completely different from the birth narrative that is found in Matthew. The two gospels agree on the fact that Jesus was born of a virgin (Matthew 1:18–21; Luke 1:26–38), that Joseph was Mary's husband (Matthew 1:18–19; Luke 2:5; 2:33), and that the birth took place in Bethlehem (Matthew 2:5–6; Luke 2:4). Yet even in those instances where the two gospels agree, there are major differences. Most obvious is the fact that in the Gospel of Matthew the family already lived in Bethlehem where Jesus was born. From Bethlehem they traveled to Egypt and then went to Nazareth rather than back to the family home in Bethlehem, following a warning to Joseph in a dream. Luke, on the other hand, locates the family home in Nazareth and then devised the Roman census as the reason for their traveling to Bethlehem, because according to the prophecy in Micah 5:2 and 2 Samuel 5:2 the Messiah had to be born in Bethlehem, the city of Israel's great king David. As in Matthew, the author of the Gospel of Luke traces Jesus' title "Son of God" back to Mary's conception: The angel said to her, "The Holy Spirit will come upon you, and the power of the Most High will overshadow you; therefore the child to be born will be holy; he will be called Son of God" (Luke 2:35).

To complete the picture, the author of the Gospel of John traces Jesus' divine Sonship back to a time before creation, the "highest" Christology that we find in the New Testament. He refers to Jesus as the incarnation of the divine *logos*, the *word* of God or the *divine reason*: "And the Word (*logos*) became flesh and lived among us, and we have seen his glory, the glory as of a father's son, full of grace and truth" (John 1:14). In the short space of about seventy years Jesus' divine Sonship was pushed backward in time from his exaltation (in Paul and Acts), to his baptism (in Mark), to his birth (in Matthew and Luke), to a time before creation (in John).

In the course of this chapter I have shown how early Christian tradition regarding the events surrounding the life, death, and exaltation of Jesus of Nazareth was informed not only by historic memory, but perhaps more importantly by the church's searching diligently through the Hebrew scriptures to find passages or "proof-texts" that might impart meaning to a life that ended abruptly and apparently unexpectedly in a way that left Jesus' followers puzzled and disillusioned about the meaning of what had transpired. We are so accustomed to thinking of the cross as a symbol of Christianity that we usually fail to recognize the shame and disgrace associated with Jesus' ignominious execution.[62] Imagine instead that Jesus had been executed in an electric chair and that Christians today wore gold electric chairs rather than crosses around their necks, and you will then understand better the disgrace and ignominy associated with Jesus' death in the minds of his earliest disciples. It is no wonder that Jesus' followers had to search through the Hebrew scriptures to find some meaning in what otherwise seemed to be a meaningless event—no, rather a disgraceful event.

I have clearly not attempted to examine exhaustively all of the passages in the New Testament that were formulated or informed "according to the scriptures." I have looked at a few strategic and decisive passages, and in doing so I have touched only the surface of the subject. The Hebrew scriptures informed the church's teaching and writings regarding virtually every stage in Jesus' life and ministry, death and resurrection in the gospel tradition, and presumably also in the oral tradition and in the earliest written documents in the history of the church. Many of those early documents were lost, probably for all time: early Christian sayings collections, early Christian catechisms, one or more versions of a passion narrative that may have been composed originally for the celebration of a church liturgy during the week leading up to the celebration of Jesus' crucifixion and resurrection.

There can be no question that the primary purpose of the Gospels was *not* to record what we would consider objective history. There is nothing objective or detached about the Gospels. They do not pretend to be history, as we understand that word; they are rather confessional compositions; they are proclamation. The Gospel of Mark begins with the words: "The beginning of the good news of Jesus Christ." The word translated here as "good news" is the Greek word *euangelion* or "gospel." For the earliest Christian communities the *gospel* was the *good news* that was preached first orally and then later written in books to proclaim that Jesus is the Messiah, the Son of God, the Lord. As the Gospel of John so appropriately states, the Gospels were written that "you might believe that Jesus is the Messiah, the Son of God, and that through believing you might have life in his name" (John 20:21).

If Christian stories about the life and ministry of Jesus have been so colored by the beliefs of the early church and so colored by a Christian reading of the Hebrew scriptures, how then can we know anything about Jesus of Nazareth? It is to that difficult task that we now direct our attention.

---

62. See in this regard Deuteronomy 21:22–23: "When someone is convicted of a crime punishable by death and is executed, and you hang him on a tree, his corpse must not remain all night upon the tree; you shall bury him that same day, for *anyone hung on a tree is under God's curse*. You must not defile the land that the LORD your God is giving you for possession" (italics mine).

Chapter 6
JESUS OF NAZARETH

*J*esus occupies a central role in Christianity. It is that focus on Jesus that clearly distinguishes Christianity from the other monotheistic religions. Jews, Christians, and Muslims appear, at least on the surface, to worship the same God. Although Jesus is an important prophet in Islam, he is, of course, just one more prophet leading up to the final revelation by God to Mohammed, the last and most important of God's prophets. Jesus occupies no role whatsoever in Judaism, although he is mentioned briefly in the Talmud.

Jesus also plays no role in the great religions of Asia: Hinduism, Buddhism, Taoism, Confucianism, and Shinto. Those religions were well established before the first European Christian missionaries traveled to Asia to proselytize.

The Councils of Nicaea (325), Constantinople (381), Ephesus (431), and Chalcedon (451) together define the place of Jesus in orthodox Christianity. The statements of these councils produced the major statements of faith regarding Jesus in Roman Catholic, Protestant, and Eastern Orthodox Christianity. The dogmatic decree of the Council of Chalcedon states this position as follows: "We teach . . . one and the same Christ, Son, Lord, Only-begotten, known in two natures, without confusion, without change, without division, without separation."

In other words, Jesus is the Messiah of Israel, the divine Son of God, who is of one substance with the Father. Jesus is wholly God and wholly human. He is the Deliverer, the Savior, and a whole host of other titles that define his role as the mediator between humanity and God the Father (who is, in fact, Jesus' own father). Jesus is the incarnation of the divine Logos, the Word of God. He is Holy Widsom.

These claims of traditional orthodox Christianity are the very essence of what we need to examine and question in light of the contributions of the Renaissance and the Enlightenment. If the quest for God is a serious problem in the twenty-first century, then so, too, is the quest for the Jesus of history, the Jesus devoid of the myth and legend of two thousand years of excessive Christian piety. Can we reach back through the sources to recover the Jesus of Nazareth who walked the Galilee and preached briefly around 30 CE? Can we retrieve the man free from the overlay imposed by the first Christians and the series of additional overlays imposed upon him by Christian theologians at the councils of the church and throughout the ages? That is the challenge.

THE QUEST FOR THE HISTORICAL JESUS: THE SOURCES

Beginning with the pioneering work of Richard Simon in the seventeenth century and J. D. Michaelis in the eighteenth century, the spirit of the Enlightenment began to shine on the Bible. Serious historical inquiry into the life of Jesus began with Hermann Samuel Reimarus, who had accepted the principles of English Deism.

The presuppositions of any historical inquiry are crucial. Nineteenth-century Liberal Protestantism often focused on the ethical component of Jesus teaching even as it suppressed the supernatural element in the Gospels. David Friedrich Strauss' two-volume *Life of Jesus* (1835–36) recognized that the Gospels contained religious ideas in the form of story (or myth), only appearing to be history. Scholars began to recognize important differences between John and the synoptic Gospels and to work on solutions to the synoptic problem, establishing thereby the priority of Mark. Some scholars have even questioned whether Jesus ever existed.

The history of those early efforts to recover the Jesus of history is contained in detail in Albert Schweitzer's amazing classic *The Quest of the Historical Jesus*.[63] It may be worth quoting a portion of Schweitzer's conclusion:

> The Jesus of Nazareth who came forward publicly as the Messiah, who preached the ethic of the Kingdom of God, who founded the Kingdom of Heaven on earth, and died to give His work its final consecration, never had any existence. He is a figure designed by rationalism, endowed with life by liberalism, and clothed by modern theology in an historical garb. (398)

Schweitzer went on to say that the failure of the quest for the historical Jesus was that nineteenth-century historians ascribed their own thoughts and ideas to a Jesus of their own making. Rather, Schweitzer maintained, "The historical Jesus will be to our time a stranger and an enigma" (399). He recognized that the one clear thing about Jesus that had been overlooked by those who had tried to modernize him was the eschatological character of his preaching. Following the lead of Johannes Weiss' *Proclamation of the Kingdom of God* (1892),[64] Schweitzer recognized that

---

63. Albert Schweitzer, *Von Reimarus zu Wrede* [from Reimarus to Wrede] (1906), English translation by W. Montgomery (1910), *The Quest of the Historical Jesus*, with a new introduction by James M. Robinson (Macmillan Company, 1968).

64. Johannes Weiss, *Die Predigt Jesu vom Reiche Gottes* [*The Proclamation of the Kingdom of God*] (Göttingen, 1892; second revised and enlarged edition, 1900); Eng. Translation, Mifflintown, PA: Sigler Press, 1999.

Jesus had been conditioned by first-century Jewish expectations about the end of history and the inauguration of the new age of God's rule. Jesus was, not surprisingly, a first-century Jew.

Schweitzer's exhaustive study effectively brought to a close the so-called original or old quest for the historical Jesus. However, biblical criticism has come of age, and there is less of a tendency today, at least in professional scholarly circles, to project into the Jesus of the Gospels the thoughts and ideas of this generation.

It has been clear to scholars for a long time that we know about Jesus of Nazareth only from the ancient sources that tell us about him, but scholars have not always understood how to read these ancient sources with a critical eye. To reconstruct the life of any person who lived long ago, historians have had to devise, develop, and refine criteria to sort out what we can and cannot know about the past. In recent decades we have learned to ask the right questions and to ask them better.

1. Ideally, we should examine sources that come from a time as close as possible to the events themselves; early sources are presumably less likely to have been influenced by myth and legend.
2. We should also look for several sources that were produced independently of one another in order to be in a position to compare the testimony of different individuals.
3. We would obviously hope that our sources would not seriously contradict one another and that they would be internally consistent.
4. Ideally, our sources should be unbiased, and our authors should have no vested interest in the subject matter at hand.[65]

Think of a court of law, and think of a prosecuting attorney or a defense lawyer questioning key witnesses. The credibility of the witnesses is critical for convincing an impartial jury. The historian is no different as he or she examines the evidence, the data, and is involved, so to speak, in the process of examination and cross-examination of the ancient witnesses.

It generally surprises Christians to learn that we know virtually nothing about Jesus from early non-Christian sources. Jesus himself had little impact on his own generation or on the generation immediately following him. His direct impact on both Jewish and Roman society was insignificant. In 112 CE Pliny the Younger, the Roman governor of Bithynia-Pontus, provided us with the earliest pagan reference to Jesus. Writing about eighty years after Jesus' death, Pliny mentioned that Jesus was worshiped by his followers as a god. Pliny was actually not interested in Jesus, but the governor was very concerned about what Emperor Trajan would have him do about the Christians who were living in his province.

---

65. Of course, it is unrealistic to expect our ancient gospels to be objective and to have no vested interest in the subject, but that is the very problem we face in using the canonical gospels as the only real sources for a reconstruction of the life and ministry of Jesus.

A few years later, the Roman historian Seutonius reported about riots in Rome during the reign of Emperor Claudius (41–54 CE). Seutonius noted that these riots were instigated by a certain "Chrestos." Did he mean "Christ"? That is not clear. And, if Seutonius did mean Christ, then he was mistaken, because Jesus was already dead some twenty years before the riots. Perhaps he was referring to Jesus' followers, the Christians, but that, too, is unclear.

About the same time (115 CE) the Roman historian Tacitus identified Christianity as a "superstition," meaning a religion that was not sanctioned by the established religion of the Roman Empire. Tacitus reports that when Nero burned Rome, he blamed the Christians for having started the fire and used them as scapegoats. In spite of this morsel of probable misinformation, we do, nevertheless, find in Tacitus the first piece of historical information about Jesus from a non-Christian writer: "Christus, from whom the Christians derive their name, was executed during the reign of Tiberius at the hands of one of our procurators, Pontius Pilate."

These three men, Pliny the Younger, Seutonius, and Tacitus, provide the only references to Jesus in pagan writings from the century following his death. The testimony is meager, unreliable, and basically useless, except for the fact that it confirms that there was a man named Jesus of Nazareth who had a following some eighty years after his death. We learn from them absolutely nothing about what Jesus taught and did, only that he was executed under Pontius Pilate. We do not even learn the reason for Jesus' execution.

The situation is not much different when we look into contemporary Jewish literature. During the century following Jesus' death, there is only one Jewish writer who made any mention of him. In book 18 of *The Antiquities of the Jews*, the historian Josephus wrote:

> At this time there appeared Jesus, a wise man, *if indeed one should call him a man.* For he was a doer of startling deeds, a teacher of people who receive the truth with pleasure. And he gained a following both among many Jews and among many of Greek origin. *He was the Messiah.* And when Pilate, because of an accusation made by the leading men among us, condemned him to the cross, those who loved him previously did not cease to do so. *For he appeared to them on the third day, living again, just as the divine prophets had spoken of these and countless other wonders about him.* And up until this very day the tribe of Christians, named after him, has not died out (*Antiquities* 18.3.3).

When we realize that Josephus was a devout Jew and that he never converted to Christianity, we need to be suspicious about the authenticity of his testimony, especially with respect to the words printed above in italics. These words sound like the testimony of a believer. When we understand that it was Christians, and not Jews, who copied and preserved Josephus' writings through the ages, it is increasingly clear that a Christian scribe probably added these confessional words to the work of Josephus. They make no sense coming from the pen of Josephus. Accordingly, Josephus has little value as an independent source for a reconstruction of the life and ministry of Jesus of Nazareth, except for the words printed above in nonitalics, which may be original.[66]

When we turn to Christian sources outside the canonical New Testament, the situation is no better. The noncanonical gospels are of questionable value. The sayings Gospel of Thomas may afford us some independent insight into Jesus' teaching, but that is by no means clear. Scholars disagree as to whether the author of Thomas was early and independent of the canonical gospels, or whether he, in fact, knew and used the canonical gospels as sources for his gospel. Some scholars have also argued for an early date for the Gospel of Peter, but that, too, is unclear. It is by no means apparent that these extracanonical sources are independent witnesses.

Much to the surprise of students of the New Testament, Paul, the earliest Christian writer, is also of little help in reconstructing the life and ministry of Jesus. We glean the following information from Paul: Jesus was "born of a woman" (Galatians 4:4); he was "born under the law," meaning he was born a Jew (Galatians 4:4). Jesus had "brothers" (1 Corinthians 9:5), one of whom was named "James" (Galatians 1:19). He had "twelve" disciples (1 Corinthians 15:5). He instituted the Lord's Supper (1 Corinthians 11:23–25). Jesus "was betrayed" (1 Corinthians 11:23), although the Greek word in this verse may mean "was handed over." And Jesus was "crucified" (1 Corinthians 2:2). As for Jesus' teaching, Paul provides little detail: Christians should not get divorced (1 Corinthians 7:10–11) and should pay preachers of the gospel (1 Corinthians 9:14). Apart from these few passages, Paul tells us virtually nothing about the life, ministry, and teachings of Jesus of Nazareth. If Paul's letters were the only available source in our effort to write a life of Jesus, we might be able to come up with one short paragraph, and even that paragraph would be trite in its detail.

Apart from the writers of the four canonical gospels, other New Testament authors tell us even less. In other words, we have little choice but to turn to the Gospels of Matthew, Mark, Luke, and John to begin the task of learning about the life and ministry of Jesus. In acknowledging that, we must be extremely careful in the way in which we use these gospels. They frankly meet none of the criteria we identified as essential for a reconstruction of the life of any figure from antiquity.

1. The Gospels do not come from a time close to the life and ministry of Jesus. Jesus died around 30 CE; the Gospels were probably written sometime between about 67 and 90 CE, forty to sixty years or two to three generations following Jesus' death.

2. Neither were the Gospels produced independently. As we have already seen, at least three of the four Gospels—Matthew, Mark, and Luke—show a clear literary relationship, with Matthew and Luke likely to have made direct use of Mark. In addition, the Gospel of John presents serious prob-

---

66. That, indeed, is the thesis of John Meier, *A Marginal Jew: Rethinking the Historical Jesus*, vol. 1 (New York: Doubleday, 1991), p. 61.

lems of its own and cannot be regarded as a credible source for historical investigation.

3. The four Gospels show a great deal of inconsistency in their portrayal of Jesus. There are serious differences between the Gospel of John and the synoptic Gospels; there are serious differences among the synoptic Gospels; and there are even serious internal inconsistencies within individual gospels.

4. Clearly our sources are *not* unbiased and make no claim to be. The Gospel of John was clearest when the author wrote in 20:31: "These [things] are written that you may come to believe that Jesus is the Messiah, the Son of God, and that through believing you may have life in his name." The gospels are admittedly and unashamedly Christian propaganda. They were written by Christians for Christians to propagate Christianity.

How then can documents whose purpose was religious rather than historical, that were written to propagate the faith rather than to present a historical account of Jesus of Nazareth, serve as sources for reconstructing the life and ministry of Jesus? This is a pressing problem. For without the canonical gospels, we have nothing.

THE QUEST FOR THE HISTORICAL JESUS: THE CRITERIA

We have already identified some of the methodologies used in biblical studies, and these tools provide the foundation for all historical investigation of the Gospels. In addition, scholars have devised several criteria to assist in the effort to determine what in the Gospels is historical and, therefore, what likely happened during the course of the life and ministry of Jesus. More specifically, what exactly did Jesus teach his followers? The following criteria have emerged as being useful in any such investigation.

Dissimilarity. A saying of Jesus or a tradition about Jesus in the Gospels that does not reflect the teachings of the early Christian church has a greater claim to historicity than a saying or tradition that merely mirrors the church's preaching.[67] Such a saying or tradition would not likely have been fabricated by the church. Why, after all, would the church preserve a saying of Jesus or a story about Jesus that contradicts the church's teaching unless that saying or teaching was otherwise genuine? Although this criterion has its limitations, it is a useful tool for assisting scholars in distinguishing between the teaching *of* Jesus and the early church's teaching *about* Jesus. Scholars call this tool the criterion of dissimilarity.

Multiple Attestation. For any testimony to be considered credible, it should be attested by several independent witnesses. In a court of law, the testimony of just one

---

67. The previous chapter "According to the Scriptures," makes it eminently clear why scholars are suspicious of material in the Gospels that suits the theological interests of the early church. The criterion of dissimilarity is a reasonable response to the dilemma.

witness, without additional collaborating evidence, is obviously less compelling than the testimony of many witnesses. In the case of the gospel tradition, we do, in fact, have multiple independent witnesses. I do not, of course, mean the Gospels of Matthew, Mark, Luke, and John, because two of the gospels are not independent witnesses: the Gospels of Matthew and Luke copied freely from the Gospel of Mark. I refer, rather, to the independent witnesses L, Q, Mark, and M, as illustrated in the chart below:

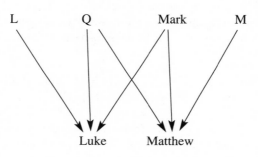

The diagram illustrates that Luke and Matthew are not independent witnesses. However, if a saying of Jesus is found in two or more of the four truly independent witnesses (the Gospel of Mark, and the three hypothetical sources apparently used by Matthew and Luke, namely Q [the sayings source common to both Matthew and Luke], M [special Matthean material], and L [special Lukan material]), there is a greater likelihood that the saying reaches back to the historical Jesus, or at least to the earliest stage in the development of oral tradition about Jesus. Scholars call this the criterion of multiple attestation or independent attestation.

Contextual Credibility. Documents must be consistent with the political, social, religious, and historical contexts to which they belong. This means that any reconstruction of the life and ministry of Jesus must fit and conform to the situation in first-century Palestine. Jesus was first and foremost a Galilean Jew. He conducted his ministry in Roman Palestine for a brief period around 30 CE. Scholars must, therefore, make every possible effort to set Jesus within the context of his own time and place. Tradition that sets Jesus in a different context has less claim to authenticity. Accordingly, much of the subject matter of the Gospel of John fails to conform to this criterion. Scholars call this the criterion of contextual credibility.

Aramaisms. Inasmuch as Jesus and his disciples spoke Aramaic as their mother tongue, sayings tradition that reflects, exhibits, or displays Aramaic or Semitic qualities or tendencies has a greater claim to authenticity than material that makes sense only in Greek. Although this criterion does not necessarily lead us directly to Jesus, it may minimally take us back to Jesus' earliest followers, who also spoke Aramaic. Scholars call this the criterion of Aramaisms or Semitisms.

Coherence. A sayings or teaching of Jesus that is similar to material whose reliability has already been established by one or more of the other criteria may be considered reliable because it is consistent with other presumably authentic material. Scholars call this the criterion of coherence.

In using these criteria, it is essential to admit that the historian of the New Testament can do no more than establish probabilities in reconstructing what Jesus may have said and what may actually have happened during the course of Jesus' life and ministry. Historical criticism is not an exact science with mathematical proofs and absolute certainty. It is impossible to authenticate the past with total confidence. Nevertheless, by employing these criteria, scholars are beginning to gain a better glimpse into the life, ministry, and teaching of Jesus of Nazareth.

THE QUEST FOR THE HISTORICAL JESUS: A NEW LOOK AT SOME OLD TEXTS

I propose in this section to look at a few passages in the synoptic Gospels (Matthew, Mark, and Luke) to show how the above-mentioned criteria for authenticity can be applied to gospel traditions in a way that affords us meaningful insight into the teachings of the historical Jesus.

1. An Example from Mark. The first of the passages I propose to examine is a cluster of sayings in Mark 8:34–9:1:[68]

> 8:34He called the crowd with his disciples, and said to them, "If any want to become my followers, let them deny themselves and take up their cross and follow me. 35For those who want to save their life will lose it, and those who lose their life for my sake, and for the sake of the gospel, will save it. 36For what will it profit them to gain the whole world and forfeit their life? 37Indeed, what can they give in return for their life? 38Those who are ashamed of me and of my words in this adulterous and sinful generation, of them the Son of Man will also be ashamed when he comes in the glory of his Father with the holy angels." 9:1And he said to them, "Truly I tell you, there are some standing here who will not taste death until they see the kingdom of God has come with power."

This passage contains five or possibly six independent sayings that relate to the theme of personal sacrifice and loyalty to Jesus. These sayings have been collected into one place by the author of the Gospel of Mark, or more probably by an earlier

---

68. This material in Mark 8:34–9:1 is part of the triple tradition and was incorporated into Matthew 16:24–28 and into Luke 9:23–27. The saying in Mark 8:35 (= Matthew 10:25 and Luke 9:24) is found also in the hypothetical source Q (= Matthew 10:39 and Luke 17:33), which will be examined later in this chapter. This saying is also found in a slightly modified, but typically Johannine form in John 12:25. In addition, the saying in Mark 8:38 (= Matthew 10:27 and Luke 9:26) is found also in the source Q (= Matthew 10:32–33 and Luke 12:8–9), which will also be examined later in this chapter.

author whose collection of these sayings was known to and used by the author of the Gospel of Mark. Let us examine the sayings individually and see what results when we apply to them the criteria for authenticity.

Mark 8:34. The saying in verse 34 poses some interesting problems: "He called the crowd with his disciples, and said to them, 'If any want to become my followers, let them deny themselves and take up their cross and follow me.'" In this saying, the words "take up their cross" fail the criterion of dissimilarity. In this form the saying clearly reveals the church looking back at Jesus' crucifixion from its vantage point, and likely reflects the church's understanding of the Crucifixion as the saving event of early Christian preaching.

There may, however, be no need to discard the entire saying as unauthentic. Eliminating only those words that fail the test of dissimilarity may be sufficient. The resultant saying would be, "If any want to become my followers, let them deny themselves and follow me." In this form the saying may, indeed, reflect a genuine call by Jesus to his disciples to follow a life of denial of the material values of this world in preparation for the future time of God's rule. This simpler form of the saying has more balance than the version with the added offending words "take up their cross":

> If any want to become my followers,
> let them deny themselves and follow me.

"Any" in the first line is balanced by "them" in the second line. "Want to become" is balanced by "deny themselves," and "my followers" is balanced by "follow me." This kind of parallelism is a common feature of Hebrew poetry and is evident throughout the Old Testament, as well as in many of the passages from the Old Testament quoted in the previous chapter. In this case, we have what scholars call synthetic parallelism; the second line repeats and reinforces the substance of the first line. The saying in this amended form meets the criterion of Aramaisms or Semitisms, meaning that Jesus could definitely have spoken these words to his followers in Aramaic. The fact that a saying that fails the criterion of dissimilarity can, with only minor revisions, satisfy the criterion of Aramaisms both validates the amended form of the saying and corroborates the methodology that scholars have devised to address the matter of authenticity.

Mark 8:35. The second saying, which appears in verse 35, poses a number of interesting problems: "For those who want to save their life will lose it, and those who lose their life for my sake, and for the sake of the gospel, will save it." In this saying in Mark, two phrases fail the criterion of dissimilarity: "for my sake" and "and for the sake of the gospel." "For my sake" clearly implies the church's belief in Jesus' special role as the messenger of God, the savior;[69] whoever dies for Jesus'

---

69. It is also worth noting that the phrase "for my sake" does not appear in several ancient manuscripts, raising the question of whether it actually appeared in the autograph of Mark or was added by a later scribe.

sake will save his own life. That phrase echoes early Christian preaching. The same is also true of the phrase "and for the sake of the gospel." The "gospel" was the "good news," the preached message of the early Christian community. When these two offending phrases are removed, we have the following couplet:

> For those who want to save their life will lose it,
> and those who lose their life will save it.

Once again the two lines balance each other:

> Those who save will lose,
> those who lose will save.

As was the case in the saying in verse 34, this parallelism is a feature of Hebrew poetry evident throughout the Old Testament. In this case, we have what scholars call antithetical parallelism; the second line states the opposite, the antithesis, of what is stated in the first line. The saying in the revised form meets the criterion of Aramaisms. Once again, the fact that a saying that initially failed the criterion of dissimilarity has, with minor modifications, met the criterion of Aramaisms speaks well for both the amended form of the saying and for the methodology that scholars have devised to address the issue of authenticity.

Mark 8:36–37. The saying or sayings in verses 36 and 37 are somewhat more enigmatic: "For what will it profit them to gain the whole world and forfeit their life?" "What can they give in return for their life?" Verse 36 is an example of what in the Old Testament is incomplete antithetical parallelism, meaning that (1) not every item in the first line is balanced by an item in the second line (hence, incomplete), and (2) the second line states the opposite, the antithesis, of what is stated in the first line:

> For what will it profit them to gain the whole world
> and forfeit their life?

"Gain the whole world" stands in contrast, in antithesis, to "forfeit their life." Once again, as in the sayings in verses 34 and 35, this parallelism is a feature of ancient Hebrew poetry and is found throughout the Old Testament. The saying in its form in Mark 8:36, therefore, meets the criterion of "Aramaisms" and may, indeed, be authentic.

The saying in verse 37 is more problematic: "What can they give in return for their life?" This saying may just be a Markan gloss or an elaboration on verse 36. It adds little to the text and seems to just dangle with no meaningful connection to the other sayings.

Mark 8:38. The saying in verse 38 is particularly interesting: "Those who are ashamed of me and of my words in this adulterous and sinful generation, of them the Son of Man will also be ashamed when he comes in the glory of his Father with the holy angels." This saying appears to meet two of the criteria: the criterion of Aramaisms and the criterion of dissimilarity. Once again we have two lines in parallel, a feature of Hebrew poetry:

| Those who | are ashamed of me and of my words | in this adulterous and sinful generation, |
| the Son of Man | will also be ashamed of them | when he comes (in the glory of his Father with the holy angels). |

I have shifted the order of the words "of them" in the English translation to illustrate more clearly the parallelism between the two lines and to show what might have been the form of the saying in the Aramaic original. The dissimilarity in this verse is evident in the fact that Jesus is speaking not of himself in the second line when he uses the words "Son of Man," but rather of someone else, presumably the eschatological Son of Man known from contemporary Jewish literature. Jesus is clearly announcing, as did others of his generation, the imminent arrival of the end of history and the inauguration of God's rule, which would be ushered in by God's messenger, "the Son of Man." This saying also meets the criterion of contextual credibility. It is very likely an authentic saying of Jesus on the basis of fulfilling at least three criteria: Aramaisms, dissimilarity, and contextual credibility.

The final words of this saying, "in the glory of his Father with the holy angels," may be a Christian interpolation into the text. In fact, the saying may have survived largely intact because, following Jesus' death, early Christians interpreted the saying in light of their belief that Jesus would, within their lifetimes, return in glory as the eschatological Son of Man. Efforts to deny that Jesus is referring in this saying to someone other than himself are theologically motivated and not based on the evidence. The meaning of the passage is quite clear: Jesus expected the imminent arrival of the eschatological Son of Man.

Mark 9:1. The saying in Mark 9:1 is also very interesting: "Truly I tell you, there are some standing here who will not taste death until they see the kingdom of God has come with power." This saying clearly meets the criterion of contextual credibility, and it coheres with the previous saying in Mark 8:38. The imminent arrival of God's rule will take place during the lifetime of some who are listening to Jesus' teaching. The fact that the end did not come, as Jesus predicted, is testimony to the saying's dissimilarity with popular early Christian teaching.

Following Jesus' death the church began to proclaim that Jesus had been raised from the dead and exalted to God's right hand and that it was, in fact, he who would return as the supernatural Son of Man to usher in the age of God's rule.

Summary of Mark 8:34–9:1. During the period of early oral tradition, followers of Jesus apparently remembered these five independent sayings separately until someone likely grouped them into this cluster because of their similar content. The original form of this written cluster of sayings may have looked something like this:

If any want to become my followers,
let them deny themselves and follow me.

Those who want to save their life will lose it,
and those who lose their life will save it.

What will it profit them to gain the whole world
and forfeit their life?

Those who are ashamed of me and of my words in this adulterous and sinful generation, the Son of Man will also be ashamed of them when he comes.

Truly I tell you, there are some standing here who will not taste death
until they see the kingdom of God has come with power.

This may have been the form of five authentic sayings of Jesus collected into a
written source that was available to the author of the Gospel of Mark. The sayings
in this form are dissimilar from the preached message of the early church, which is
to say they meet the criterion of dissimilarity. They reflect a clear familiarity with
ancient Hebrew poetry and must have taken form either in the teaching of Jesus or
possibly in the very earliest period of the Aramaic-speaking church, long before
Jesus' teaching was stripped of its original Semitic form and transformed for a
Greek-speaking, Greek-thinking audience.

The sayings fit nicely into the context of first-century Judaism, and they cohere;
that is, they afford a single consistent picture of what Jesus probably preached.
These sayings also meet the criterion of multiple attestation because they are similar
in form and in content to apparently authentic sayings of Jesus from other independent sources, as we shall see below.

From this analysis of this cluster of five sayings, there emerges a picture of
Jesus as an eschatological prophet who preached the imminent end of history and
the coming of the Son of Man, who would soon usher in God's rule. These events
would transpire within the lifetime of many of those who were listening to Jesus'
message. To prepare for these impending events, Jesus called upon his followers to
renounce the values of this world and to live their lives as if God's rule had, indeed,
already arrived. Jesus may have believed that he was already setting the process in
motion through his teaching and his action.

2. Examples from Q. Let us turn now to two sayings from the Q source and
examine them using the same criteria. The reader is reminded that Q was apparently
a written sayings source available to Matthew and Luke, but not to the author of the
Gospel of Mark. The first of these Q passages is found in Matthew 10:32–33 and
Luke 12:8–9, the other in Matthew 10:39 and Luke 17:33.

Q (Matthew 10:32–33 = Luke 12:8–9)

Matthew 10:32–33

Luke 12:8–9

	And I tell you,
Everyone who acknowledges me	everyone who acknowledges me
before others,	before others,
I will also acknowledge	the Son of Man will also acknowledge
before my Father in heaven;	before the angels of God;
but whoever denies me	but whoever denies me
before others,	before others
I will also deny	will be denied
before my Father in heaven.	before the angels of God.

total # words in Matthew: 30	total # words in Luke: 32 (excluding intro)
# words in Matthew underlined: 19	# words in Luke underlined: 19
% words in Matthew underlined: 63%	% words in Luke underlined: 59%

The agreement between Matthew and Luke in this Q passage is very high, 63% in Matthew and 59% in Luke.[70] The only significant difference between the two texts is the first person "I" in Matthew where Luke has the third-person "the Son of Man," and "my Father in heaven," which appears twice in Matthew, where Luke has in both instances "the angels of God." These differences are, however, significant. Was Jesus at the center of his own teaching, as Matthew's text clearly indicates, or was Jesus rather pointing to the coming of someone other than himself, "the Son of Man," as Luke's text unmistakably implies? With regard to this saying, does Matthew or Luke follow more closely the wording of the hypothetical Q, their common written source?

Applying the criterion of dissimilarity, it is evident that Luke preserves the more original version of this saying and that the author of the Gospel of Matthew has changed the words of Q in order to have Jesus point not to someone other than himself, the Son of Man, as the intermediary between God and man, but rather to have Jesus point indisputably to himself as God's intermediary. It is easy to explain why Matthew would have changed the Q source, if Luke's version is more original; it is far more difficult, in fact virtually impossible, to explain why Luke would have modified Q, if Matthew's text preserves the original wording. Hence, we have here a Q saying for which Luke preserves the more original wording. In fact, Luke may have preserved Q unchanged, given the fact that Matthew supports 63% of the words in Luke.

---

70. We have done our calculations based on the text of the New Revised Standard Version of the Bible in English, hence our calculations are only approximate, although not unreasonable. Ideally, the comparisons should be made by using the Greek texts of the Gospels, not English translations.

The poetic parallelism of this Q passage is evident in the literary form of the saying, as printed below. The criterion of Aramaisms is, therefore, also satisfied.

Everyone who	acknowledges me	before others,
the Son of Man	will also acknowledge	before the angels of God;
but	whoever denies me	before others
	will be denied	before the angels of God.

Not only are the criteria of dissimilarity and Semitisms satisfied by this examination and interpretation of the data, but we now have a saying that likely satisfies all five criteria for authenticity: multiple attestation (Mark and Q), dissimilarity (Jesus points to someone other than himself as the Son of Man), contextual credibility (the Son of Man was a well-known figure in first-century Jewish apocalyptic circles), Aramaisms (the passage reflects the form of ancient Hebrew poetry), and coherence (the message of this saying is very much like the message in the collection of sayings in Mark 8:34–9:1 that we examined above).

Q (Matthew 10:39 = Luke 17:33)

Matthew 10:39

Those who find their life
will lose it,
and those who lose their life for my sake
will find it.

total # words in Matthew: 20
words in Matthew underlined: 14
% words in Matthew underlined: 70%

Luke 17:33

Those who try to make their life secure
will lose it,
but those who lose their life
will keep it.

total # words in Luke: 20
words in Luke underlined: 14
% words in Luke underlined: 70%

The agreement between Matthew and Luke in this Q passage is very high, 70% in both gospels. The differences between the two gospels is largely editorial: "find" in Matthew for "try to make secure" in Luke; "and" in Matthew for "but" in Luke; and "find" again in Matthew for "keep" in Luke. The words "for my sake" in Matthew once again destroy the poetic parallelism and are likely an addition, just as they were in Mark 8:35. These words fail to satisfy the criterion of dissimilarity. The fact that the phrase "for my sake" occurs in both Mark 8:35 and Matthew 10:39 may indicate that the phrase was in Q and that Luke eliminated it, but it is certainly not original to the earliest form of the saying as originally spoken by Jesus. The words "find," "lose," "lose," and "find" in Matthew reflect much better the probable poetic structure of the original. Luke's changes in the verbs in lines 1 and 4 destroy the poetic balance. I am inclined to propose the following as the version of this saying that was most likely in Q:

Those who find their life will lose it,
but those who lose their life will find it.

3. Examples Found in Both Mark and Q. When we compare the versions of the sayings discussed above that appear in both Mark and Q, it is not entirely sure what lies behind these two versions:

Q (of Matthew 10:32–33 and Luke 12:8–9) and Mark 8:38

<u>Q of Matthew 10:32–33 and Luke 12:8–9:</u>	<u>Mark 8:38:</u>
Everyone <u>who</u> acknowledges me before others, <u>the Son of Man</u> will also acknowledge before the angels of God; but whoever denies me before others	Those <u>who</u>
	are ashamed of me and of my words
	in this adulterous and sinful generation,
of them <u>the Son of Man</u> <u>will</u> be denied	<u>will</u> also be ashamed when he comes in the glory of his Father
before <u>the angels</u> of God.	with <u>the</u> holy <u>angels</u>.
total # words in Q: 32 words underlined in Q: 8 % words underlined in Q: 25%	total # words in Mark: 39 words underlined in Mark: 8 % words underlined in Mark: 21%

The incidence of verbal agreement is not sufficient to prove that these are actually two versions of the same saying, although one could probably make that case. The saying in Q has two parts in parallel balance; the saying in Mark parallels only the second part of the Q saying. However, the appearance of "Everyone who" in the first portion of Q and of "Those who" in Mark, as well as the appearance of "the Son of Man" in the first portion of Q and in Mark, would enable us to reconstruct a single version that combines portions of both, such as:

Those who acknowledge me before others,
the Son of Man will also acknowledge before the angels of God;
but those who deny me before others
will be denied before the angels of God.

Although possible, this reconstruction is highly speculative and proves very little. What is clear is that we have two very similar accounts of a saying, both versions of which have strong independent claims to authenticity. There are three possible explanations of the data: (1) either the two versions (Mark and Q) stem from a single saying in oral or written form; (2) they are two distinct and independent sayings, both of which were remembered in the oral tradition; or (3) Jesus' sayings were not always remembered verbatim, hence the variation in the two forms.

There is something to be said for all three explanations. First, even if the essence of Jesus' teaching was remembered by his followers, no one was taking stenographic notes when Jesus spoke. Repeating the tradition during the period of oral transmission obviously resulted in both accidental and deliberate changes to what Jesus actually said. Second, Jesus probably had a consistent message, but he would not necessarily use exactly the same words every time he delivered that message. The differences between the saying in Mark and the saying in Q may reflect quite accurately two distinct versions of the teaching delivered by Jesus. Third, maybe few or none of the so-called sayings of Jesus in the synoptic Gospels report verbatim what Jesus actually said. I suspect that there is some truth to all three explanations, but we cannot be sure which addresses best this particular saying tradition in Mark and Q.

We will never know definitively whether this is one or two sayings. We will never know exactly how much the saying has suffered in transmission. We will never know exactly what reflects accurately the words that Jesus actually spoke and what was changed by the early church during the period of oral and written transmission. Nevertheless, I do believe that we can be confident that the substance of the saying(s) is an authentic teaching of Jesus, because it meets several of the criteria for authenticity identified above.

Q (Matthew 10:30 and Luke 17:33) and Mark 8:35

Q (Matthew 10:39 and Luke 17:33)   ## Mark 8:35

Those who try to make their life secure will lose it, but those who lose their life will keep it.	For those who want to save their life will lose it, and those who lose their life will save it.
total # words in Q: 20	total # words in Mark: 20
total # words underlined in Q: 15	total # words underlined in Mark: 15
% words underlined in Q: 75%	% words underlined in Mark: 75%

The verbal agreement between the Q version of this saying and the version in Mark is very strong: 75 percent. The parallelism in Mark—*save, lose, lose, save*—seems more balanced and more poetic than Q's *make secure, lose, lose, keep*. The Markan form of this saying is certainly more original, because it resembles more closely the literary form of ancient Semitic poetry.

4. An Example from John. Very similar to this saying in Mark and Q is a saying in the Gospel of John 12:25:

Those who love their life
lose it,
and those who hate their life in this world
will keep it for eternal life.

The form of this saying in John is quite similar to the synoptic versions, the major difference being the addition of the words "in this world" in the third line and the typically Johannine phrase "for eternal life" in the fourth line.[71] Apart from this characteristically Johannine expression, we have in John the same saying that we have examined already in Mark and in Q. We, therefore, have multiple attestation for this saying in three independent sources: Mark, Q, and John.

The pre-Johannine version of this saying may have read:

Those who love their life
(will) lose it,
and those who hate their life
will keep it.

Notice once again the formal structure of what may be the original parallelism of the Aramaic poetry that likely underlies the Johannine version of this popular saying.

5. Miscellaneous Sayings. Other sayings of Jesus in the synoptic Gospels also reflect this representation of Jesus as an apocalyptic prophet. Among them are:

Mark 1:15: "The time has been fulfilled, the kingdom of God is near; repent and believe in this good news."

Mark 13:32–37: "But about that day or hour no one knows, neither the angels in heaven, nor the Son, but only the Father. Beware, keep alert; for you do not know when the time will come. It is like a man going on a journey, when he leaves his home and puts slaves in charge, each with his work, and commands the doorkeeper to be on watch. Therefore, keep awake—for you do not know when the master of the house will come, in the evening, or at midnight, or at cockcrow, or at dawn, or else he may find you asleep when he comes suddenly. And what I say to you I say to all: Keep awake."

Mark 13:26–27: "Then they will see the Son of Man coming in clouds with great power and glory. Then he will send out the angels, and gather his elect from the four winds, from the ends of the earth to the ends of heaven."

---

71. John uses the phrase "eternal life" nine times in his gospel: John 3:15; 4:36; 5:39; 6:54; 6:68; 10:28; 12:25; 17:2; 17:3. Matthew, Mark, and Luke together use the phrase only six times (Matthew 19:16; 25:46; Mark 10:17; 10:30; Luke 10:25; 18:18), and even then in passages that reflect Matthew and Luke's literary dependence on Mark.

This collection of passages is by no means exhaustive, but these passages do afford a clear and consistent representation that Jesus, devoid of the overlay of early Christian theology, was an apocalyptic prophet. In fact, Jesus' teaching strongly resembles the teaching of John the Baptist, who was Jesus' predecessor and perhaps his mentor. Many of the parables in the Gospels of Matthew, Mark, and Luke also reflect Jesus' teaching that God's rule was coming very soon, or that it was already growing and breaking into history whenever anyone does God's will.

Jesus' radical ethical teaching was likely grounded in his apocalyptic world-view. Jesus believed that the end of history, as we know it, was coming very soon and that his followers should prepare for this cataclysmic event by loving God unconditionally with their entire being and by loving their neighbors (meaning "everyone") as themselves. This appears to have been Jesus' single commandment, because for Jesus it was not possible to love God without loving one's neighbor.[72]

Jesus taught his followers that there should be no division, no discord, no hatred, no discrimination among people. Those who were rich should sell everything to support the poor. Unconditional love of humankind was more important than the command of the Mosaic Law to observe the Sabbath. Dietary laws were meaningless in the new order. God was not concerned about what food went into the body of a person but with what actions came from that person. Not only should Jesus' followers prepare themselves for the imminent judgment; they should also proclaim this message and this ethic to other people. The occasion for this radical ethic was Jesus' belief in the imminent arrival of God's rule, which would be ushered in by God's mediator, the eschatological Son of Man, who in Jesus' teaching was clearly someone other than himself.

There is nothing in the authentic sayings tradition to support the idea that Jesus was ever the subject of his own teaching. That position is a perversion of early Christianity and most particularly of the Gospel of John. It is difficult to know exactly what Jesus thought his role was in the unfolding eschatological drama. He likely understood himself to be the final precursor of the Son of Man, a herald who would prepare the people for the arrival of God's final messenger, whose coming would signify the end of history, as we know it, and the arrival of the new age of God's eternal rule.

Not only Jesus' words, but also his actions suggest that he thought of himself as an eschatological prophet: his baptism by John the Baptist; his call of twelve disciples, likely representing the twelve tribes of Israel; his association with tax collectors, women, sinners, lepers, the outcasts of society; his ceremonial cleansing of the Temple shortly before his arrest and crucifixion; and perhaps even his apparently willing execution at the hands of the Jews and the Romans, thereby pronouncing his (and God's) judgment on the current religious and political order.

---

72. In a famous pericope in Mark 12:28–34 (= Matthew 22:34–40 and Luke 10:25–28), a scribe asked Jesus which is the greatest commandment. Jesus answered: the first is to love God, and the second is to love your neighbor. Jesus obviously understood that the two commandments could not be separated; they were, in fact, one commandment. His teaching consistently supports this conclusion.

Jesus lived his life as if God's rule had already arrived. Perhaps Jesus believed that he and his followers could thereby help to usher in the Age to Come, the new order of God's rule.

The Jesus painted here is a far cry from the Jesus of the Gospel of John, who said: "I am the bread of life" (6:35); "I am the light of the world" (8:12; 9:5); "I am from above" (8:23); "I am the gate" (10:9); "I am the good shepherd" (10:11, 14); "I am the resurrection and the life" (11:25); "I am the way, and the truth, and the life" (14:6). The Jesus of the Gospel of John is not Jesus of Nazareth. He is not the historical Jesus. He is rather a construct of the Christian church, a construct of the author of the Gospel of John, who bears little or no resemblance to the Jesus of history. Yet, it is this Jesus of the Gospel of John who has so dominated Christian theology down through the ages. It is time for Christians to retrieve and return to the Jesus of history and to determine how he might fit into a Christianity for the future. Christianity's ancient and long-standing misrepresentation of Jesus cannot and should not persist in the face of the truth about what kind of man Jesus actually was.

The canonical gospels themselves represent Jesus in rather different ways. In *The New Testament: A Historical Introduction to the Early Christian Writings*, Bart H. Ehrman appropriately titles his chapters on the Gospels accordingly:

"Jesus, The Suffering Son of God: The Gospel According to Mark";

"Jesus, the Jewish Messiah: The Gospel According to Matthew";

"Jesus, the Savior of the World: The Gospel According to Luke"; and

"Jesus, the Man Sent from Heaven: The Gospel According to John."

In doing so, Ehrman makes the point that what we have in the New Testament are not four independent testimonies regarding the life and ministry of the historical Jesus. Rather, we have in our four Gospels four distinct theological portraits that represent different ways in which early Christians understood Jesus. Other early Christian gospels painted still different portraits of Jesus, but the church rejected these writings and excluded them from its canon of the New Testament.[73]

What I have attempted to accomplish in this chapter is to reach behind the early church's various portraits of Jesus, using the criteria of historicity in an attempt to gain a clearer picture of what kind of person Jesus actually was. We cannot be sure of every detail in the portrait of Jesus of Nazareth that we have painted, but we can, I believe, be confident that our construct reflects a far clearer portrait of the historical Jesus than do any of the surreal portraits painted in our canonical gospels.

What can we conclude about the historical Jesus and about the Gospels from this review?

---

73. These so-called apocryphal gospels include three Jewish-Christian gospels, the Gospel of the Nazareans, the Gospel of the Ebionites, and the Gospel of the Hebrews; also the Gospel of Peter, the Gospel of Thomas, the Infancy Gospel of Thomas, and many others. Like our canonical gospels, the noncanonical gospels portrayed Jesus in ways that were consistent with the views of the communities that generated these gospels. In every instance, we probably learn more about the community that produced the gospel than about Jesus himself, a dilemma shared by canonical and noncanonical gospels alike. To deny so is to deny reality.

1. The Gospels seldom, if ever, provide us with the exact words of Jesus. They provide us with the testimonies of the second and third generations of Christians who received from earlier generations both oral and written traditions that were already influenced and conditioned by the beliefs, needs, and prejudices of nascent churches.

2. Only though a rigorous critical examination of Jesus' alleged words, using all of the best tools of historical analysis, can we hope to understand what Jesus likely said and did in the course of his ministry. It is difficult but not impossible to move from the Gospels to Jesus, using the finest and sharpest tools of historical criticism. The task is challenging, but possible, and the results are sometimes even promising.

3. Critical study of the evidence suggests that Jesus of Nazareth expected the imminent arrival of a supernatural figure, whom he and others of his time referred to as the Son of Man (or the Man), an angelic figure who would come riding on the clouds of heaven to usher in the new order of God's rule, what the Gospels sometime refer to as the Kingdom of God. Jesus was apparently an apocalyptic prophet who understood that he was the final precursor of that angelic Son of Man, and, as such, the messenger of a radical ethic that demands unconditional love of God and of one's fellow human beings in preparation for the arrival of the age of God's rule.[74]

4. This historical reconstruction is supported by all of the criteria established at the outset of this chapter: the criteria of dissimilarity, multiple independent attestation, contextual credibility, Aramaisms, and coherence.

5. Anyone who approaches the Gospels uncritically and expects to know exactly what Jesus said on any specific issue by citing individual Bible passages is involved in a futile exercise in self-delusion. Evangelical biblical fundamentalism is a misguided, self-authenticating, self-congratulating pursuit for absolute truth with no basis in history and with no long-term chance whatsoever of success.

---

74. I am confident that this portrait best serves the evidence. Other reputable scholars have represented Jesus very differently; and some have denied that Jesus ever existed.

Part 4
MYTH

Chapter 7
MYTH AS A VEHICLE OF HUMAN UNDERSTANDING

here is a pervasive belief that myth is pure and simple fantasy or invention—something that is untruthful or imaginary and that belongs to some past prescientific age. There is, of course, some truth to this popular conception of myth. The New Testament seems to support this view, when we read in 1 Timothy 1:3–4 and 4:7:

> 1:3I urge you, as I did when I was on my way to Macedonia, to remain in Ephesus so that you may instruct certain people not to teach any different doctrine, 4and not to occupy themselves with myths and endless genealogies that promote speculations rather than the divine training that is known by faith.
> 4:7Have nothing to do with profane myths and old wives' tales.[75]

In spite of this popular belief about myth as falsehood, scholars of mythology define and understand myth quite differently. Myth is rather a distinctive category of story that explains and interprets aspects of the world around us.

In his book *Myth from the Ice Age to Mickey Mouse*, Robert W. Brockway concisely summarizes a number of different scholarly ideas about the meaning of myth:

> Myths are stories, usually, about gods and other supernatural beings (Frye). They are often stories of origins, how the world and everything in it came to be *in illo*

---

75. See also 2 Timothy 4:3–4 (For the time is coming when people will not put up with sound doctrine, but having itching ears, they will accumulate for themselves teachers to suit their own desires, and will turn away from listening to the truth and wander away to myths), and Titus 1:13–14 (That testimony is true. For this reason, rebuke them sharply, so they may become sound in the faith, not paying attention to Jewish myths or to commandments of those who reject the truth). The myths and genealogies alluded to here may refer to portions of the Old Testament (as in the passage in Titus), or to Gnostic speculations common in Christian circles in the second century.

tempore [at that time] (Eliade). They are usually strongly structured and their meaning is only discerned by linguistic analysis (Lévi-Strauss). Sometimes they are public dreams which, like private dreams, emerge from the unconscious mind (Freud). Indeed, they often reveal the archetypes of the collective unconscious (Jung). They are symbolic and metaphorical (Cassirer). They orient people to the metaphysical dimension, explain the origins and nature of the cosmos, validate social issues, and, on the psychological plane, address themselves to the innermost depths of the psyche (Campbell). Some of them are explanatory, being prescientific attempts to interpret the natural world (Frazer). As such, they are usually functional and are the science of primitive peoples (Malinowski). Often, they are enacted in rituals (Hooke). Religious myths are sacred histories (Eliade), and distinguished from the profane (Durkheim). But, being semiotic expressions (Saussure), they are a "disease of language" (Müller). They are both individual and social in scope, but they are first and foremost stories (Kirk).[76]

I am not a professional student of world mythology and do not intend to explore the extensive role of myth in the history of religion. That is an enormous undertaking, even for the trained specialist. Neither will I address the role of myth in the Old Testament, although it is important for any serious student of the Bible to look seriously into the various levels of meaning contained in the creation myths of Genesis 1:1–2:4a and 2:4b–3:24. The stories of creation and the Garden of Eden are replete with meaning. So, too, are the accounts of the great flood in Genesis 6:9–9:17. Many of the myths found in Genesis 1–11 borrowed themes from the great treasure store of ancient Near Eastern mythology: Mesopotamian, Canaanite, and Egyptian.

I do, however, intend to look rather closely at the role of myth in the New Testament, because this issue speaks directly to the question of the future of Christianity. The name David Friedrich Strauss (1808–1874) comes immediately to mind. Before Strauss published his monumental *Life of Jesus* in 1835 and 1836, no one had truly grasped or consistently applied the concept of myth to the New Testament. The association of the word "myth" to pagan mythology (as found in the passages in the Pastoral Letters cited above) had effectively barred Christian scholars from applying the term to any of the tradition surrounding the life and ministry of Jesus.

For Strauss, it mattered not that so little time had elapsed between Jesus' death and the writing of the Gospels. He was convinced that those forty-plus years were sufficient for history to have become embedded in myth. Most important in this regard is the key that Strauss used to open the meaning of the word "myth" in its application to the life of Jesus. Myth for Strauss is "nothing else than the clothing in historic form of religious ideas, shaped by the unconsciously inventive power of legend, and embodied in a historic personality."[77]

For Strauss, the interpenetration of infinity and finitude, of God and man, assumed the form of God-manhood that was realized in the historic personality of

---

76. Quoted from the Web site on Myth and Legend from Ancient Times to the Space Age: http://www.pibburns.com/myth.htm.

77. Albert Schweitzer, *Quest of the Historical Jesus*, p. 79.

Jesus of Nazareth. In Jesus, the unity of godhood and manhood came together. The fact that Jesus of Nazareth brought this idea, this unity of godhood and manhood, to life for humankind introduced into the world for the first time the ultimate goal of humanity, the bringing together of the two realms, the human and the divine.

Strauss examined each and every incident in the life of Jesus, first as explained supernaturally, then as explained rationally, and then sought to afford a mythical explanation of each story. Strauss was the first to recognize that the story of Jesus' temptation was woven together out of material from the Old Testament, and that the account of Jesus' call of his disciples was modeled on the calls of Elijah and Elisha. He explained the demons' recognition of Jesus as Messiah as the evangelists' way of representing the idea that even powers from the world of evil spirits would necessarily know and recognize who Jesus really was. For Strauss, these stories did not, of necessity, correspond to incidents in Jesus' life. Rather, they encapsulated who or what the church believed this Jesus to be.

Jesus' miracles have myth written all over them. The simple fact is that for Christianity Jesus had to equal and even excel the deeds of the Old Testament prophets and Greco-Roman divinities. Many of the miracle stories in the Gospels were built on stories in the books of 1 and 2 Kings involving Elijah and Elisha. The transfiguration of Jesus was based on the story of Moses' shining countenance in Exodus. The appearance of Moses and Elijah in the story of Jesus' Transfiguration showed that the Law (Moses) and the prophets (Elijah) testified to Jesus and disclosed who Jesus really is.

For Strauss, if Jesus died, then there was no resurrection. Alternatively, if Jesus, in fact, appeared after his crucifixion, then obviously he was not dead. The ascension is pure myth: following his death, Jesus had to return to the heavenly realm from which he had originally come. Once again these gospel stories, Strauss maintained, do not necessarily conform to events in Jesus' life. They reflect, instead, the church's interpretation of who this Jesus was and is. They are simply stories that developed within the early church to establish a perceived religious truth.

What is so persuasive about Strauss is that he makes it evident that there is no reasonable explanation of the gospel tradition that does not take account of the role of myth in the formation of that tradition. David Friedrich Strauss put a stake into the heart of both supernaturalist and rationalist interpretations of the Gospels. Of course, Strauss allowed for the possibility that many of the stories in the Gospels may have had their basis in historical fact. Yet rarely are stories in the Gospels told outside a mythic framework, even in the case of those stories that likely reach back into the life of Jesus of Nazareth.

Strauss was one of the first to recognize the substantial difference between the Jesus of the Gospel of John and the Jesus of the synoptic Gospels. In doing so, he called attention to the fact that John's mythic representation of Jesus was more advanced than the mythic representation found in the synoptic Gospels. John interpreted Jesus as the divine Son of God, an understanding influenced more by Greek thinking than by the earlier Jewish-thinking storytellers. The Gospel of John is, therefore, much less reliable as a source for reaching back to the Jesus of history, because John is more influenced by theological interests than are the synoptic evangelists. It was David Friedrich Strauss who brought an end to the discussion of "the miracles" in the life of Jesus and focused attention instead on "the mythic miracle stories" of the Gospels.

For people of his generation, Strauss' work was their first glimpse at the opinion that many of the incidents reported in the New Testament were not "historically true." Many of his generation were outraged with Strauss' view that biblical stories may rest on myth rather than on historical reality. Even scholars were slow to recognize the full impact of Strauss' work and resisted the notion that the scriptures of Judaism and Christianity were laden with myth.

It was not until the time of Rudolf Bultmann in the 1940s—more than a century after Strauss wrote his fourteen-hundred-page magnum opus—that the significance of myth in the New Testament was once again fully understood. Bultmann maintained that it is through myths that cultures symbolize and objectivize their worldviews. Further, he observed that the mythical background of the New Testament is basically the mythological outlook of first-century Jewish and Hellenistic thought. The mythical framework of the New Testament is a given. It is not specifically biblical; rather, it was presupposed by Jesus, by early Christians, and by the authors of the books of the canonical New Testament. The conception of the world presupposed both in Jesus' own teaching and in the New Testament's preached message about Jesus is mythical.

Bultmann pointed to the universal belief in a three-tiered universe: humankind living in the middle tier (the earth), with the upper tier serving as the realm of God and his angels (heaven), and the lower tier the domain of Satan and his demonic spirits (hell). Much of what happens in our middle tier is the result of the intrusion or intervention of supernatural powers from above and/or below. It was impossible to understand events in the world of Roman Palestine apart from this mythical worldview, which was the universally accepted belief in that part of the world at that time.

As is evident from Brockway's composite definition of myth at the outset of this chapter, anthropologists, sociologists, historians, psychologists, and theologians have had difficulty in agreeing upon a single definition of myth. Nevertheless, Robert A. Oden Jr. has indicated that there are certain elements that most definitions of myth share:

1. the material has to be a story or in the form of story;
2. the material has to be traditional, meaning that it has been transmitted, usually orally, within a community;
3. the stories invariably deal with a character or characters who are more than mere humans; and
4. the stories generally deal with events from remote antiquity.[78]

---

78. Robert A. Odin Jr., "Myth and Mythology," *The Anchor Bible Dictionary* (New York: Doubleday, 1992): 4:949.

From this statement it is clear that whatever else it may be, a myth is a story, but not all stories are myths. What then characterizes certain stories as myths? If we look for speculative thought in the writings of the ancient Near East, we will soon recognize that there is little in the ancient documents that we might call speculative thought, at least as we would understand that term today.

It is evident that there are basically two ways of looking at the world: (1) the intuitive or visionary way, and (2) the empirical or scientific way. The former, the intuitive or visionary mode of perception, characterizes the mythical way of knowing the world. It implies knowing the world and the things in the world as a "you," or as many "yous." Martin Buber characterized such relationships as I-Thou or I-You relationships. The latter, the empirical or scientific mode of perception, began in a meaningful way with people like Descartes and Newton. It operates on the assumption of the distance and separation between me as a subject and the world as an object or a series of objects. Martin Buber characterized such relationships as I-It relationships. The world of myth, and I would contend the world of religion, is the world of I-Thou or I-You relationships. I would contend that religion is not science minus; it is rather poetry plus! Unfortunately, too, many people still continue to maintain that religion falls into the category of the empirical.

Once we acknowledge that myths are stories, which are ostensibly (but not actually) historical, whose origin is generally forgotten, and whose purpose is usually to explain some practice, institution, belief, or natural phenomenon, it is apparent that it is misleading to ask whether myths are "true." It is more important to ask how myths function in society.

In *Myths, Dreams, and Religion*, Joseph Campbell identified what he called the four functions of mythology:[79]

1. **The Ontological (or the Mystical, or the Metaphysical) Function of Myth.** Campbell describes this function as "the reconciliation of consciousness with the preconditions of its own existence" (139). By this he means the moment in human evolution when we lost our animal innocence and attained consciousness. Campbell compares this moment to the moment in the Garden of Eden when Adam and Eve ate the fruit of the tree of the knowledge of good and evil and were confronted directly with the "brutal bloody facts of life" (139). He maintains that humankind has three possible responses to the awesome mystery of life: "yes" (acceptance), "no" (renunciation), and "no" with a contingent "yes." This conditional response is the position that Campbell associates with what he calls the messianic cults of Zoroastrianism, Judaism, Christianity, and Islam. In these religions the basic myth is of an originally good creation, corrupted by a fall, followed by the

---

79. Joseph Campbell, ed., *Myths, Dreams, and Religion: Eleven Visions of Connection* (New York: E. P. Dutton, 1970), pp. 138–44. Although Campbell does not have a strong following among professional students of myth, he is well known by the public because of the PBS television series of interviews about mythology that Campbell had with Bill Moyers.

establishment of "a supernaturally endowed society" through which "the pristine state of the good creation is to be attained" (139). Accordingly, there is hope, not in all societies, but only in these especially God-designated societies, for redemption and perfection in the future.

2. **The Cosmological Function of Myth.** Campbell describes this function as "formulating and rendering an image of the universe, a cosmological image in keeping with the science of the time" (140). Within this function of myth, all things in this universe—the trees, the rocks, the animals, the sun, the moon, the stars—are all parts of "a single great holy picture" and serve as "vehicles and messengers of the teaching" (140).

3. **The Sociological Function of Myth.** Campbell describes this function as "validating and maintaining some specific social order, authorizing its moral code as a construct beyond criticism or human emendation" (140). In the Old Testament, the personal God who is the author of creation is also the author of the Law, the Ten Commandments, that he delivered to Moses and the people of Israel on Mount Sinai.

4. **The Psychological Function of Myth.** Campbell describes this function as "shaping individuals to the aims and ideals of their various social groups, bearing them on from birth to death through the course of human life" (141). Sometime between the ages of fourteen and twenty, human beings are expected to make the transition from a life of total dependence on their parents to a life of independence that requires them to respond to life's challenges with responsible social action that serves the welfare of the larger community. Puberty rites often accompany this transformation, which functions in many traditional societies as a kind of second birth.

Campbell's description of the four functions of myth, coupled with our earlier effort to propose some sort of definition of myth, lays the foundation for our discussion of Bultmann's program of demythologizing the New Testament.

For Bultmann, "myths give to the transcendent reality an immanent, this-worldly objectivity. Myths give worldly objectivity to that which is unworldly."[80] Stated simply, certain transcendent truths find human expression in indirect and sometimes obscure language. As such, myths are stories that require deeper, thoughtful, and more reflective scrutiny than simply looking at them as the factual record of actual events in the distant past. As an example, the story of Adam and Eve in the Garden of Eden is not an accurate historical account of what actually happened to our first parents. It is rather a story that points to certain truths about humankind's passage from innocence to maturity, a coming of age that obliges us to distinguish between good and evil. It is not so much a story about *them* as it is a story about all of *us*.

---

80. Rudolf Bultmann, *Jesus Christ and Mythology* (New York: Charles Scribner's Sons, 1958), p. 19.

I would like to look at just three examples of myth in the New Testament before turning again to Bultmann:

1. **New Testament Cosmology.** As I stated earlier, the New Testament assumes the cosmology of the Old Testament and the rest of the ancient Near Eastern world, specifically the tripartite division of the world into heaven above, earth between, and hell beneath. This is a prescientific, mythological conception of the universe. This view of the world was not a creation of Jesus or of the writers of the New Testament. It was a given; it was taken for granted by just about everyone who lived in Roman Palestine and the surrounding areas in the first century.

2. **The Eschatological Myth.** As part of an inheritance from ancient Persia's Zoroastrian mythology, belief in a dualism involving a cosmic struggle between the powers of good and evil entered Judaism no later than the second century BCE, and through Judaism influenced Jesus and early Christianity.[81] More specifically, this Zoroastrian mythology taught that this world order is irretrievably evil and that it will be redeemed in the end-time either by God himself or by an agent of God, who will usher in the new age of God's rule. Those Jews and Christians who, in the first century CE, believed in the imminent coming of the end-time (the *eschaton* in Greek, hence our words "eschatology" and "eschatological") generally expected that a cosmic drama would unfold and culminate ultimately in God's eternal reign. There can be no question that Jesus understood himself and was also understood by the early church against the backdrop of this mythical eschatological drama.

3. **The Christological Myth.** In order to explain the significance of Jesus' death and the church's belief in his resurrection, early Christians borrowed a number of popular images to explain who this Jesus of Nazareth was: the Messiah (in Greek, the Christ) of Israel, the Divine Son of God, the Lord, the Redeemer, the future Son of Man, the Coming Judge of the World. These for-

---

81. The dualism of ancient Zoroastrianism involved the struggle of two apparently equal powers of good and evil: the god of light, Ahura Mazda, and the god of darkness, Angra Mainyu. Scholars debate the degree of the dualism in the Persian prophet Zarathustra's original teaching and whether Zoroastrianism was, in fact, the world's first monotheistic religion. Nevertheless, once exposed to Persian thought, Judaism could not accept wholesale the more radical Zoroastrianism dualism. Certain circles in Judaism developed a modified dualism in which there was still the one God. The power of evil evolved in Judaism and Christianity into a much lesser demigod or a fallen angel, variously named Satan, Beelzebub, Beelzebul, Belial, the devil, among others. Through its infiltration into Judaism, the theology of Zoroastrianism has had an enormous influence on Judaism's daughter religions, Christianity and Islam with respect to beliefs regarding God and Satan, heaven and hell, savior, resurrection, eschatology, final judgment, and so forth. Although Zoroastrians today number little more than one hundred thousand believers, Zoroastrian beliefs influence the teachings of billions of Christians and Muslims worldwide.

mulas led to the creation of the narratives of Jesus' supernatural birth, to the legends of the empty tomb, and to the idea of Jesus' descent into Hades (hell) following his death. Old Testament prophecies, of the sort we examined in the chapter "According to the Scriptures," gave rise to mythic stories that purport to portray "events" in the life of Jesus. Reports of exorcisms and healings were transformed into "miracle stories" to illustrate the divine power of this god-man Jesus of Nazareth. His God-Manhood was assured when the church drew up its canon of sacred scriptures and adopted the creeds of Nicea and Chalcedon.

The *Symbolum Apostolorum* or the Apostles' Creed is probably the best known and most popular confessional statement used in worship by Western Christians. Legend has it that Jesus' apostles wrote this creed on the tenth day after his ascension into heaven. That is, of course, not the case, but the name Apostles' Creed endures. The earliest written version of the creed is likely the *Interrogatory Creed of Hippolytus* (ca. 215 CE). This was originally a baptismal creed that was believed to summarize the teachings of the Apostles. It was administered to catechumens at the time of their baptism in the form of a series of questions to which the catechumen gave assent indicating that he or she both understood and believed the articles in the creed. Eventually the question-and-answer format was modified into the prayer form that we have today. The current form of the creed is first found in the writings of Caesarius of Arles (d. 542).

I reproduce now the text of that creed, because it illustrates the mythical character of the Christian confession of faith. Especially evident is the mythical "movement" of God, Jesus, and the Holy Spirit among the three tiers of the triple-decker universe.

I believe in God, the Father Almighty,
    the Creator of heaven and earth,
    and in Jesus Christ, His only Son, our Lord:

Who was conceived by the Holy Spirit,
    born of the Virgin Mary,
    suffered under Pontius Pilate,
    was crucified, died, and was buried.

He descended into hell.

The third day He arose again from the dead.

He ascended into heaven
    and sits at the right hand of God the Father Almighty,
    whence He shall come to judge the living and the dead.

I believe in the Holy Spirit, the holy catholic church,
    the communion of saints,
    the forgiveness of sins,

the resurrection of the body,
and life everlasting.

Amen.

Recognizing that mythology permeates the whole of the New Testament, as well as
the preaching and teaching of the Christian church, in an important essay first published in 1941, German New Testament scholar and theologian Rudolf Bultmann
proposed his program of "demythologizing."[82]

Bultmann's challenge was to determine how to preserve the essence of Christianity without requiring Christians to accept mythology that no rational person can
reasonably believe in this scientific age. Bultmann recognized, however, that all
mythology expresses some sort of truth, although usually in an indirect way. He
understood that it is no longer possible to expect Christians to accept the mythological view of the world in which the teachings of Jesus and of the New Testament are
clad. To ask Christians to do so would require them to accept a view of the world
that has been superseded by more recent scientific models. How can anyone in the
twenty-first century be expected to believe that our world is subject to the influence
of powers from above and from beneath the earth?

Bultmann observed that the preached message of the New Testament, which
scholars generally refer to as the church's *kerygma*,[83] presupposes the ancient mythical view of the world:

> In the fullness of time God sent forth his Son, a pre-existent divine Being, who appears
> on earth as a man.[84] He dies the death of a sinner on the cross and makes atonement
> for the sins of [humankind].[85] His resurrection marks the beginning of the cosmic
> catastrophe. Death, the consequence of Adam's sin is abolished,[86] and the demonic
> forces are deprived of their power.[87] The risen Christ is exalted to the right hand of God
> in heaven[88] and made "Lord" and "King."[89] He will come again on the clouds of
> heaven to complete the work of redemption, and the resurrection and judgment of
> everyone will follow.[90] Sin, suffering, and death will then be finally abolished.[91] All
> this is to happen very soon; indeed, St. Paul thinks he himself will live to see it.[92]

---

82. Rudolf Bultmann, "New Testament and Mythology," *Kerygma and Myth*, ed. Hans
Werner Bartsch, trans. Reginald H. Fuller (London: S.P.C.K., 1957), pp. 1–44.

83. *Kerygma* is the New Testament's Greek word for both the activity of preaching and
the content of the preached message of the church.

84. 2 Corinthians 5:21; Romans 8:3.

85. Romans 3:23–26; 4:25; 8:3; 2 Corinthians 5:14, 19; John 1:29; 1 John 2:2, etc.

86. 1 Corinthians 15:21–22; Romans 5:12–14.

87. 1 Corinthians 2:6–7; Colossians 2:15; Revelation 12:7–9; etc.

88. Acts 1:6–7; 2:33; Romans 8:34; etc.

89. Philippians 2:9–11; 1 Corinthians 15:25.

90. 1 Corinthians 15:23–24, 50–57.

91. Revelation 21:4; etc.

92. 1 Thessalonians 4:15–17; 1 Corinthians 15:51–52; cf. Mark 9:1.

> All those who belong to Christ's Church and are joined to the Lord by Baptism and the Eucharist are certain of resurrection to salvation,[93] etc., etc., etc.[94]

This summary of the church's kerygma sounds very familiar. It is the same mythological message that stands at the heart of the creeds; it is what is regularly preached in churches every Sunday and daily on American TV.

The mythological content of the church's teaching is particularly evident in the following diagram, which illustrates the "movement" of characters among the various tiers of the triple-decker universe:

HEAVEN	Incarnation of the divine Logos		Jesus' ascension to heaven
EARTH	Jesus' earthly ministry and crucifixion	Jesus' resurrection and earthly appearances	Outpouring of the Holy Spirit
HELL		Jesus' descent into hell	

The diagram could very well continue with the arrival of the Son of Man, the final judgment, the resurrection of the dead, etc.; however, the point is sufficiently clear: the content of the gospel is cast in language that involves mythological movement among the three spheres of the prescientific universe.

It is evident by now that the worldview of the New Testament is an outdated and, therefore, unbelievable cosmology. Accordingly, Bultmann proposed that the ancient biblical mythology should no longer be interpreted *cosmologically*, as has been the case for the past two thousand years. The message of Christianity should not be that Christians are required to accept a prescientific mythological view of the cosmos. Yet, that is effectively what is expected of Christians, even in mainstream denominations. That ancient cosmology is simply assumed by Jesus and the early church; it is the *framework* for Jesus' teaching and the church's teaching. It is, however, not the *content* of the church's teaching. Or it ought not to be, if it is.

Bultmann has proposed that the New Testament should be interpreted *anthro-*

---

93. Romans 5:12–14; 1 Corinthians 15:21–29, 44b–49.

94. Quoted from Rudolf Bultmann, "New Testament and Mythology: The Mythical Element of the New Testament and the Problem of Its Re-interpretation," *Kerygma and Myth*, ed. Hans Werner Bartsch, trans. Reginald H. Fuller (London: S.P.C.K.), p. 2.

pologically, or, better yet, *existentially*. In other words, the ancient mythology does not present an accurate picture of the universe; that was actually never its intention. However, within the structure of that ancient cosmology, the New Testament offers its teaching about humankind, its message about the meaning of human existence. The nature of man and the meaning of human existence are the essence of the biblical message, not an outdated pre-scientific view of the world. To clarify Bultmann's position even further, the real subject matter of the New Testament is not God and the transcendent realm of God's otherworldliness. The real subject matter of the New Testament is humankind and human self-understanding. In a famous passage in *Jesus Christ and Mythology*, Bultmann states this position succinctly:

> [Man] has a relation to God in his search for God, conscious or unconscious. Man's life is moved by the search for God because it is always moved, consciously or consciously, by the question about his own personal existence. The question of God and the question of myself are identical.[95]

With one sweeping blow, Bultmann restated the Christian agenda. It was not God who was the subject of Christianity, neither was it Jesus. The real subject matter of the New Testament, the real subject matter of Christianity is *humankind*. The real message of Christianity is its claims regarding the meaning of human existence. That is what Bultmann meant when he said that "The question of God and the question of myself are identical."

Christianity cannot expect its followers in this third millennium of its history to continue to accept a mythical view of the world. That is not an option. Bultmann says that

> To do so would be both senseless and impossible. It would be senseless, because there is nothing specifically Christian in the mythical view of the world as such. It is simply the cosmology of a pre-scientific age. Again, it would be impossible, because no man can adopt a view of the world by his own volition—it is already determined for him by his place in history.[96]

The problem is compounded by the fact that philosophy and psychology have exposed us to entirely new and different views of human self-understanding. Despite Hollywood and whatever we may have been taught in Sunday school, most of us cannot believe that we are in actual fact victims of the intrusion or the invasion of supernatural forces from above and below the earth.

Bultmann ridicules the absurdity of some of the church's core teachings when he writes:

---

95. Rudolf Bultmann, *Jesus Christ and Mythology* (New York: Charles Scribner's Sons, 1958), p. 53.

96. Rudolf Bultmann, "New Testament and Mythology," p. 3.

The idea of original sin as an inherited infection is sub-ethical, irrational, and absurd. The same objection applies to *the doctrine of atonement*. How can the guilt of one man be expiated by the death of another who is sinless—if indeed one may speak of a sinless man at all? What primitive notions of guilt and righteousness does this imply? And what primitive idea of God? . . . What a primitive mythology it is, that a divine Being should become incarnate, and atone for the sins of men through his own blood![97]

Christianity must henceforth focus its efforts on humankind. It is in that context and only in that context that it is possible to discuss the question of God. Using the best that science has to offer, it is time to try to reach *behind* or *through* Christian mythology to uncover its enduring relevance for humankind in the new millennium.

Once the power of myth has been unleashed and its meaning unlocked and understood, we can then look at the myths of Genesis and the mythology of the New Testament and focus on the existential content and timeless truth that are enshrined in the teaching of Jesus and the teachings of the Old and New Testaments. What will that involve? What will it mean?

Primarily, it will mean turning the cosmological model upside down. It will mean focusing on humanity and the question of the meaning or meaningfulness of human existence. Christian models usually begin by looking first at God, Jesus, creeds of the church, and so forth. There has already been considerable discussion about Bultmann's program of demythologizing the New Testament.[98] I do not intend to rehearse the issues of that discussion here.

Suffice it to say, a Christianity for this new millennium will have to reinterpret ancient mythology to address the questions of God, the Bible, and Jesus. That is the focus of the four sections of this book. Presumably, Christians will want to wrestle with all three of these historically central features of Christianity to determine where we go from here on each of these issues.

It is no longer clear that God exists, at least not in the way in which Christians have generally believed. Our popular view of God is laden with mythology, and we should probably understand that God cannot and should not be understand apart from the human experience of what it means to be human and how we ought to respond to our experience of the universe and our encounter with all life on this planet.

It is essential to address the question of what role the Bible will play in this exercise. It can no longer serve as the single authoritative written record of the human encounter with God's revelation, first of all because revelation means something very different to us today than it did two thousand years ago, and secondly because Christians need to look increasingly to many different so-called inspired writings as avenues to understand the relationship between God and humankind.

---

97. Ibid., p. 7.

98. One place to begin a review of those issues might be the theological debate about Bultmann's program in the two volumes of *Kerygma and Myth*, ed. Hans Werner Bartsch, trans. Reginald H. Fuller.

Jesus' total humanity is uncompromisable. Christians, therefore, need to ask whether there is anything unique in the person of Jesus or in his teaching. Is he qualitatively different from other great prophetic figures? Does his message to humanity represent a better way than what we find in the teachings of Moses, Buddha, Mohammed, and Lao-tzu?

The stakes are high, and the challenge is enormous, but to survive, Christianity needs to speak openly and honestly to these and other issues. It is essential to keep one's eyes to the future and look back toward the past only for an occasional point of reference.

CONCLUSION

$\mathscr{O}$n the day that I wrote the first words of the first draft of this concluding section, an article by Frank Bruni, titled "Faith Fades Where It Once Burned," appeared in the *New York Times* (October 13, 2003). In this article, Bruni discusses the shrinking role in Europe of both Roman Catholic and Protestant Christianity, primarily because the church is viewed as being out of step with this changing world. Everything I have written in this book supports that claim that Christianity has lost much of its relevance and faces a future of diminishing influence.

Christianity is, however, booming in the developing world, especially in Africa, where it is competing successfully with Islam. But, Bruni observes, "Europe already seems more and more like a series of tourist-trod monuments to Christianity's past." Among developed countries, the United States is the anomaly. Although about 5 percent of French adults attend church once a week, more than 30 percent of Americans claim to do so. Even former Communist countries, which experienced a brief religious resurgence following their liberation, have settled back into religious indifference.

Increasingly, Christians from what Americans generally consider mainstream denominations (Roman Catholics, Presbyterians, Episcopalians, Methodists, etc.) still show up at church for Christmas and Easter, and for baptisms, weddings, and funerals, but few of the faithful regularly attend Sunday services or heed their church's teachings and admonitions on such matters as birth control, abortion, and other timely social issues. Europe is already light-years ahead of the United States on gay and lesbian rights, with several countries already recognizing same-sex civil marriages.

Although fewer and fewer Christians regularly attend church, sizable majorities say that they still believe in something they continue to call God. There is, however, among Christians a disconnection between believing and attending church. Studies show that as people grow wealthier and are better educated, they gradually fall away from their ancestral faiths. Once again, Americans, or at least evangelical American Christians, may be the anomaly, the exception to the rule.

Yet, even in America, where membership of mainstream Christian denominations is shrinking to dangerously low levels, there is phenomenal growth among evangelical fundamentalist denominations, especially among those denominations where worshipers speak in tongues, witness faith healings, clap their hands, and cry out "Hallelujah." People who are disconnected from family and even from themselves are apparently looking for intense experiences in tight-knit supportive communities. But what has this need for tight-knit communities and intense experiences got to do with Christianity? Could the same experience be duplicated by joining a local bowling club?

People are drawn to churches with programs of rousing song and dance and the promise of health, hope, prosperity, and a place in heaven. If you're going to pay your $5 a week, or whatever the going rate is these days, you want to know that when you die, you are going to be with God and Jesus in heaven. A quarter of Christians in the world today are Pentecostals, swept up in sects that promote religious ecstasy, guaranteed salvation, and individual and mass hysteria.

Most of the growth in Pentecostalism is centered in the Southern Hemisphere, in Africa, where Christianity and Islam are in fierce competition, and in South America, previously a stronghold of Roman Catholicism. Peripheral religious cults have strong appeal to oppressed people, who, unable to make it in this highly competitive world, look forward to a better tomorrow in the next. Among developed nations, the United States is once again the exception, because, unlike their European brethren, Americans in large numbers are swept up in the Pentecostal frenzy. Again the appeal, even in the United States, is largely to less well-educated and poorer whites and oppressed minorities. There is strong appeal to Pentecostalism, where people come to understand that God affirms those whom society has tended to leave behind.

It appears that Christianity is moving in two very different directions at the same time. The movement to the Religious Right is especially evident in the United States, in Africa, and in South America, and also in immigrant populations in Europe. Mainstream denominations are in trouble as church attendance continues to fall off, either through conversion to movements on the right, or through movement right out the door.

Is right-wing religious fundamentalism the wave of the future? I certainly hope not, and I do not believe that it is. It is a short-term aberration, popular with people who are still content with living in the innocence of some previous century, people who are yearning for meaning and affirmation in a world that has failed to understand them or to address their personal needs. In fact, this was the appeal of Christianity in its first decades in the first century.

The clue to Christianity's future may be found in some of the speculation as to why Pope John Paul II was passed over in 2003 for the Nobel Peace Prize, which was awarded instead to an obscure Iranian woman, Shirin Ebadi, for her efforts for democracy and human rights in Iran. Pope John Paul may have been passed over, so say the gossip mills, for his poor handling of sexual abuse by Roman Catholic priests, his continued insistence on relegating Catholic women to second-class status in the church, and his persistent hostility to the civil rights of gay men and lesbians. At least in the minds of the liberal Norwegian selection committee, the pope, in spite of his remarkable role in the liberation of Eastern Europe from communism and his far-reaching efforts to expunge anti-Semitism from Roman Catholicism and to build a bridge of understanding and mutual respect to Judaism, was too conservative. He had one heavy foot cemented in the past and one lighter foot trying to tiptoe gently into the future. Insufficient!

Capitulating to the enemy, the Religious Right, is not the solution. There is nothing to suggest that there is a long-term future in right-wing religious and political extremism, for the Religious Right in the United States has also developed an extreme political agenda. If we measure time in centuries, no less millennia, we have no choice but to acknowledge that the growing movement on the Religious Right is a temporary, if currently highly successful, reaction to implications and repercussions of the Enlightenment and dramatic social change within the last generation or two.

What mainstream Christianity needs to do is to address itself not to the groups that attempt to run backward in time to recover religious and political extremism, but rather to the group that headed for the door, that group of Christians who are disconnected from the church, because it is perceived as being out of step with the many of this generation, particularly our youth. Quite frankly, the church is no longer relevant to this group of mainstream Christians because it fails to address the future needs and challenges of society. That group of stay-at-home Christians must be reengaged by addressing issues of the future, not by moving further to the right, back to the past. I predict that there will be—in fact there already is—something like a civil war waging for the heart of Christianity. The battle is bitter, and it will likely get even bitterer in the decades to come before victory is in sight for either side. The stakes are enormously high.

The title of this book is *The Future of Christianity*. I have not tried to predict what Christianity will look like a thousand years from now. I am, however, confident that it will be very different from what it is today, and I have ventured to propose some ways in which Christianity can and must change, for unless Christianity changes dramatically, I am confident that it will continue to wither and perhaps even disappear, probably long before the end of this millennium. This is not a time for new fundamentalisms, for retreat into Christianity's dark past. It is a time to step courageously into the future, with all of its uncertainties. The same might be said of the rest of the world's major religions, none of which is currently postured to meet confidently the challenges of the future.

I have proposed that in the new millennium, Christians must further open the door—no, rather throw the door wide open—and question the meaning of their belief in the one God, not because there are many gods, as some religions claim, but because the very concept of God in Christianity is too limited. It is time to have the faith to doubt what we have been taught since early childhood.

I have proposed that Christians may find in Taoism, in Thomas Jefferson, in science, in Martin Buber, and elsewhere some of the clues needed to understand better what (or possibly who) it is that is the cause or source of the universe and that affords meaning to human existence. The discussion must be wide open and not hindered by what is and is not, what has and has not been, Christian orthodoxy. Christians should be involved in a quest for Truth, wherever they find it, because in the end it is Truth that sets us free.

I have also proposed that Christianity's understanding of the Bible must be challenged and reexamined. The Christian canon was fixed by ancient church fathers, based on certain assumptions of the time regarding orthodoxy and heresy, and definitely on issues involving the acquisition of power. I would ask once again what is meant by inspiration and whether only these books are inspired (whatever that may mean). Are there other ancient (and modern) writers who were also inspired and whose writings are suitable for study and reflection? By that, I do not mean that we should look at just the Gospel of Thomas or the Teaching of the Twelve Apostles (also known as the Didache). Shouldn't we also return to the teachings of Plato and Aristotle, the Stoics, the Epicureans, and others?

Shouldn't we also look at the teachings of other ancient "prophets," such as Buddha, Confucius, Lao-tzu, Mohammed, and others, and consider what they have contributed to the question of the meaning of the universe and of human existence? Can any of these religious traditions contribute meaningfully to a Christianity for the new millennium? I believe that they can, and will. Are these men (and women, if we can identify any) more or less inspired than were Moses, Amos, Isaiah, and Jesus? We cannot really answer that question until we are prepared to take the question itself more seriously.

And what about more contemporary thinkers? I think here not only of Luther, or Calvin, or Roman popes. I think also of poets, philosophers, scientists, and others who may have glimpsed what Christians have historically chosen to name as "God." Might we not also learn from some of the perceived enemies of the church: not only from Copernicus and Galileo, who have already been vindicated, but from Darwin, Nietzsche, Freud, and even Marx, all of whom have had a glimpse into issues that matter most to humankind.

I am convinced that Christians can no longer confine their study to the canon of sixty-six books, except by regarding them, perhaps, as the historical core of inspired writings. I am not, of course, proposing to reopen the canon to add additional books, but I am proposing that Christians will have to understand their canon in new ways. Minimally, the canon is a historical fact; these are the books that the church has historically considered the heart of its teaching. Maybe that is all that we can say about the Bible in the new millennium. These books gave definition to our faith nearly two thousand years ago. They continued to speak meaningfully to later generations of Christians. They are still worth studying, but they do not contain the last and, certainly, the only word.

In recent centuries, we have learned to look at the books of the Bible critically. The challenge now is to find the timeless message within those ancient books, the "truths" that are not conditioned and limited by time and place, the insights that are not dictated by culture and bias, but rather to look for those ideas, those truths, that reach more deeply into the universal spirit of all of humankind, not only those who call themselves Christians. Perhaps, in the process, we can make Christianity a truly universal religion.

It will be a challenge for Christians to deal seriously with the question of the canon, but they must address that challenge, or the Bible will by the end of this millennium surely be relegated to the status of one more collection of religious books that served as authoritative for millions or even billions of people for a brief time in the long history of humankind. We need to understand what it means to call the Bible the Word of God, especially since we have already made the point that the Christian concept of God is itself dead and needs to be reexamined and updated, and that God maybe even need to be renamed.

Jesus was without doubt one of the most important persons in human history, and there must be a reason for that. Jesus is important not only because he was invested with importance by later Christians, who equated him with God. Jesus is important in his own right. He is one of many individuals in history whom people have identified as a mediator between the human and the divine. It was Jesus' apprehension of what he called God that drove him to a life of self-sacrifice. Jesus gave new meaning to the word "love," when he called for his followers to love unconditionally not only their neighbors, but everyone, even their enemies. Following Jesus' radical social ethic and his personal example might just lead to a greater respect for this planet, to a dramatic redistribution of the world's wealth, and to universal enjoyment of human rights. It is time to understand Jesus in our own time, stripped of the theological overlay of earlier centuries.

Jesus would have understood that there is no room for second-class citizenship on this planet if we are, indeed, all equal. There can be no discrimination between male and female, black and white, gay and straight, slave and free. Until everyone is free and equal, none of us is free and equal. In substantial respect, this is an economic issue. Capitalism is in itself not evil, but the accumulation of excessive wealth and human greed are evil. Everyone climbing the ladder of success needs only to reach back and lend a hand to uplift by one step someone who is on a lower rung on that ladder. And to claim that we are all equal does not, of course, mean that we are all the same.

In trying to recover Jesus in his total humanity there should be no concern that we will thereby diminish Jesus. We will only wonder all the more at how one man was able in his brief lifetime to incarnate that which Christians call God. I am, of course, speaking poetically, not literally, when I speak of Jesus here as the incarnation of God. I do so to illustrate ways in which we might acknowledge and pay respect to the past, even as we reach for the future. It is our individual responsibility to see that the world is a better place because we have walked its face, and Jesus, if nothing else, may be an example worth imitating. Do we in any way diminish Jesus by saying this? By no means! What we do is make Jesus more human and make his message come alive in ways that enable us to focus both individually and collectively on a better tomorrow.

The hardest question for Christians to answer may be whether what we create for tomorrow is in any way faithful to our past. The answer lies, at least in part, in the fact that the church has changed in every generation, in every century, sometimes subtly and sometime more dramatically. I am, of course, calling now for very dramatic changes, but many of the changes I am calling for are currently within our reach. Just as Jesus called upon his followers to act as if God's rule was about to break into history, so, too, we can and must act in the same way in this generation. Jesus understood that the moment of God's judgment is the eternal now. We can and must begin to act now in the same way, and we must begin to behave in each new situation as if we were living in the immediate shadow and judgment of the moral imperative.

We can and must break down the barriers of discrimination and oppose evil and injustice wherever we find them. We must be careful, however, about what it is that we call evil. We cannot call evil everything that our grandparents called evil, although that is the position that many Christians comfortably embrace. Neither can we call something evil simply because we don't like it. We must discover the timeless principles on which we are prepared to base our lives, and then live not for yesterday, but for tomorrow.

I am reminded in this regard of an e-mail that circulated a few years ago about Dr. Laura Schlesinger, a radio personality who used to dispense sex advice to people who phoned in to her radio show. She once said that, as an observant Orthodox Jew, she believed that homosexuality was an abomination, citing Leviticus 18:22,[99] and that it should not be condoned under any circumstances. The following is an open response to Dr. Laura penned by an anonymous writer and posted on the Internet:

Dear Dr. Laura:

Thank you for doing so much to educate people regarding God's Law. I have learned a great deal from your radio show, and I try to share that knowledge with as many people as I can. When someone tries to defend the homosexual lifestyle, for example, I simply remind them that Leviticus 18:22 clearly states that homosexuality is an abomination. End of debate! I do need some advice from you, however, regarding some other Bible laws and how to follow them.

   a) When I burn a bull on the altar as a sacrifice, I know it creates a pleasing odor for the Lord (Leviticus 1:8–9).[100] The problem is my neighbors. They claim the odor is not pleasing to them. Should I smite them?

   b) I would like to sell my daughter into slavery, as sanctioned in Exodus 21:7.[101] In this day and age, what do you think would be a fair price for her? She's 18 and starting University. Will the slave buyer continue to pay for her education by law?

---

99. You shall not lie with a male as with a woman; it is an abomination.

100. Aaron's sons the priests shall arrange the parts, with the head and the suet, on the wood that is on the fire on the altar; but its entrails and its legs shall be washed with water. Then the priests shall turn the whole into smoke on the altar as a burnt offering, an offering by fire of pleasing odor to the LORD.

101. When a man sells his daughter into slavery, she shall not go out as the male slaves do.

c) I know that I am allowed no contact with a woman while she is in her period of menstrual uncleanliness (Leviticus 15:19–24).[102] The problem is how do I tell? I have tried asking, but most women take offense. I'm sure you have found a way to do this and can share it with me.

d) Leviticus 25:44[103] states that I may, indeed, possess slaves, both male and female, provided they are purchased from neighboring nations. A friend of mine claims that this applies to Mexicans, but not Canadians. Can you clarify? Why can't I own Canadians?

e) I have a neighbor who insists on working on the Sabbath. Exodus 35:2[104] clearly states he should be put to death. Am I morally obligated to kill him myself, or should this be a neighborhood improvement project?

f) A friend of mine feels that even though eating shellfish is an abomination (Leviticus 11:10-11),[105] it is a lesser abomination than homosexuality. I don't agree. Can you settle this?

g) Leviticus 21:20[106] states that I may not approach the altar of God if I have a defect in my sight. I have to admit that I wear reading glasses. Does my vision have to be 20/20, or is there some wiggle room here? Would contact lenses help?

h) Most of my male friends get their hair trimmed, including the hair around their temples, even though this is expressly forbidden by Leviticus 19:27.[107] How should they die?

i) I know from Leviticus 11:7–8[108] that touching the skin of a dead pig makes me unclean, but may I still play football if I wear hemp gloves?

---

102. When a woman has a discharge of blood, that is her regular discharge from her body, she shall be in her impurity for seven days, and whoever touches her shall be unclean until the evening. Everything upon which she lies during her impurity shall be unclean; everything upon which she sits shall be unclean. Whoever touches her bed shall wash his clothes, and bathe in water, and be unclean until the evening. Whoever touches anything upon which she sits shall wash his clothes, and bathe in water, and be unclean until the evening; whether it is the bed or anything upon which she sits, when he touches it he shall be unclean until the evening. If any man lies with her, and her impurity falls on him, he shall be unclean seven days; and every bed on which he lies shall be unclean.

103. As for the male and female slaves you have, it is from the nations around you that you may acquire male and female slaves.

104. Six days shall your work be done, but on the seventh day you shall have a holy Sabbath of solemn rest to the LORD; whoever does any work on it shall be put to death.

105. But anything in the sea or the streams that does not have fins and scales, of the swarming creatures in the waters and among all the living creatures that are in the waters— they are detestable to you and detestable they shall remain. Of their flesh you shall not eat, and their carcasses you shall regard as detestable.

106. (For no one who has a blemish shall draw near [the altar of God], one who is blind or lame,) . . . or a hunchback, or a dwarf, or a man with a blemish in his eyes or an itching disease or scabs or crushed testicles.

107. You shall not round off the hair on your temples or mar the edges of your beard.

108. The pig, for even though it has divided hoofs and is cleft-footed, it does not chew the cud; it is unclean for you. Of their flesh you shall not eat, and their carcasses you shall not touch, they are unclean for you.

j) My uncle has a farm. He violates Leviticus 19:19[109] by planting two dif-
    ferent crops in the same field, as does his wife by wearing garments made
    of two different kinds of thread (cotton/polyester blend). He also tends to
    curse and blaspheme a lot. Is it really necessary that we go to all the trouble
    of getting the whole town together to stone them? (Leviticus 24:15–16).[110]
    Couldn't we just burn them to death at a private family affair like we do
    with people who sleep with their in-laws? (Leviticus 20:14)[111]

I know you have studied these things extensively, so I am confident you can help.
Thank you again for reminding us that God's word is eternal and unchanging.

Well, clearly not all of God's word is eternal and unchanging. I have quoted this
bogus letter to Dr. Laura Schlesinger in its entirety, and even provided in footnotes
the relevant biblical passages, in order to drive home the point: quoting individual
verses of holy books out of context is nonsensical. Yet, it is common practice among
fundamentalist Christians (and, I might add, fundamentalist Jews and fundamentalist Muslims, as well). This letter points to the absurdity of this practice. Yet, this
very practice is regularly used today to justify discrimination against homosexuals,
and it has been used and is still used to justify second-class status for women. In the
relatively recent past, the Bible was used by many Christians in the United States to
justify the legitimacy of slavery and the segregation of the races.

The same practice is used by Jewish extremists to justify their claim to land in
the occupied West Bank and Gaza, because God gave this land to the Jews, and it is
not theirs to negotiate away. This concept of God as a real estate broker is obscene
and self-serving. Similarly, Islamic extremists justify murder and acts of terrorism
against "infidels" through a reading of the Quran that justifies their own political
agenda. Christianity does not have a monopoly on quoting holy writings out of context to justify unholy acts.

Opposing evil and injustice and promoting and celebrating human diversity can
and must be a cornerstone of Christianity in the new millennium. Jesus' life and
teaching are a model of acceptance and tolerance and can and should serve as a suitable standard in developing a Christian ethic for which unselfish and unconditional
love is the measure of the moral imperative. Jesus walked in the footsteps of Israel's
prophets, who were especially eloquent in their condemnation of a religion that
focused narrowly on ritual and formal observances and who made it clear what they
believed constitutes true religion.

---

109. You shall not sow your field with two kinds of seed; nor shall you put on a garment
made of two different materials.

110. And speak to the people of Israel saying: Anyone who curses God shall bear the
sin. One who blasphemes the name of the LORD shall be put to death; the whole congrega-
tion shall stone the blasphemer. Aliens as well as citizens, when they blaspheme the Name,
shall be put to death.

111. If a man takes a wife and her mother also, it is depravity; and they shall be burned
to death, both he and they, that there may be no depravity among you.

Following the tenth-century BCE civil war that left Israel divided into two kingdoms, Israel in the north and Judah in the south, Amos prophesied[112] by delivering a scathing indictment of northern Israel in about 750 BCE. One of his most derisive oracles is recorded in Amos 5:21–24:

21 I hate, I despise your festivals,
and I take no delight in your solemn assemblies.
22 Even though you offer me your burnt offerings and grain offerings,
I will not accept them;
and the offerings of well-being of your fatted animals
I will not look upon them.
23 Take away from me the noise of your songs;
I will not listen to the melody of your harps.
24 But let justice roll down like waters,
and righteousness like an ever-flowing stream.

True religion and faithful worship of Israel's god Yahweh are summarized by Amos in verse 24 in Yahweh's demand for justice and righteousness.

A few years later, Isaiah of Jerusalem, the great Judean prophet, delivered an equally sarcastic denunciation of religion to the southern kingdom, when he spoke, sometime after 738 BCE, the oracle found in Isaiah 1:10–17:

10 Hear the word of the LORD, you rulers of Sodom!
Listen to the teaching of our God, you people of Gomorrah!
11 What to me is the multitude of your sacrifices? Says the LORD;
I have had enough of burnt offerings of rams and the fat of fed beasts;
I do not delight in the blood of bulls, or of lambs, or of goats.

12 When you come to appear before me,
who asked this from your hand?
trample my courts no more;
13 bringing offerings is futile;
incense is an abomination to me.
New moon and Sabbath and calling of convocation—
I cannot endure solemn assemblies with iniquity.
14 Your new moons and your appointed festivals
my soul hates;
they have become a burden to me,

---

112. Prophecy is often popularly understood as predicting the future. Nothing could be further from the truth. The prophets of ancient Israel and Judah understood that they were spokesmen for the Word of Yahweh in their own generations. They pronounced God's judgment on his people and spoke uncompromisingly to the present situation. To the extent that there is a futuristic element in Israelite prophecy, it is because the prophets understood that the future is a necessary consequence of the present. Evildoing in the present would necessarily lead to destruction in the near future.

> I am weary of bearing them.
> 15 When you stretch out your hands,
> I will hide my eyes from you;
> even though you make many prayers,
> I will not listen;
> your hands are full of blood.
> 16 Wash yourselves; make yourselves clean;
> remove the evil of your doings from before my eyes;
> cease to do evil,
> 17 learn to do good;
> seek justice,
> rescue the oppressed,
> defend the orphan,
> plead for the widow.

Isaiah understood well the vainglory and the ostentatious boastfulness that often accompany the outward manifestation of pompous and hypocritical religiosity. For Isaiah, true religion is summarized in those bullet points at the very end of his oracle:

> cease to do evil,
>   learn to do good;
> seek justice,
>   rescue the oppressed,
> defend the orphan,
>   plead for the widow.

Micah, who prophesied in the southern kingdom of Judah just a few years later during the last quarter of the eighth century BCE, delivered bitter oracles against Jerusalem. One such oracle is found in Micah 6:6–8:

> 6 "With what shall I come before the LORD,
> and bow myself before God on high?
> Shall I come before him with burnt offerings,
> with calves a year old?
> 7 Will the LORD be pleased with thousands of rams,
> with ten thousand rivers of oil?
> Shall I give my firstborn for my transgression,
> the fruit of my body for the sin of my soul?"
> 8 He has told you, O mortal, what is good;
> and what does the LORD require of you
> but to do justice, and to love kindness,
> and to walk humbly with your God?

An anonymous prophet, the so-called Third Isaiah or Trito-Isaiah (Isaiah 56–66), writing two hundred years later in about 520 BCE, delivered a similar admonition, recorded in Isaiah 58:3–9:

3 "Why do we fast, but you do not see?
    Why humble ourselves, but you do not notice?"
    Look, you serve your own interest on your fast day,
    and oppress all your workers.
4 Look, you fast only to quarrel and to fight,
    and to strike with a wicked fist.
    Such fasting as you do today
    will not make your voice heard on high.
5 Is such the fast that I choose,
    a day to humble oneself?
    Is it to bow down the head like a bulrush,
    and to lie in sackcloth and ashes?
    Will you call this a fast,
    a day acceptable to the LORD?

6 Is not this the fast that I choose:
    to loose the bonds of injustice,
    to undo the thongs of the yoke,
    to let the oppressed go free,
    and to break every yoke?
7 Is it not to share your bread with the hungry,
    and bring the homeless poor into your house;
    when you see the naked, to cover them,
    and not to hide yourself from your own kin?
8 Then your light shall break forth like the dawn,
    and your healing shall spring up quickly;
    your vindictor[113] shall go before you,
    the glory of the LORD shall be your rear guard.
9 Then you shall call, and the LORD will answer;
    you shall cry for help, and he will say, Here I am.

Amos, Isaiah of Jerusalem, Micah, and Trito-Isaiah all dispensed with the wide-spread focus on the external display of individual and group religiosity: what would be today's attending church regularly on Sunday in your new best suit, saying more frequent novenas, wearing your ashes on your forehead on Ash Wednesday for all to notice, fasting regularly during Lent as a sacrifice to God, and heaping up more and more empty prayers for each and every religious festival. These prophets focused instead on the social component of true religion: the doing of justice and righteous and the loving of mercy and kindness. Micah 6:8 summarizes better than any single verse in the Old Testament the essence of prophetic religion, the heart and soul of the Hebrew Bible: do justice, love mercy, and walk humbly with God.

There is clear and unambiguous continuity between Israel's prophetic religion and the message of Jesus of Nazareth. Christians need to rediscover that continuity and to make it the focus of a transformed and better Christianity. Like the prophets who pre-

---

113. Or *vindication*.

ceded him, Jesus, too, dismissed the empty hypocritical religiosity of his time: "Beware of practicing your piety before others in order to be seen by them. . . . Whenever you give alms, do not sound a trumpet before you, as the hypocrites do in the synagogues and in the streets, so that they may be praised by others. . . . And whenever you pray, do not be like the hypocrites; for they love to stand and pray in the synagogues and at the street corners, so that they may be seen by others. . . . And whenever you fast, do not look dismal, like the hypocrites, for they disfigure their faces so as to show others that they are fasting" (Matthew 6:1–5, 16). Jesus is totally faithful to his prophetic precursors and should be understood as part of that movement.

Evangelical Christians in the United States have sought to capture not only the religious agenda. They have also advanced a radical political agenda consistent with their narrow and often narrow-minded religious agenda. They have worked feverishly at the local, state, and national levels to turn back the clock on the Enlightenment, on individual liberties, and on reform and renewal within Christianity by advancing the teaching of creationism in public schools, by promoting prayer and the reading of the Bible in public schools, by turning back the clock on women's reproductive rights and gay and lesbian rights, and by diminishing the constitutional protection of religious liberty and the separation of church and state. They would hijack not only Christianity, but also our American democracy and constitutionally based liberties.

Unlike the Amish, who have been content to withdraw from society and impose their values only on their own small group, evangelical Christians have attempted for decades to make their agenda the American agenda. They practice and promote not only a form of Christianity that is dead on arrival, but, with their fanatical political agenda, they pose a serious threat to individual liberty. Evangelical Christians are what some have called the American Taliban.[114]

I have painted the broad strokes of the future of Christianity as being very different from what Christianity is today. I have called for a Christianity that is consistent with reason, consistent with science, consistent with individual liberty, and consistent with basic human rights. I see no other possibility for the future, unless Christians are so wedded to the past that they are prepared to accept responsibility for the demise of Christianity because of its increased irrelevance. In saying that Christianity must be consistent with reason and consistent with science, I do not intend to imply that everything that Christians believe must be rational and scientific; I do, however, mean that Christianity must dispose of everything that is illogical, unreasonable, irrational, groundless, and absurd. We must be prepared to recognize the legendary and mythological elements in Christianity for what they are and be willing to reinterpret them for future generations.

Is there a place for churches in this Christianity for the new millennium? Pos-

---

114. The following Web site is produced by a group called Theocracy Watch, a project at Cornell University. It describes the degree to which the Religious Right has infiltrated the American political agenda in an effort to Christianize America: http://www.4religious-right .info/index.htm.

sibly, although the church will necessarily have to function in roles much different from the roles in which they have served to date. The church should be on the cutting edge of change and should be leading, not following, the people in forging ahead in asking the difficult questions and in learning to live with the uncertainty of not knowing all of the answers.

There will continue to be an essential role for clergy to carry out the priestly, the ministerial, and the prophetic functions that they have historically performed, but they, too, must live up to the challenge or face the likelihood of becoming irrelevant and obsolete. The clergy must be broadly educated and intellectually honest with the people at all times. In many mainstream Christian denominations, members of the clergy already know and agree with much of what I have written in these pages, but they lack the courage to share their doubt and uncertainty with their congregations and continue, instead, to preach little more than that Old Time Religion, repackaged from one year to the next. Christians will continue to want their clergy to celebrate and officiate at those ceremonies that anthropologists call human rights of passage: birth, puberty (or the transition to adulthood), marriage, and death. Clergy will continue to minister to their congregations, looking after, caring for, and attending to the needs of the people, especially in times of sickness, trouble, and uncertainty. Clergy must also serve as prophets to the community by articulating the call to action in the service of humankind. The changes I am proposing are subtle but essential. Should there be weekly services on Sunday? I'm not sure, but that is something for the church itself to decide. And if there are regular services, they will certainly need to be transformed and invigorated to suit the changes I have proposed.

Is there hope for life after death? I doubt it, but the promise of rewards and punishments either in this life or beyond should not be the basis for human behavior. We must be particularly wary of Christians who are so heaven-bound as to be of no earthly good. We need to live our lives as if this life is all that matters for ourselves and for our loved ones, and we must begin to live with greater attention to the next generations, and to the future of this fragile planet. Unless we care for the earth, our only home, we may destroy this planet, or more likely we will destroy ourselves first, and the planet will survive and adapt to whatever changes we have forced upon it.

I do not have a clear vision of what Christianity will look like at the end of its third millennium, if, indeed, it survives. But now is the time for Christians to develop an imaginative agenda for the future, because Christianity a thousand years from now, and even a hundred years from now, must be measurably different from what it is today. Extinction is really not an acceptable option.

Now is the hour to begin the renovation, the adaptation, the revolution, the transformation, and the renewal that are essential to the future of Christianity. It is time to identify and to address the issues and challenges that face all of humankind, not only Christians, in the foreseeable future, if Christianity is truly to serve as a world religion.

There is, I am convinced, a creative, an imaginative, an essential role for Christianity to play in this third millennium of its history, and maybe in the next, but only if Christians want there to be. The question is whether in the face of the enormous challenges that our world faces, Christians will simply entrench themselves even more deeply into a past that should already be behind us. That choice will surely bring demise. Or will Christians have the vision and the courage to look and to act for the future?

INDEX